TIMELY VOICES

To James Britton and James Moffett — always timely voices

TIMELY VOICES

English Teaching in the 1980s

Edited by Roslyn Arnold

Melbourne
OXFORD UNIVERSITY PRESS
Oxford Auckland New York

OXFORD UNIVERSITY PRESS

Oxford London Glasgow New York Toronto
Delhi Bombay Calcutta Madras Karachi
Kuala Lumpur Singapore Hong Kong Tokyo
Nairobi Dar es Salaam Cape Town
Melbourne Auckland
and associates in
Beirut Berlin Ibadan Mexico City Nicosia

National Library of Australia
Cataloguing-in-Publication data:

Timely voices: English teaching
in the 1980s

ISBN 0 19 554363 7.
1. English Language — study and teaching —
Addresses, essays, lectures. I. Arnold,
Roslyn M., 1945-.

420'.7'1

Designed by Susan Kinealy
Typeset in Hong Kong by Graphicraft Typesetters
Printed by Kings Time Printing Press Ltd
Published by Oxford University Press, 7 Bowen Crescent, Melbourne

Acknowledgements

My thanks to Ken Watson, Paul Richardson, Marjorie Aldred and Robert Hogan for their advice, and many favours. I would also like to thank Joyce Cook and Jonyth Burton for typing the manuscript. My thanks too to my editor Diana Giese. A portion of James Moffett's article was originally written for, and included in, a position paper commissioned by the Agency for Instructional Television.

Roslyn Arnold
Sydney, 1983

Contents

1 JAMES BRITTON   Reading and writing poetry   1

2 BRUCE BENNETT   The necessity of metaphor   17

3 DOUGLAS AND DOROTHY BARNES
Cherishing private souls? Writing in fifth year
English classes   35

4 JOHN DIXON   English Literature — a course
in writing   52

5 NANCY MARTIN   Contexts are more
important than we know   64

6 MARGARET GILL   Three teachers: defining
English in the classroom   78

7 C.T. PATRICK DIAMOND   How to succeed
in composition: 'Large as life, and twice as
natural'   96

8 JAMES MOFFETT   Excerpts from an
educator's notebook   111

9 ROSLYN ARNOLD   How to make the
audience clap: children's writing and self-esteem   123

10 MARGARET MEEK   How do they know it's
worth it? The untaught reading lessons   138

11 ROBERT E. SHAFER   Pushing the pendulum:
new perspectives for teacher education in
the eighties   154

12 PAUL K. BROCK   Processes involved in
curriculum change: a case study of New South
Wales, Australia   174

13 IAN PRINGLE   English as a world language —
right out there in the playground   187

NOTES   209

Contents

...
NOTES ... 209

Contributors

ROSLYN ARNOLD lectures in English Method and Drama in the Department of Education at the University of Sydney. She was director of the Third International Conference on the Teaching of English held in Sydney in 1980.

DOUGLAS BARNES taught English in secondary schools in England for seventeen years until he moved to the University of Leeds, where he is Senior Lecturer in Education. From 1967-9 he was chairman of NATE. Although he now lectures mainly in curriculum theory, his research interests earlier led to the publication of *Language, the Learner and the School* (with James Britton and Harold Rosen, 1971) and *From Communication to Curriculum*, 1976 (both Penguin Books).

DOROTHY BARNES is Research Fellow at the University of Leeds School of Education. She has raised a family and taught English in secondary schools and in further education in England for nineteen years. For four years she was a member of the development team of the Schools Council project *English 16-19* with John Dixon. *et. al.*

BRUCE BENNETT is Senior Lecturer in English at the University of Western Australia. He was Director of a three-year pilot project on the development of writing abilities in the senior years of Western Australian high schools. He is co-editor of the literary journal *Westerly*.

JAMES BRITTON was director of the Schools Council project, *The Development of Writing Abilities 11-18* and was formerly head of the English Department, Institute of Education, London University. He is a distinguished scholar in the teaching of English and has contributed to its development in

England, Canada, the United States and Australia through his writings, teaching and influence.

PAUL BROCK lectures in the Department of English at the University of New England, Armidale. His special interests are the teaching of literature and the processes of curriculum change. He is also active in in-service teacher education.

C.T.P. DIAMOND is Senior Lecturer in Education at the University of Queensland and a former research editor for *English in Australia*. His interests include composition, personal construct psychology, teachers' professional perspectives and ways to implement them, and classroom research.

JOHN DIXON has recently been involved with the Schools Council project *English 16-19*: 'The Role of English and Communication'. He is the author of *Growth Through English*, Oxford University Press, 1967, is well known for his writings and contributions to conferences in England and abroad.

MARGARET GILL lectures in curriculum and teaching at Victoria College (Rusden campus) and is editor of *English in Australia*.

NANCY MARTIN is former head of the Department of English Education at the Institute of Education, London University. She has spoken and conducted workshops on English education in England, Canada, the United States and Australia.

MARGARET MEEK is Senior Lecturer in English at the Institute of Education, London University. She is well known as co-editor of *The Cool Web*, Bodley Head, 1977; as a critic of children's books, and review editor of the *School Librarian*. She is also a regular contributor to the *Times Educational Supplement*.

JAMES MOFFETT is an author and consultant in education. His best-known scholarly books are *Teaching the Universe of Discourse*, Houghton Mifflin, 1968, *Student-Centred Language Arts and Reading, K-13* (with Betty Jane Wagner), Houghton Mifflin, 1976, and, recently *Coming on Center* and *Active Voice*, 1981 (both Boynton/Cook). He is acknowledged as one of the most original thinkers in the theory and practice of English teaching.

IAN PRINGLE is Chairman, Department of Linguistics, Carleton University, Ottawa. He was co-director of the 1979 CCTE Conference *Learning to Write* and co-editor with Aviva Freedman of the conference publication, *Reinventing the Rhetorical Tradition*, Canadian Council for the Teaching of English, 1981.

ROBERT E. SHAFER is Professor of English and Director, English Education, at Arizona State University. He is director of the Greater Phoenix Area Writing Project and was formerly chair of NCTE Assembly on International Research and Exchange in English. He has spoken and written widely on English education.

Introduction

We are at a time in the development of English education when the traditional concerns of teaching language and literature of necessity involve larger social, political and psychological issues than we have recognized before. Some of the dilemmas of the past, such as finding suitable classroom methods or resources, have been taken over by present dilemmas such as social pressures for public accountability, multicultural classrooms, conflicting research findings and opposing methodologies. We are recognizing that influences, issues and concerns larger than the immediate classroom have to be acknowledged for their powerful influence on the dynamics of teaching-learning contexts. Yet even as we look outwards to the bureaucracies and groups which influence curriculum development, we find we know very little about the processes operating within classrooms, very little about the relationships between the teachers and their students, and even less about the internal processes of thinking, learning, feeling and knowing going on within individuals. The present challenge is to look more deeply into those aspects of English education which are traditionally part of the English teacher's domain, such as the teaching of literature, reading, and writing, as well as aspects with more innovative overtones: the personal constructs of teachers and students; the influences of societal expectations, historical contexts, and political forces, and the nature of change and personal relationships in teaching and learning.

This book attempts to provide some insights into the extremely complex nature of teaching English in contemporary classrooms. It does not attempt to cover the whole spectrum but to pinpoint through its points of view and examples, fruit-

ful areas for further analysis and for consideration in the
development of worthwhile classroom experiences. The contributors are drawn from England, the United States, Canada
and Australia in the recognition that national concerns are
often also international. Sometimes specific examples are
local, but all the contributors are aware of many of the
particular and universal features of teaching English in the
modern English-speaking world. In many instances this awareness arises from their personal experiences of teaching and
researching beyond their home grounds. The contributors
were asked to write about an aspect of English education they
felt strongly about at present. The result could have been an
eclectic group of discordant chapters, but, because of the
preoccupations of the writers and the interrelatedness of many
current issues, there are a number of complementary themes
throughout the book.

One of these is the strategies students employ to make sense
of the world. James Britton and Bruce Bennett separately
explore the nature of metaphor in poetry and in everyday life.
When Britton speaks of 'a pattern of feeling' in poetry, and
Bennett of 'the necessity of metaphor', we can sense a turn of
the circle back to the eternal quest for meaning in existence.
Yet their points of view are new because they are shaped by
personal perspectives, informed by contemporary knowledge
and spoken in the language of extended metaphors. These
chapters have special resonances which call for a quiet revolution in learning processes. The logic of English curriculum
must bond with the supra-logic of metaphor lest we ignore a
major influence upon our construing of the world.

In investigating students' understanding of the criteria for
writing in the senior years, Douglas and Dorothy Barnes ask
'What view of the world is being communicated to young
people?' through the writing topics set, their treatment by
teachers and their interpretation by pupils. Their investigation
led them to conclude that one of the problems of all schooling
'is the detachment of what goes on in classrooms from the
urgent concerns of the world'. This is reflected in the too-
narrow range of rhetorical functions required, and the limited
range of topics offered. In these contexts students cannot
perceive an option to engage creatively in their own development.

John Dixon offers some guidelines for developing written
responses to literature which are implicitly linked to the

dilemmas outlined by the Barnes. He suggests that narrative, with its 'beautifully flexible and rich range' can open up powerful options for student writers and develop deeper responses to literature than the writing of examination papers. Dixon provides textual evidence of students' written narratives in response to literature and survey evidence that 'you don't have to appreciate literature to pass the exam'.

Drawing upon her recent work in Western Australian schools Nancy Martin examines the role of contexts in teaching and learning, specifically the influence of personal constructs, individual intentions, and the managerial system. The methods of enquiry she outlines offer a model for school based research which promises a clearer insight into the conflicting and colluding influences in school contexts than is usually available to researchers or observers. Most importantly, she concludes that while contexts are significant, the beliefs and attitudes of teachers 'are the most powerful of all the features in the context of learning'.

Margaret Gill looks closely at how three English teachers construct definitions of their subject and their teaching. Her argument and examples point again to the need to understand the reality of everyday classroom practice, and the influences upon it. Ultimately, she concludes, teachers need to develop sufficient professional confidence to develop their own curriculum.

This point is elaborated by Patrick Diamond in the context of the teaching of composition. He argues that teachers' personal constructs often work against the successful teaching of composition, and that students perceive their composition experiences as 'fairly bleak and often conflicted'. The encouraging point he makes is that students can engage in theorizing and experimenting where their own construing of the world is recognized and encouraged as essential for their self-development.

In a chapter which implicitly draws together many of the concerns of this book, Moffett offers a triptych, including a fine miniature of an aspect of narrative, 'Tally Me a Story'; a larger landscape depicting the characteristics and learning needs of early high school students; and a highly evocative and metaphoric reflection on the nature of language and thought. The educator best known for his innovative theory and practice of English curriculum attests to the value of observation, reflection and the internalizing of experience through writing and thinking. These examples offer practical and theoretical insight into how his ideas about education develop.

From my own research with late primary and early secondary school children, I argue for tapping children's innate abilities to develop language and construe experience by providing them with writing contexts which they can perceive as self-enhancing and realistic.

Margaret Meek considers in depth the nature of children's reading and response to literature. She argues that we need to look at 'not what young readers don't understand but how they ignore what does not make the story work for them'. Her point of view suggests a need to reconceptualize even our most up-to-date notions of how children learn to mean through reading. We need to make sense of the many ways children make sense of literature before we can be of assistance to them in their reading processes. At the heart of the matter is the reader's valuing of that process. What is it that helps them think it is worth it? Margaret Meek offers some valuable insights from research into an important and often unacknowledged aspect of reading.

In the final chapters of the book, the focus shifts to the wider contexts of English teaching: teacher education, English as a world language and the processes of curriculum change. Robert E. Shafer examines teacher education across a broad span of time and place, discovering such important universals as the need for individual teachers to seek self-knowledge and to develop openness to experience.

Paul Brock's case study of the factors influencing English curriculum change in New South Wales is an example, like Nancy Martin's, of a research methodology we are at last recognizing as particularly valuable in English teaching — a close analysis of a particular process in order to understand better larger clusters of processes. He also makes a number of points reiterated in preceding papers about the influence of the individual and the nature of change.

Ian Pringle takes up a critically important aspect of English teaching, and one many of us feel reluctant and ill-prepared to face: the relationships between first-language teaching and learning and the second-language field. He argues that those working in the second-language field 'have made discoveries and elaborated theories which serve to corroborate, strengthen and expand recent tendencies in English education'. Pringle's perspectives and conclusions make thought-provoking reading for teachers of English as a first or second language, and those struggling to teach both in the same classroom.

It is interesting that from whatever starting point or within whatever context these writers work, they draw similar conclusions about the potential problem-solving capacities of teachers and learners. Whether the research is based in a number of schools or classrooms; whether it is largely empirical or observational and reflective, anecdotal or speculative, there is a sense of powerful optimism guiding the conclusions.

We know that students and teachers carry into the classroom conscious and unconscious beliefs, attitudes and expectations which have to be acknowledged and orchestrated in some mutually beneficial way if any worthwhile learning is to occur. We can no longer ignore the powerful defences students can employ against the uncertainty of new experiences and the discomfort of feeling ignorant or wanting. We still need to understand more about our own capacities to act as a temporary support between the safe old ground of the known and the uncertain new ground of the future. When students perceive the teacher as willing to take calculated risks in the teaching and learning process, and willing to analyse, understand and be realistic about that process, then they will often co-operate, at least long enough for the task or experience to make its own impact. When the teacher's defences collude with the student's defences, chaos ensues. We know from the ways children learn language that they have the need, wish and power to learn, and can master extremely complex cognitive processes. In spite of all the defences against learning which can develop over the years, it is still necessary to believe that somewhere inside these processes can still be tapped and developed. It is not only the timely voices of educators we hear in this book, but in many examples the timely voices of our students.

All the writers show a willingness to probe the reality of education contexts and to listen to the sometimes uncomfortable truths students will reveal. While we cannot define a global representation of the nature of English teaching, we can engage in a search for approximations of it by constant reviews of existing knowledge and aspirations. The task of being critically aware, even sceptical, does not necessitate defeatism, but a confidence that seeing things as they are promotes development. For all the variety of experiences cited, here there is a similarity of insight at the core of each writer's argument. It centres around acknowledging the capacities, metaphors, constructs and conflicts students and teachers bring with them to the classroom, and the power of the complex relationships between and within the participants in teaching and learning contexts. The effectiveness of those contexts to promote personal insight and knowledge about the world depends largely on a belief in the learning process, and sustained curiosity about its analytic and imaginative nature.

The arguments and insights offered here may contribute to the shaping or re-shaping of a reader's theory and practice of English teaching. While they are based largely on practical classroom teaching and research experience, the reader's creative and critical engagement with the points of view is essential for the development of a personal construct of English teaching. The voices are timely because in an age of diversity and complexity, a belief in the power of the individual is an encouraging re-discovery of an old truth. Timely voices should resonate harmoniously while retaining their intrinsic qualities as instruments of experience. It is hoped that the reader finds the orchestration effective.

My warmest thanks to all the contributors for their enthusiasm and commitment to this book. To each person I owe gratitude for advice and support. The motivation for compiling this edition stems largely from my own valuing of writers, thinkers and educators with that special capacity to share themselves, their uncertainties, their beliefs and their developing wisdoms with others, no matter what the context.

Roslyn Arnold

1 JAMES BRITTON

Reading and writing poetry

I think it is part of our human nature that we seek constantly to reduce disorder to order. In all our perceptions we look for a satisfying pattern, 'a meaning', and in further contemplating what we have perceived we look for a deeper relatedness between phenomena, patterns that lie below surface appearances and serve to explain why they are as they are. Michael Polanyi,[1] scientist and philosopher, suggests that the kind of discomfort that makes us blink our eyes when we are not seeing clearly is paralleled by an intellectual discomfort when we meet difficulties in our understanding.

The search for satisfying patterns in what we know and feel and believe about the world takes many forms. The practice of the arts is one of those forms. What I want to do in this paper is to consider the role of poetry, in our lives and in the school curriculum, against the background of that search for order that constitutes artistic endeavour — a search which is at times passionate enough to deserve Wallace Stevens' phrase, 'a rage for order':

> Oh! Blessed rage for order, Pale Ramon,
> The maker's rage to order words of the sea,
> Words of the fragrant portals, dimly-starred,
> And of ourselves and of our origins,
> In ghostlier demarcations, keener sounds.[2]

Scene 1: Enter THE POET

Poetry is an intoxicating topic. Even sober writers are led to make extravagant claims, and when the poets themselves turn to commenting on it their exuberance is liable to be less controlled than it is in their poetry itself. Here is Robert Graves making 'an observation on poetry':

1

The nucleus of every poem worthy of the name is rhythmically formed in the poet's mind, during a trance-like suspension of his normal habits of thought, by the supra-logical reconciliation of conflicting emotional ideas. The poet learns to induce the trance in self-protection whenever he feels unable to resolve an emotional conflict by simple logic.[3]

Extravagant, but certainly interesting. 'Conflicting emotional ideas' recalls Vygotsky's claim for all art that it is 'the work of the intellect and of very special emotional thinking'.[4] 'Supra-logical' is something of a riddle. We are familiar enough with the idea that in our logical thinking we have to ensure, as far as we can, that our conclusions are not influenced by what we hope or what we fear but would be capable of confirmation by somebody else whose hopes and fears were different from our own. Is there a sense, then, in which our 'very special emotional thinking' could be *superior* to our logical thinking?

To make a broad generalization, I think language provides us with two alternative modes of making sense of our experience. The goal of the first is to arrive at an accurate picture of what the world is like. We use it for practical purposes — buying and selling, identifying a lost object, prescribing a treatment, arranging a rendezvous — and for theoretical purposes, for it is the language of philosophy and history and science. In relatively simple form it is the language of stating facts and in more complex form it is the language by which we arrive at theories to relate those facts. Our moods, attitudes, feelings enter into and affect all our experiences, but if we are to put together an accurate picture of what the world is like we must try to eliminate those effects in order to state facts and describe theories that have a general application, regardless of our own or other people's feelings at the time. Clearly, then, this is a logical mode of organization, a way of organizing the *objective* aspects of our experiences.

The alternative mode of language is one that aims at organizing our experiences *in toto*, as they come to us — without, that is to say, excluding the unique and personal aspects, our moods, attitudes, feelings. We owe to Susanne Langer[5] the recognition that this mode of organization in its developed form produces *works of art* — is in fact common to all the arts, including literature. It is this 'language as art' that achieves 'the supra-logical reconciliation of conflicting emotional ideas'.

What is 'supra-logical' about the reconciliation process is, paradoxical though this may sound, that it involves the *sub-conscious*. Robert Graves goes on to say that the poet, 'if able to continue until the draft is completed will presently come to himself and wonder: was the writer really he?'

The element of surprise comes, I suggest, from the fact that in his 'trance-like' state he has *listened to himself more deeply* than our normal habits of mind permit. The full value of the 'supra-logical' mode emerges only as we move to the next stage in Graves' account:

> As soon as he has thus dissociated himself from his poem, the secondary phase of composition begins: that of testing and correcting on commonsense principles, so as to satisfy public scrutiny, what began as a private message to himself from himself — yet taking care that nothing of poetic value is lost or impaired. For the reader of the poem has to fall into a complementary trance if he is to appreciate its full meaning.

My point is that the language of poetry is 'supra-logical' above all in that it allows the unique and personal experience to be *shared*. Discursive language, the language of facts and logical inference, builds cumulatively a commonwealth of knowledge about the nature of the world: it is above all through poetry and the products of the other arts that our unique, personal, emotionally charged experiences become *social*, make their contribution to a pattern of culture by which we order our lives.

Robert Graves was speaking specifically of poetry and that is the topic I have chosen to pursue. It is worth noting, however, that much that is true of poetry is likely to be true, sometimes in diminishing degree, of other forms of literature.

Scene 2: Enter THE CHILD

Many thinkers, representing diverse schools of thought, have subscribed to the notion that a child's play and the arts have much in common. This is surprising when we bear in mind the sophisticated nature of the patterning that creates a work of art, gives it internal coherence and a unity that isolates it from the traffic of everyday existence. The intricacy of this patterning is well illustrated in an anecdote told by Tolstoy about a Russian painter called Briullov:

> As he was correcting the sketch of a pupil, Briullov gave it a few touches here and there, and the dull, drab sketch suddenly came to life. 'But you've *scarcely* touched it, and everything has

changed!' said one of his pupils. 'Art begins where *scarcely* starts,' replied Briullov, expressing the most characteristic trait of art ... Thus, the 'intoxication' with the art of music ... occurs only when the performer succeeds in finding those infinitely small instants necessary for a perfect interpretation. The same applies to all the arts: in painting, scarcely lighter or darker, scarcely higher or lower, slightly more to the left or right; in drama, the slightest increase or decrease of stress, or a minute acceleration or delay; in poetry, the slightest understatement, overstatement, or exaggeration — and there is no intoxication.[6]

The ability to make these fine distinctions must certainly come with experience and we cannot expect young children to have acquired it. How then account for the fact that their spontaneous playful behaviour has anything in common with a work of art?

A young child's directness of perception has often been remarked upon. Particularly vivid and stable visual images, known as 'eidetic images', have been found to occur in sixty per cent of children but only seven per cent of adults.[7] I.A. Richards has argued that children up to the age of ten make free and direct emotional responses to the objects and people and events of their environment whereas after that age they are likely to respond in accordance with stereotyped attitudes, shaped by 'social suggestion and by accidents which withdraw us from actual experience, the one force which might push us further'. 'The losses incurred by these artificial fixations', he goes on, 'are evident. Through them the average adult is worse, not better adjusted to the possibilities of his existence than the child'.[8]

Then, with the art of poetry in mind, we must attach some importance to the psychological finding that young children relate words to each other on the basis of their *sounds*, whereas adults in normal circumstances look through the sounds and relate in terms of meaning.[9] Add to this the well-known fact that children early develop a strong sense of rhythm, and we are ready to accept what Michael Oakeshott has to say about young children's speech:

Everybody's young days are a dream, a delightful insanity, a miraculous confusion of poetry and practical activity in which nothing has a fixed shape and nothing has a fixed price. 'Fact' and 'not fact' are still indistinct... And to speak is to make images. For although we spend much of our early days learning the symbolic language of practical intercourse ... this is not the

> language with which we begin as children. Words in everyday use are not signs with fixed and invariable usages; they are poetic images. We speak an heroic language of our own invention, not merely because we are incompetent in our handling of symbols, but because we are moved not by the desire to communicate but by the delight of utterance.[10]

A directness of perception — a sharper awareness of 'the thing-ness of things' — a responsiveness to the sounds made by words and to rhythm in all its manifestations; a directness of emotional response; a propensity for delight in utterance — we may recognize all these as characteristic of early childhood; yet I don't think we have arrived at the major affinity between play and the arts. It has to do, I believe, with pattern-making, make-believe and the world of stories. I have often been amazed at the readiness with which a young child enters into the alternative worlds offered by stories and nursery-rhymes; how quickly he makes himself at home in those worlds, adapts them to his liking; and how, without losing his grasp on reality, he creates in make-believe play and in story-telling his own alternatives to that reality. He seems astonishingly free to pattern the possibilities of experience — a freedom owed in part no doubt to his inexperience, his ignorance of the social and cultural recipes by which adults interpret the world and regulate their behaviour in it.

It is, I believe, this aspect of a child's development that Vygotsky refers to, somewhat enigmatically, in the following passage:

> There are remarkable phenomena in the art of children. First there is the early presence of a special structure required by art, which points to the fact that for the child there exists a psycho-logical kinship between art and play. 'First of all,' says Bühler, 'is the fact that the child very early adopts the correct structure, which is alien to reality but required by the fairy tale, so that he can concentrate on the exploits of the heroes and follow the changing images. It seems to me that he loses this ability during some period of his development, but it returns to him in later years.[11]

Vygotsky gives us a further hint when he points out that in his drawings a child 'draws patterns, not events or phenomena'. This 'special structure' referred to above is perhaps a psycho-logical 'set' which enables a child to pattern reality, first-hand experience, in one mode, and the story world in another; without feeling the need (as he will at a later stage) for the one mode to challenge the other.

It is an inevitable part of growing up that children should lose some of their freedom. They must, for example, to some degree organize their emotional responses if they are to meet the increasing social demands made on them. There is a sense in which the rat-race begins early and if they are not to be losers they must develop a utilitarian knowledge and know-how at the expense of perceptual pleasure, see through the corporeal qualities of words to their meanings, develop a concern for communication at the expense of delight in utterance — and in other ways adjust to the 'shades of the prison house' that 'begin to close upon the growing boy'.

If this were in no sense a true picture of development, we should surely be tempted to regard the adult poet as a Peter Pan, a child who never grew up. Clearly, the major difference between the creative acts of an adult and those of a child lies in the sophistication of the patterning techniques the adult employs. He has two reasons for doing so: first in order to recover, as a special activity among all his other modes of behaviour, the directness of perception and emotional response he had as a child; and secondly in order to communicate the unique subjective experiences so gained to others — themselves no longer children. His artistic development might be seen to parallel in some respects the spiritual development described by Thomas Traherne. Rounding off an ecstatic description of what the world was like to him as a young child, he goes on:

> The Skies were mine, and so were the Sun, Moon and Stars, and all the World was mine, and I the only Spectator and Enjoyer of it. I knew no Churlish Proprieties, nor Bounds nor Divisions: but all Properties and Divisions were mine: all Treasures and the Possessors of them. So that with much adoe I was corrupted; and made to learn the Dirty Devices of this World. Which now I unlearn, and becom as it were a little Child again, that I may enter the Kingdom of GOD.

Intermission

Ten minutes ago, as I sat idly musing (it was in the bath, but I don't have to tell you that), three words and a cadence drifted into mind. The words were 'but not this . . .', spoken in a certain way, quiet yet portentous. I soon completed the phrase, 'but not this peace no bird could contradict', but still could not identify the poem. That gave me the opportunity to play a kind of game I have often indulged in: to try to say all I could, based on the fragment, about the poem from which it is drawn. In this case I knew the poem was by Auden; it felt like a closing phrase, a finishing point. I thought that, curiously enough, what 'it' was *not* rather than what it *was* dominated the mood. A complex mood, part nostalgic, part fulfilled — and an underlying sense of something threatening. I did not know what the poem was about, what events were narrated, but I did have a strong sense of its mood.

The last time this happened to me it was the words, 'Break your heart, but not Orion his (something)' that drifted into mind. I did not know how to fill in the last word and I had no idea who wrote the poem or what its 'subject' was; once again, what I did recover was above all a sense of a mood. I imagined a starlit sky, remote, unchanging, inscrutable; and the mood was a stern one — not of despair but of resolve — a 'down to the bone' feeling without which the mood might have been mere self-pity.

The final stage of the game is, of course, to identify the poem at the bookcase and check one's recollections against the text. The Auden poem I have found without difficulty. It is the poem that begins 'Taller today, we remember similar evenings . . .' and ends:

But happy now, though no nearer each other,
We see the farms lighted all along the valley;
Down at the mill-shed the hammering stops
And men go home.

Noises at dawn will bring
Freedom for some, but not this peace
No bird can contradict: passing, but is sufficient now
For something fulfilled this hour, loved or endured.[12]

It took me some while to trace the second poem — since it turned out unexpectedly to be one I wrote myself in Egypt during the Second World War — thirty-eight years ago. The line I recalled begins the poem:

Break your heart, but not Orion his silence.
Not his god-like sword will strike the rock.
As the day when Adam laughed to see him
Shines he now upon your broken luck.

O splendour, splendour of the bright procession!

7

Turn your eyes to earth, you mortal man.
Break your heart, but not Orion his splendour.
Guard your grief, he will not intervene.

O splendour. Breaking hearts and broken empires:
Eyes like stars that will not shine again.
Starry gems that dust of kings has buried,
While the splendid stars shine on, in vain.

Seeing the whole piece, I can sense the underlying conflict of emotion: a desire on one hand to preserve and on the other to forego a sense of a presiding deity, watching, father-like, over the affairs of men; over my affairs as an individual and over the destiny of nations — though the attempt to link individual concerns with the fate of empires clearly does not come off.

But the point of this digression — time off before getting into school — is to suggest that what is stored from the experience of a poem — reading it or writing it — is above all a *mood*; not a story, not a theme, but, in some complexity, a pattern of feeling.

Scene 3: Enter THE TEACHER

I recall a picture of a tree painted by a girl in the kindergarten class of a Vancouver school. It was a fairly typical picture, for her age — a firm green goblet of foliage resting on a firm brown stem. But underneath it the child had written. 'I saw a tree and then I walked away from it for ever'. In that sentence, I believe, the writer had dredged beneath the surface of a commonplace event to remark, intuitively, on the nature of experience itself. She was able to do so on that occasion because she felt free to use a poetic mode of utterance.

Perhaps the most important inference to be drawn from all we have said about poetry in the early years is to notice how the freedom to use that form of utterance *provides a depth to what can happen in the classroom*. I have sat in elementary school classrooms successfully organized to provide a great deal of purposive activity and busy learning and yet have felt a lack, a failure to engage those undercurrents of feeling that make learning a rich and personal experience. Teachers can produce this, of course, by the use they make of music, of painting and other forms of activity, but since language is the normal currency of exchange in the classroom, the means by which teachers and children become a community, it seems to me that poetic speech and writing have a very special importance.

It is not that we can *teach* children to make their intuitive poetic utterances, but, by reading poetry, by having it around the walls, and by showing that we value it in the responses we make to what they say and write, we can encourage them to be free to use it in our classrooms.

A teacher in a Grade 4/5 class in a Toronto school was taking a lesson on the day before Armistice Day. He read a poem in which a mother is speaking of her dead son, and he went on to talk about the debt we owe to men and women who died in the two World Wars. Then the children were invited to write or draw something related to what had been said. One of the boys in the class drew the kind of cross that suggests a war-memorial and wrote:

> Why didn't you try to stay alive? You are gone for good. But you have bought my life, that is fine for me. But I am sad that you died for me, I would have liked to see you around.

I am not sure how I feel about what the teacher was doing; perhaps the truths about war, about sacrifice and about survival, are too complex to handle entirely honestly with children of that age. But I find the boy's response fascinating in the way it embraces conflicting emotions. He seems in the first sentence to resist the attempt to implicate him, to make him feel in some way responsible: 'Why didn't you try to stay alive?' — brought to a manageable level by its concreteness, addressed not to a generation but to a single soldier. Then comes 'You are gone for good', implying, 'There is nothing I can do about it now'. This is followed by a restatement of what is asked of him, 'But you have bought my life, that is fine for me. But I am sad that you died for me'; and finally, in a language that is entirely appropriate to everyday realities, 'I would have liked to see you around'. It is typical of the deeper penetration made possible by poetic utterance that it should involve an attempt to reconcile conflicting emotions — as we saw in discussing Robert Graves' statement.

One further comment could be made — tentatively. Are we perhaps observing in the words of this ten-year-old a stage in the very process Richards referred to, the taking on of a conventional mode of feeling in place of a direct emotional response? Both are present in his response and the conflict between them is unresolved. When the voice of poetry is welcomed in the classroom conversation, there is no telling what chance effects its deeper penetration may yield.

That the writing and reading of poetry should go hand in hand seems to me important. It is not that the poems read are seen as models in any direct sense, though over time they may have an enormous influence on the way children tackle their own writing. I believe the satisfied reading of a poem, or listening to it, provides the best stance from which to write one's own poem. This was illustrated for me when, some years ago, I presented a series of poetry programmes for nine and ten-year-olds on the BBC and invited listeners to send in their own poems. In a programme on 'Indoors and out', I read a poem by Elizabeth Coatsworth called 'On a Night of Snow'. Her first stanza shows the owner tempting the cat to stay indoors on a wild winter's night, while the second stanza gives the cat's reply — let me out! A nine-year-old boy sent in a piece under the same title that had nothing to do with cats. He had responded in fact to the symbolic meaning for which I had chosen the topic: it has always seemed to me that indoors and out of doors symbolize a young child's conflicting needs — the need to be adventurous and the need for a secure home base. Here is nine-year-old Bernard's poem:

On a night of snow

On a night of snow
As thick it lay
Nothing to show
But the shepherd's way,

Wandering the hill side
Seeking a stray,
Dog by his side
To keep fox at bay.

Families by fires sit
Laughing and warm.
Shepherd, lamp lit,
Keeps on till the dawn.

The quality of our input as teachers is, of course, crucial; crucial that what we present should be genuinely poetic. Comic poetry and narrative in verse may serve as an occasional livener, but the mainstream should be genuinely poetic, and there is a wide range of lyrics, lullabies, songs and nursery rhymes to choose from. The quality of the children's listening will guide our choice, and we are further likely to learn from experience those areas of concern that make the strongest appeal — the areas in fact where conflicting emotions are likely to be involved. We find, for example, that poems about old people and eccentrics appeal to many children of elementary school age, and it is easy to relate this interest to the conflict between the desire for autonomy and the demands of society. The pressure to conform, conform, conform that comes from parents, teachers etc., finds relief in imaginative encounters with non-conformers — grandparents, old soldiers, tramps, old sailors, gypsies.

Our aim in all that we present is to build up, by degrees, a class repertoire of familiar and well-liked poems. Given that our choice is right, repeated readings will serve only to enhance response. In this connection, some of the most successful professional development work I have ever taken part in has been in the form of voluntary poetry-reading sessions with the staff of an elementary school. In the early sessions there has been more listening on the part of the teachers than presenting, but that balance does improve with time. The focus has been upon poetry *for ourselves* rather than poems to read in class. Elementary school teachers are in danger of subscribing to the widely-held view that poetry is a closed language accessible only to the initiated — including notably graduates in English; we have worked together on that to disprove the notion. In schools organized on a class-teaching basis, it is the class teacher's own poetic sensitivity that we rely on.

Scene 4: Enter THE ADOLESCENT and THE ENGLISH TEACHER

If the earlier years of childhood constitute a golden age for poetry, an opportunity that must not be missed, what do we do about poetry as children move into adolescence? Do we bow to the inevitable?

In society in general comparatively few adults are poetry readers and fewer still will ever write it. We have first to accept, then, that as adolescents develop their individual life-styles, some will move further into poetry and many will move out of it altogether. So it is with adults — the kind of satisfaction I get from reading and writing poetry, some of my friends get from painting, from music, from novel-reading, from drama; and they have as much right to be critical of my level of concern and my sophistication in these arts as I have to criticize their neglect of what poetry could offer.

11

What matters is that the modes of perceiving and organizing our experiences that are peculiar to the arts should, in some form or other, be maintained as widely as possible. It is my conviction, first, that whatever has been achieved with poetry in 'the golden age' will contribute to later activity in any of the arts, and second, that in the succeeding stages whatever arts are represented in the curriculum should collaborate in achieving that common goal.

The move from artlessness to art will involve a search for techniques of expression and of interpretation. How do we handle this in the classroom? I think it must first be clear that the search for techniques of expression is an individual matter and not one for direct class instruction. It is a search for the particular technique which will serve an individual's particular intentions at a given moment — though, of course, our experience as teachers and as craftsmen is at all times a resource upon which the student can call. The major resource for techniques of poetry writing will, however, always be reading and listening to poems. The quality of the reading aloud here is, again, crucial, creating as it does the sound patterns a student will internalize.

We must make allowances for apprentice work, be patient in responding to pieces marred by too conscious an imitation of a poetic form, or to the student who loses his own voice in his admiration for somebody else's. As Auden has put it:

> A would-be poet has to pretend to be somebody else; he has to get a literary transference upon some poet in particular . . . He serves his apprenticeship in a library. Though the Master is deaf and dumb and gives neither instruction nor criticism, the apprentice can choose any Master he likes, living or dead, the Master is available at any hour of the day or night, lessons are all for free, and his passionate admiration of his Master will ensure that he works hard to please him. [13]

But, yes — the teacher has an invaluable role to play as mediator and catalyst. He can encourage the writer to have confidence in his own intentions, to realize that concentrating upon the verbal object he intends to create may be the best way of finding words — having them alight on the page rather than trying to winkle them out with a pin! He can help the writer to understand the value of incubation, and, on the other hand the need to work on a poem once it is in existence. He can help him to be ready to seize upon a line or a phrase that promises a poem even before he is aware that there is here'a poem he wanted to write.

One of the rewards of the patient teacher will be the variety of the voices that adolescents discover. Here is a piece written by a Grade 11 girl in Northern Alberta:

The child in me
Cupped her hands
To bring the water
To her dry lips;
(Just as the woman
Had grasped at love
To comfort
Her bruised heart,
And like a fool
Loosened her clasp
And let love
Slip away).
The water
Spilled from her
Young, inexperienced hands
And fell,
Like tears of sorrow
On the sands.

The opening words, 'The child in me' allows us, by an ambiguity that I am sure was intended, to relate the following section (in parentheses) to 'the woman in me', and the closing section brings about the fusion of the two. And the following was written by a Grade 12 boy in the same school:

I'm into it

I'm into Dylan
Last week I was into Stones
And their screams
And their shouts
And their wild taunts to promiscuous humanity
And their sociological innuendoes.

Next week I'll get into artsy art
And artsier art
And especially avant-garde art
And monolithic sculpture that makes final statements about life
And death

And everything before and after.

And sooner or later I know I'll get into politics
And peace
And war
And power
And crimes of injustice against humanity
And after I've gotten into everything that a decent intellectual
    conscientious white North American wasp can only be expected
    to get into
I hope I can get out.

A fifteen-year-old in an English school writes:

Lonely Beach

Walking hand in hand
Along that lonely beach,
The sand, the stones, the sea, the air
Everything was there.
But now as I walk
Along on my own,
There's only me there,
With only the sea, the sand, the air.

The winding/unwinding effect of the move from 'everything'
to 'only' serves to show how deceptively simple this statement
is.[14]

Curtain

I want in conclusion to examine a little more closely I.A.
Richards' claim that 'the average adult is worse not better
adjusted to the possibilities of his existence than the child'. As
we have seen, young children, in homes that are sympathetic to
their activities, spend a great deal of their time in 'supposition',
make-believe, the story world. They pursue such activities with
seriousness and energy. As masters of these alternative worlds
they can control the kinds of demands that are made within
them. An essential part of growing up consists in learning to
inhibit some of the emotional responses characteristic of
existence in alternative worlds in order to respond more
adequately to the demands of the real world — the need to
arrive on time, for example, and in other ways to behave
responsibly. This introduction of selective emotional response,

response in accordance with some predisposition, sets up what Richards referred to as 'fixations of attitudes', or what the psychologist Denys Harding has called 'sentiments', defining a sentiment as 'an enduring disposition to evaluate some object or class of objects in a particular way'.[15]

Given that this is a necessary part of achieving maturity, two important questions remain: what is the basis on which these ways of organizing emotional responses are developed? And is there any area of activity in which the adolescent continues to explore imaginatively the possibilities of experience with the emotional directness and freedom he or she enjoyed in childhood?

There can be no doubt that poems and stories, listened to and read, are important embodiments of the ways of feeling that form a part of our pattern of culture. They operate, as it were, as a primer from which a child learns. In poems and stories he finds his own emotional responses re-echoed, confirmed, modified, extended. Part of the process of developing attitudes must thus be seen as a means by which individual responses become socialized, acculturated.

The ways of feeling represented in our pattern of culture owe a great deal, of course, to the individual adjustments to experience made by creative artists throughout the generations. (In an ideal society they would owe more; in any real society they have to contend with easier, short-term answers to questions about values). When important changes occur in a society — such as the invention of the atom bomb — creative artists give the lead in adjusting to those changes. But it is only insofar as their adjustments are given currency — by lesser artists, by the men and women who make up their audience, their readers, that they can become a part of our pattern of culture.

What Richards has underestimated, I believe, in the statements of his we have quoted, is the extent to which the organization of an individual's attitudes may be based upon the genuine and sensitive responses to experiences of creative artists — the extent to which poetry for example does in fact function as a primer of our socially developed ways of feeling. Richards does, of course, restrict his statement to 'the average adult'; and he goes on to suggest that the average adult forms attitudes on the basis of current 'easy answers' and the commercially-conditioned products of the mass media — 'bad literature, bad art, the cinema, etc'.[16] Those of us who are average adults teaching average children (for what those terms are worth) are in my opinion justified in taking a more optimistic view of society.

As to my second question, the answer is at this stage of my argument perfectly obvious. It is in the practice of the arts, in interpreting and originating art objects, that the adolescent and the adult devote a part of their time, among their more practical concerns, to preserving the directness of perception and emotion that came naturally to them as children and occupied much of their time. Richards is quite right in maintaining, as he does, that if we take our stock responses, our fixed attitudes, into the practice of the arts we shall rob of their power the most powerful means by which, individually and socially, we become the sort of people we are and create the sort of society we live in.

2   BRUCE BENNETT

The necessity of metaphor

As if, as if, as if the disparate halves
Of things were waiting in a betrothal known
To none, awaiting espousal to the sound

Of right joining, a music of ideas, the burning
And breeding and bearing birth of harmony,
The final relation, the marriage of the rest.
Wallace Stevens, Study of Images II.[1]

Between Wallace Stevens's neo-romantic espousal of metaphor
as the consummation of all our linguistic activity and the outlook of the classical rhetoricians, on whose precepts much of our
teaching still rests, a great gulf seems fixed. I.A. Richards has
summarized the rhetoricians' standard outlook on metaphor:

> Throughout the history of Rhetoric, metaphor has been treated as
> a sort of happy extra trick with words, an opportunity to exploit
> the accidents of their versatility, something in place occasionally
> but requiring unusual skill and caution. In brief, a grace or
> ornament or added power of language, not its constitutive form.[2]

Richards himself, of course, demonstrated the centrality of
metaphor in thinking, speaking and writing. No use of
language, he argued, can be entirely 'plain' or 'straightforward' or 'conceptual': metaphors are required to even make
these claims. Metaphor, claimed Richards, is the principle of
all language. Yet many of us who profess to teach the language
have not properly considered this proposition, or examined its
implications.

   Although the primacy of metaphoric thinking in the making
of myth and poetry has been convincingly demonstrated,[3] these
activities are usually assumed to be peripheral to the concerns
of technologically advanced societies, with the result that the
thinking which informs them is underestimated. The philo-

sopher Ernst Cassirer[4] has challenged this assumption with his persuasive argument that our most fundamental and formative conceptions derive from the kind of metaphorical thinking which we see most clearly exemplified in poetry and myth. If this is true, the consequences of a civilization's preoccupation with rationality, literalness and quantitative measurement may be the loss of a whole dimension of mind; and with it the capacity to converse in a language which retains its necessary roots in human experience. But before losing ourselves in such dismal speculations, we should first define our subject.

The chief function of metaphor is suggested by the parts of the Greek word *metaphora*: 'meta' meaning 'over', and 'pherein' 'to carry'. Hence the notion of aspects of one object being 'carried over' or transferred to another object, so that, as Terence Hawkes[5] observes, 'the second object is spoken of as if it were the first'. (Thus, the essential form of metaphor is apparent in constructions such as 'The mind is a machine' or 'Love is a journey'). Metaphor is commonly considered generically as the fundamental form of all 'figurative language': in the discussion which follows the two terms will be used interchangeably.

Definition may be enhanced by contrast; hence metaphoric uses of language may be defined by contrast with literal uses, though if we accept I.A. Richards' assumption that metaphor is the principle of *all* language, the distinction can not be absolute. Hawkes states that

> Language which means (or intends to mean) what it says, and which uses words in their 'standard' sense, derived from the practice of ordinary speakers of the language, is said to be *literal*. Figurative language deliberately *interferes* with the system of literal usage by its assumption that the terms literally connected with one object can be transferred to another object. The *interference* takes the form of *transference*, or 'carrying over', with the aim of achieving a new, wider, 'special', or more precise meaning.[6]

Although this distinction between literal and metaphoric language is generally helpful, it presents problems of interpretation and application, especially in the distinction between 'standard' and 'new' usage. The notion of 'standard' usage is notoriously difficult to apply across different societies, institutions and age groups. If considered within a developmental context, 'standard' usage is an especially perilous notion: as any teacher knows, one student's cliché is another's discovery.

Some of these difficulties will be considered later, in relation to actual students and their writing. We need not be detained here by the various sub-categories of figurative language: personification, synecdoche, metonymy, oxymoron and the like; to further analyse such terms would be to contribute to the mistaken view of metaphor as ornament.

Instead of encouraging writers to enjoy metaphor and experiment with it, pedagogues and critics all too often begin with the hazards. Northrop Frye,[7] for instance, warns writers of the dangers of using metaphor, and its close cousin analogy, and in doing so suggests somewhat misleading distinctions between science and imagination, poetry and reason:

> You'll find that analogy, or likeness to something else, is very tricky to handle in description, because the differences are as important as the resemblances. As for metaphor, where you're really saying 'this *is* that', you're turning your back on logic and reason completely, because logically two things can never be the same and still remain two things. The poet, however, uses these two crude, primitive, archaic forms of thought in the most uninhibited way, because his job is not to describe nature, but to show you a world completely absorbed and possessed by the human mind.[8]

The injunction to 'take care' is of course appropriate in some respects — creating good metaphors is at least as difficult as creating good logical propositions — but the adoption of a stance and manner like Frye's is likely to inhibit the risk-taking experimentation with language from which good metaphors will emerge. Moreover, poets are not devoid of reason, nor scientists of imagination when they engage in making metaphors and analogies.

The question of how necessary metaphor is can be tested most rigorously in the physical sciences, where, if anywhere, a metaphor-free, conceptual language would seem to operate. However, Gerald Holton[9] has effectively demonstrated the primacy of imagination and the importance of metaphor in scientific discoveries. His study of themata in scientific thought shows the recurrence of metaphoric thinking in the creation of hypotheses and explanations. Holton has noted the prevalence of 'thema-anti-thema' couplings throughout the history of modern science, for example in the changing relations of images of order and chaos in the writings of physicists from Newton to Einstein. Furthermore, at moments of discontinuity, when logical reasoning seems to take a scientist no further, the breakthrough has often occurred through meta-phoric thinking: the transference of the image of sound 'waves' to light was one such breakthrough. Root metaphors of this kind often provide a basis for theory. Clearly, adventurous, risk-taking thought is as important in science as in the arts; and in a time of rapid turnovers of theory and fashion it is more necessary than ever to be aware of the metaphors which under-lie our thinking, and their implications.

Metaphor in everyday discourse

An understanding of the role of metaphor in science as well as the humanities is important, but just as important is an under-standing of its role in everyday discourse. This question is tackled in an outstanding collaborative work by George Lakoff and Mark Johnson[10] a linguist and a philosopher. The authors argue, with a variety of well-chosen examples, that metaphor not only pervades our everyday language, but informs our thought and action: the concepts which give direction to thought are largely metaphorical, however unconscious we may be of this. A good example is the metaphor *argument is war*: we frequently talk about argument in terms of war (we 'attack a position', or find another 'indefensible', perhaps even 'gain ground', or 'fall back', 'fighting a losing battle'). This metaphor is not mere ornament: it strongly influences the way we think about, and participate in, argument. The force of such metaphors varies from culture to culture. (It is possible to imagine the metaphor *argument is conversation* prevailing in certain cultures, though not, the authors assert, in America). Another metaphor which is claimed to work powerfully in American life is *time is money* ('You're *wasting* my time'; 'This gadget will *save* you hours'; 'I don't *have* the time to *give* you'). Such a metaphor structures experience, so that we conceive time as a valuable commodity, and act as if it were. The persuasive argument that such metaphors in a culture are not random or arbitrary occurrences but are systematic, suggests great benefit in understanding them better.

Metaphor and culture

How, if at all, do these studies touch on Australian culture and society? First, they serve as a reminder of a well-documented tradition of pragmatic 'realism', which trusts literal versions of the 'truth' but is deeply distrustful of its metaphoric transformations. Patrick White drew attention to this characteristic of the Australian psyche, and he, and a number of younger writers have, to an extent, reversed the trend in literature, if not in society at large. Reflecting these wider trends, Australian education has been pragmatic rather than speculative or imaginative, and the predictable result has been achieved: generations of students who play safe. The picture is clearest in the senior years of high school, where curricula, for the most able students at least, are dominated by the sciences and social sciences, wherein a myth of objectivism prevails and scant attention is given to the transforming and problem-solving powers of language. As an index of this, writing tasks are usually mere copying of others' work, short-answer exercises or report writing in the transactional mode.[11] The 'use it or lose it' philosophy may prevail in sexual matters, but does not apply to the imagination.

Some interesting studies which bear on the Australian situation of the role of the metaphoric imagination in education have been carried out in Britain and the United States. The most suggestive of the British studies is Liam Hudson's investigation[12] of the 'contrary imaginations' of arts and science-biased adolescent English schoolboys, from which he made the broader observation that:

> . . . the arts man is free to use his imagination just because he is not committed to being practical; while the scientist's practical commitment precludes his thinking about any use for an object other than the right, the most conventional one.[13]

The obvious place to test Hudson's hypothesis of 'convergent' and 'divergent' thinkers, and other theories of the imagination in education is in students' language in different subject areas; the locus of such studies might be expected to be metaphor. As Janet Emig commented in 1972:

> If comprehending and creating metaphor form 'one of the pillars of human cognition' such a major mode for learning would seem to be an essential subject for research, perhaps particularly by those of us in English education.[14]

Yet few have taken up her challenge. While the functions of metaphor are regularly debated by philosophers, and a growing interest in the subject is apparent among psychologists, the significance of metaphor in education is seldom explored at any depth.

21

Metaphor in education

A significant exception to this tradition of neglect is a book by Howard Pollio, Jack Barlow, Harold Fine and Marilyn Pollio,[15] which analyses and comments upon recent studies of figurative language in psychology, psychotherapy and education. Much of the research described in this book deals with the measurement of metaphor comprehension and production in interaction with various psychological tests. However, some synthesizing generalizations are attempted. The first one which concerns us here is the attempt to place children's understanding and use of metaphor in a developmental context. Interpreting the results of a number of studies, the authors conclude that children can and do produce both 'novel' and 'frozen' figurative language as early as the American third grade (age 8), although an ability to explicate this language may not be present.[16] Adolescents appear to produce a higher total rate of metaphoric usage on similar composition and comparisons tasks than do comparable elementary school children.[17] These findings are placed in a Piagetian framework of intellectual development and a 'genuine discontinuity in figurative language production' is postulated 'somewhere between the ages of eleven and sixteen'.

Attempts have also been made to differentiate 'high metaphorizers' from 'low metaphorizers' and to describe the former in terms of their intelligence and 'cognitive style'. Again, the empirical basis for generalization is sparse. However, several studies indicate that intelligence, while related to the perception of metaphor is not related to its production. (Motivation, task and situation are clearly important factors in the kind of language 'produced'). In a study by Chapman,[18] a significant correlation was found between the ability to communicate with metaphorical expression and one measure of an individual's cognitive style: the more flexible the person's style the more metaphor was produced. On the basis of Chapman's work and other related studies, the Pollio team outline a very favourable profile of the 'high' metaphorizer':

> He or she is a flexible individual. He or she is perceptually open and notices and responds to more than other individuals. He or she is able to attend to several diverse things at one time and to integrate and organize these diversities effectively. He or she shows a preference for complexities and is able to tolerate ambiguities and confusion. He or she is unafraid of the unusual and the new, and is therefore willing to experience things in new ways and to be

open to change and growth. Such flexibility allows the person to be immature and childlike when desired, but able to respond in a logical, adult manner when needed. Such a person is in touch with him or herself and with his or her own feelings and desires. The metaphorizer can respond to emotion because repression is not used as a defence. He or she can be uninhibited, but can also delay gratifying needs and wishes. Because such a person is not afraid of what is not understood, he or she has access to unconscious and relatively immature, primary process thinking. However, while the person can regress, he or she has sufficient personal strength to 'return to reality' when such is wanted or needed. It is this flexible but controlled cognitive style that allows the person to be creative, to produce novelty.[19]

This identikit would require detailed case studies to return it to the realms of the human, but it is interesting to find an apparently empirically realized alternative to the image of the brow-clutching, hysterical creator of metaphor in the high Romantic tradition.

Perhaps the most important area touched on by Pollio and his colleagues concerns the institutional context in which learning activities (including writing) occur. Referring to the data of Pollio and Pollio (1974), they comment that, in the elementary school context (in Knoxville, Tennessee) 'compositions seem best construed not as a task in creative writing but rather as a task in the control of grammar and word choice'.[20] The competitive atmosphere of upper middle-class schools led to a 'don't rock the boat' philosophy which depressed the use of novel figurative language, such suppression occurring to a much lesser extent in lower to lower middle-class schools.[21] Taking into account the results of other studies, Pollio's team concluded that the educational process in the public school system as a whole 'appears to suppress the use of novel figurative language'. The significance of such a situation should be clear in the light of the previous discussion. But how typical is it? What does it mean for individual learners? And what are its implications for society at large?

An investigation

Figurative language was one among a number of topics investigated in the University of Western Australia's writing research project.[22] This was a three-year investigation of the process of writing and the development of writing abilities of fifteen to seventeen-year-olds at four Western Australian high schools. Although the research contained surveys, questionnaires and statistical analysis, case studies of individual writers and their writing were an important part of the work.[23] The study of metaphor in this research occurred as part of an investigation of features of free writing in response to newspaper photographs. (These responses were 'free' in the sense that students were asked: 'Please write about the photograph in any way you like' and they were advised that the composition would not be used in any way for school assessment). Since the frequency of figurative usage has been shown to vary with different writing tasks, it is necessary to show the distribution of main writing forms chosen by the students (Table A).

Forms of Writing	Year 10 N = 307	Year 11 N = 144	Year 12 N = 145
Description:			
Literal	4	8	8
Interpretive	7	6	9
Story	70	55	43
Essay	4	14	26
Poem	10	12	8
Other	4	10	1

Table A: Choice of main writing forms over four schools according to year, expressed as percentages of scripts in each year

The most interesting feature of this table is the dominance of the story category (which however diminishes as students move further up the school) and the corresponding increase between years 10 to 12 of the essay category. Previous research indicates that the rate of novel metaphoric production is significantly higher on 'self-referent' than on 'objective' compositions;[24] and writers tend to use more metaphor in narrative than in essays, possibly because they view narrative as more unstructured and as offering more freedom of expression for creative writing.[25]

A subset of 86 of the above scripts was analysed for eleven different features, including figurative language.[26] (The other features were: engagement with the task, fluency, presentational skills, humour, feeling for the whole, appropriateness and control of style, originality, reader interest, vocabulary and speculation). Three members of the research team rated the scripts on a scale of 0-3 for degrees of figurative usage.

Major differences of opinion (i.e. two points or more) were discussed and if they could not be resolved in this way the majority opinion on the appropriate score for a script prevailed. A high degree of agreement was achieved. The main difficulty occurred in the interpretation of 'dead' metaphors. Some examples: expressions such as 'the tears streaming down his face', 'escape the clutches of' and 'in the doldrums' were generally rated 0, since they were considered in their context to represent no sense of comparison in the mind of the writer. (The difficulty is obvious however: the mind of the writer was apparent to us only on the page, and who knew what vital images might or might not have flashed through the mind of the writer who had his character 'in the doldrums'?) Self-conscious images and those which were not dead but were certainly not original (like 'a trail of death and destruction') enabled a script to be rated 1. At the other end of the scale a script was sometimes figurative in a structural as well as a textural way: such a script (composition A, quoted later, is an example) rated 3. Thus kind and frequency of metaphoric usage together with its structural significance in the piece as a whole formed the basis of this rating scale. Table B shows the distribution of ratings on figurative language usage:

Year 10					Year 11					Year 12				
Schools					Schools					Schools				
A	B	C	D	Total	A	B	C	D	Total	A	B	C	D	Total
4	6	5	3	18	6	9	7	8	30	19	9	3	7	38

Frequency: Script rating	Year 10 No.	Year 11 No.	Year 12 No.
0	17	14	11
1	9	10	8
2	3	4	6
3	1	4	6

Table B: *Figurative Language (rated 0-3)*

The salient feature of this table is the overwhelming majority of scripts rated at 0 for figurative language. Even when they were offered an open invitation to write in any way they liked, few fifteen to seventeen-year-olds chose to write metaphorically. Nevertheless, the results did show slight increases in metaphoric usage with age. The sample is too small and the method too unsystematic for large conclusions, but the findings seem more suggestive when considered in relation to the low ratings also obtained for the features of speculation and originality and the increasing power of the essay as a model for extended writing activities in the senior high school years. The natural adolescent desire to push the language boat out into foreign waters appears to be inhibited by the school context; to repeat the metaphor applied to Tennessee schools, a 'don't rock the boat' philosophy inhibits risk-taking in writing and thinking done at school.

Two case studies

Quantitative analysis can take us only so far in the study of language. What is needed is closer observation of individuals reading, writing, learning and reflecting on their experience.[27] With this in mind I have chosen samples of writing by two sixteen-year-olds, 'Wendy' and 'Caroline'[28] and will discuss the question of figurative language in relation to wider aspects of these students' experience. One reason for choosing two girls is that some previous research has claimed sex differences in imagery vividness.[29] Another is that the two girls were close friends attending the same high school in an Australian country town, where I visited and interviewed each of them seven times between 1977 and 1979, as well as collecting numerous samples of their writing. Certain aspects of their school experience were therefore similar and I knew something of them and their context. Although both girls were of generally high ability, as reflected in teachers' estimates and examination results, Caroline was somewhat stronger in Mathematics and Science and was taking the standard science-biased course at this level (Chemistry, English, Geography, Maths II, Maths III, Physics), while Wendy was considered slightly stronger in English and was taking a somewhat more linguistically-oriented course (Biology, Economics, English, English Literature, History, Maths I). The differences between these two friends interested me and I gradually formed the opinion that they thought, felt, imagined and wrote in different, perhaps fundamentally different, ways.

The reader might like to guess which of the following pieces of writing was produced by which girl. Both pieces were composed in the same classroom during a forty-minute school period, in reponse to a photograph which showed a male figure, back to camera, facing a fire which is consuming a large object. As mentioned earlier, students were invited to write in any way they liked in response to the photograph. For ease of later reference, the major instances of figurative language are italicized.

A   *Fire*

I love fire but then again I hate it. Somehow a burning log fire has a great fascination for me. It's so viscous — all those red, orange, purple flames jaggedly *lashing* up the chimney. And those incandescent coals glowing, radiant. I feel like picking one out of the fire and holding it so I can blow on it and watch it's colour flicker from red to black to red. But I can't. That's what I don't like about fire — it's unapproachable: *tempting, welcoming but unapproachable.*

I love melting and burning things in a fire. A plastic bottle for instance looks so much nicer all mangled and distorted reflecting flames in its clear almost liquidity. And a burning magazine — page by page crinkling, browning and breaking up into indecipherable pieces of black nothingness. A half squeezed lemon amidst the coals — *how it cries*! The bitter juices *explode* in the grate. The singed skin hardening and shrinking in the heat.

They tell me the smell of burning flesh is repulsive. A lot of sheep died in a drought and there was nothing to do with the carcasses except to burn them. So while the fire spitted and choked *as if digesting* a meal the stench arose choking everyone around it. There must have been another way, they thought, instead of burning the sheep.

In bushfires, the trees are not always fully *cremated*. Sometimes they are left half scorched: their black gnarled trunks and the orange, lifeless leaves contrasting against the blueness of the sky. There is no green except for the olive blackness of the impenetrable black-boy — the *witness* to the fire. It saw the flames *snatching up* at the dark sky. Their red tips *dancing* against the indigo. And it saw the animals scramble for safety their eyes reflecting glazed fear. The trees and those creatures that could not escape *perished*.

'We should do this more often' my friend said as we crouched around the campfire. 'It's going to be cold in the tent, we could sit out here all night and watch the sparks extinguish as they hit the cold air'.

I stabbed the coals looking for the half baked potato I intended to have for tea.

'It's *like a little village* in there isn't it?' I said waiting for my friend's reaction.

'Yes, they've all got *lights in their windows*'.

'Well, we'd better switch them off' I said yawning and tired from the heat, 'otherwise we won't get up in the morning'.

I tipped the billy over the coals. In a sissing angry *reply* the village lights *went out*. Destructive as it was *the fire was dead*.

B

I stood and watched as the last remains of that awesome construction blazed against the blackened sky. I felt a sense of satisfaction as I watched it, and, after all this time, I felt safe.

Turning, I walked towards the helicopter which was waiting for me, my job was complete.

Never had I experienced such a day. Everything was in a turmoil. People were running all over the building, and I'm not even sure if they knew where they were going or why. I certainly hadn't given them any cause to being going at such a terryfying pace. I just wished my secretary would get back from where-ever she had run off to and get on with some of my work. There were reports due in in a few days, correspondence to see to and *a mountain of other jobs*.

'Where is she! That damn phones ringing; I'll have to answer it'.

'Hello, this is headquarters can I please be put onto Dave'.

Oh no not another case. I was *up to my eyeballs* in 'cases'.

'Yes this is Dave Marks' I answered.

'Mr Marks', I recognized the chief inspectors voice. Wow this must be important for him to be contacting me personally.

'We have an extremely important case which has come up and we would like you to drop everything and come over to our office to find out details, no ifs, there will be a large sum of money coming to you if you oblige us. Be here by 11am. Good day'. and he hung up. I stood for a moment *collecting my thoughts* then hurriedly scribbled a letter to my secretary.

> Please get someone to cover for me,
> May not be back for a while.
> Bye. Dave.

She would be hysterical when she got back. She's one of those types that can't do a thing for herself. I'll have to seriously start thinking of finding myself an new secretary.

Anyway, I finally arrived at the chief's office *dead on 11am* to my utter amazement, I'm usually hours late or hours early.

I was ushered into the room by a police constable. There were guards outside the door. I sarted to get worried.

This must be top secrect or why all the secruity.

'Mr Marks', he said. No hi or hello, just 'Mr Marks'.

'You have been choosen for this job because you are an unknown detective'.

Thanks, I said sarcastically in my mind. That really was nice of him.

'The Germans are planning to blow up the nuclear power station that has just gone into construction on the Canadian border. They have set up a missile in a deserted part of Canada and it is set to go on the 17th which is ten days from now'. Well I thought how exciting could you get *my day had actually come.* And who said these things only happened in the movies!

'And what I refuse to become involved'.

'You will not refuse as you have been thoughoughly investigated and we have knowledge that you need the work'. I've got news for you I felt like saying.

'You're job is to go to this missile, dismantle it and then blow up the whole construction'.

'Well, that's not much to ask', I said considering I've never dismantled a bomb before'.

'You will be trained in this field and everything will be supplied for you'.

'When do I start this training', I asked.

'Tomorrow morning', he replied full of authority. Well, there went my plans for the next fortnight, I watched them *float out the window.*

'Right, I'll be there in the morning Sir. Is that all?'

'Yes, you will be given further instructions as the coarse continues. Goodbye Mr Marks'.

'Goodbye Sir', and I turned and worked towards the door.

'Oh, and Mr Marks. This is top secret. Don't breath a word to anyone. You are the only other person outside of this office who has any knowledge of this'.

'Yes Sir', and then I did walk out. The full impact of what I had to do *struck* me that night. This was in a way like spying and all of a sudden I felt scared in fact, I was frightened *out of my wits.*

I managed though, *to pull myself together* and I did get through the coarse OK. I also did a good job, it was completed satisfactorally and on time. It had been a real experience. Perhaps the experience of my life.

It would be interesting to know if most readers guessed correctly that the more humanities-oriented Wendy was the author of A and the science-oriented Caroline of B.

In some respects A suggests Hudson's 'diverger' (linguistically inventive, entertains emotions, impractical) and B his 'converger' (stereotyped language, does not entertain emotions, practical, 'getting the job done'). But in order to complicate, and then clarify this dichotomy we need to consider more closely these compositions and their composers.

Differences in figurative language

Figurative language is a useful initial focus. The two stories reveal significant quantitative and qualitative differences: although the faster-writing Caroline's story (B) is almost twice as long as Wendy's, it contains fewer instances of figurative usage and these are less deeply embedded; another way of putting this is that in Wendy's story (A), metaphoric usage is 'foregrounded', while in Caroline's it is 'backgrounded'. But we need to consider more carefully the purposes of metaphor in the two stories. Wendy's 'Fire' is a contemplative, introspective piece and Caroline's (B) is full of externalized action and talk in the manner of the popular espionage story.

The two kinds of story draw on different modes of metaphoric expression. Wendy's central metaphor of fire as a person, with its dual characteristics of violent destructiveness and a nurturing warmth is supported by a number of finely-rendered sensuous images which show the writer's eye and ear for poetic effects ('those red, orange, purple flames jaggedly lashing up the chimney'; 'A half squeezed lemon amidst the flames — how it cries!'). In Caroline's story, on the other hand, action and dialogue and the male narrator's voice are dominant: figurative language here does not play a transforming imaginative role but characterizes the racy, superficial style of the speaker and his genre ('a mountain of other jobs', 'my day had actually come', 'I watched my plans . . . float out the window'). A mere count of the figures of language in the two stories would not adequately describe these differences.

A more thorough investigation of the imaginative qualities of these two writers might also consider the personae in their stories in relation to the writers themselves. Wendy's poetic depiction of a dreamer recalls other poems, stories, letters, diary entries of hers, which show a genuine 'literary' sensibility at work, experimenting with (for her) new images, vocabulary, rhythms, sounds. What are the sources of this rare concern for language? Perhaps it has something to do with the encouragement of teachers: Wendy remembered with pleasure a primary school teacher who started word games — tongue twisters, puns, poetry and inventive expressions — and other teachers since who have encouraged her to 'try things out'. A more consistent influence, however, has been Wendy's mother: an only child on a wheat and sheep farm some twenty miles from her school in a country town, Wendy had developed with her mother a close and apparently fruitful relationship, at least as far as her writing was concerned; the mother would listen and comment helpfully on things written by the daughter. A wider variety of audiences was provided by Wendy's fifteen pen pals in different parts of the world, to whom she would write from her bedroom in the farmhouse. Her isolation contributed to a social gaucheness ('my schoolfriends think I'm a bit of a loony'), but she achieved another kind of satisfaction in her writing: 'I write because I don't feel so embarrassed when someone reads my work as I do when I'm telling them something . . . Specially in stories I get really emotional but I'd never be able to say things like that'. Wendy's sense of humour is apparent in a quote from Thurber in one of her letters: 'Better to have loafed and lost than never to have loafed at all'. It expresses a serious point for her: the need for time to reflect on experience ('I hate writing under pressure'). For her, reflection on what she is writing implies much editing and redrafting, until it 'sounds right'. She tries to put herself in the position of her reader and rewrites what seems wrong and 'words that jar'. Her major difficulty was in adapting to scientific report writing: 'I write emotively, but I can't write scientifically really well. I find that hard 'cos it's sort of not like I'm speaking. It's like I'm writing down an encyclopedia . . .' She found science writing inhibiting: 'You can't really say well I think this, 'cos you're not a really qualified scientist and what you say is probably wrong anyway'.

Caroline's choice of a male persona in her story is interesting. Does it indicate an acceptance of the view that the world of action and excitement is reserved for men? Perhaps so, for many of Caroline's ideas are informed by a respect for the conservative values of her provincial country town; yet she also feels constrained to be 'modern'. Caroline's is a social and academic success story: as head prefect and dux of her school she excelled in the qualities which her school system encourages: social poise, athleticism, modesty and academic superiority, particularly in mathematics and the sciences. There is no class element in this. Caroline's father was a professional fisherman who lived with her mother and three younger sisters and brother some eighty miles from her school; Caroline lived in a hostel adjoining her school, where she slept in a dormitory with five other girls and did her homework in a communal study. This communal life (broken at weekends sometimes by visits home) is important. Caroline had the sense of being continually busy and always having people around her; she confided in one of our discussions that she felt pressured by a sense of being watched and judged by teachers and fellow students and of how she had burnt her diary in case someone should read it. Behind the surface assurance of this eldest child and image of her parents', teachers' and society's success lay a deep uncertainty. Yet this uncertainty seldom revealed itself in her school work or her writing, which she saw in practical terms rather than as a pleasure or as a means of self-exploration: 'The more advanced your writing is the more people are going to think of you. When you go for a job . . . you're going to have a better chance if you can write properly and speak properly'. That adverb 'properly' indicates a scale of values against which a more private sense of self only occasionally collided. Caroline's honesty and clarity of observation were remarkable, but she herself remarked, with a laugh, 'I haven't got a very good imagination'. The main point of writing for her was communication, 'to express yourself more clearly . . . so people will understand exactly what you say'. She prefers writing in science and social studies to English because 'it's all common sense', you have some 'specific thing' to write about and 'all you have to do is get your facts together'.

Wendy and Caroline epitomize many of the skills, attitudes and values of Hudson's arts 'diverger' and science 'converger' respectively. But even these glimpses from the case notes and transcribed discussions are enough to show that an investigation which begins in metaphor should not end in stereotypes of the imagination. The additional problem with psychological stereotyping is that it tends to omit the motives of people for doing things (e.g., writing, thinking imaginatively) and the social context and specific situation in which behaviour occurs. Moreover, the dynamics of the activity (thinking, writing imaginatively) is often left out of account too.

Investigations of metaphor can be taken further, then. One of the main questions to be asked of the social context is why a high metaphorizer such as Wendy should be so rare in Australian education. If Wendy's mode of exercising the imagination is rare, and becoming rarer, whilst Caroline's is encouraged and is becoming predominant, what are the implications for society at large? What is it in the wider social fabric which conditions teachers and students towards rationalist goals and a distrust of the metaphoric imagination? Has the literary sensibility had its day, to be allowed to exist only on the outskirts of Australian (and perhaps Western) civilization? If so, that would be civilization's loss, and a loss for the sciences as well as the arts, as Gerald Holton indicated.

But research should not remain at a general, social level. At a more intensive, individual level the cases of Wendy and Caroline indicate the importance of 'inner voice' and its relation to 'audience' in thinking and writing imaginatively. Some highly suggestive and helpful research on audience has been published by the London University Institute of Education writing research team.[30] More recently, James Moffett[31] has emphasized Vygotsky's notion of writing as 'revision of inner speech' and the long-range problem for writers as 'how to best develop the highest quality of inner speech'. (Moffett believes that meditation is a way of enhancing that quality). Jerre Paquette[32] has demonstrated the role of the adolescent writer's 'interior dialogue' with an imagined audience before and during writing. What is crucial, he claims, is 'the enabling capacity of the writer's available internalized audience'. While Moffett stresses the need for occasional aloneness and the value of meditation exercises and Paquette stresses the need for a range of sympathetic audiences, both recognize the need for what Nancy Martin[33] has called 'scope for intentions': the development in individual writers of a sense of purpose and a chance to envisage themselves as authors, not as mere regurgitators of others' material.

If we take into account these insights and theories of the writing process, it seems that of the two case studies I have referred to, Wendy was more fortunately placed, physically, socially and psychologically, for the development of a flexible, deeply-embedded metaphoric habit of mind. Her reading habits, the range of audiences available to her, her relative isolation from peer groups, her opportunities to be alone and reflect upon experience and, above all, perhaps, her enjoyment of writing wherein her imagination shaped itself, all this provided her with a set of conditions within which what I have called a literary sensibility might incubate. Ironically, these conditions existed chiefly outside her school life.

The circumstances and conditions in which Caroline lived and worked were less propitious for the development of this mode of imagining. More closely associated with the prevailing ethics and pragmatic outlook of her school environment, she closed off certain areas of emotional and intellectual development in response to an audience which she thought was scrutinizing her critically, while nevertheless retaining, for the most part, a clear-headed and commonsense approach to her work. Since success in Australia is usually measured in male terms, she armed herself with a typically male set of values and responses — which may account for her choice of the male persona in her story.

This brings us to the crunch question. If metaphor is a crucible of the imagination, how should we, as teachers of English, the sciences and social sciences treat it? The first option seems to be the most popular: to ignore the figurative language all around us and press ahead in educating our students towards a literal-minded truthfulness and reasonableness. An opposite approach would be to teach metaphor directly, either in the old rhetorical tradition, or as suggested by Pollio and his colleagues, with a graduated series of exercises in understanding, applying or creating figurative language.[34] But much figurative language occurs, and is best understood, intuitively: to expose this process to a relentless sequence of exercises might halt its development or reduce it to a clever trick. If metaphoric thinking is to lodge itself in the inner voice which controls our spoken and written utterances a more delicate, tactful and indirect approach seems called for, especially in the years of adolescence, when the ferment of physical and emotional change can itself contribute to the metaphoric process of making the familiar strange and the strange familiar.

If I seem to have argued for some ideal value in the metaphoric imagination, I do not mean to. I believe that flexibility, emotional openness and the ability to create and understand experience in its multiplicity rather than as a single track are important qualities. But they do not lead to predictable social results. The metaphoric mind may drift into a harmless dilettantism, or apply itself to a radical rethinking of personal, social and political goals (as was the case with Shelley, the most political thinker of the highly metaphoric Romantic period).[35] The metaphoric mind will seldom remain in stasis, satisfied with where it is. It will often be unpopular, for we generally prefer our rulers and fellow citizens to be 'straight', single-track and practical; the ability to imagine alternatives, or new connections, is commonly perceived to be obstructive, inimical to action. But the potential inventiveness of the metaphoric imagination, its capacity for perceiving and making new connections, and for solving problems, must be stressed again and again in the face of a social order which seeks its solace in conformity.

3   DOUGLAS AND DOROTHY BARNES

Cherishing private souls? Writing in fifth year English classes

English is sometimes described as 'a subject without a content', but this is far from being the case, as observation of secondary school English lessons soon shows. Most English teachers when they ask pupils to write, spend a good deal of time preparing them by preliminary reading and discussion which displays possible topics and approaches, and perhaps enacts the presence of a concerned and sympathetic audience. This is true even of the fifth year examination classes which we have been studying in the 'Versions of English' project.[1] Pupils in such classes need to learn the criteria by which their writing will be assessed.

Surface and deep criteria
This criteria of assessment can be thought of as falling into two groups. 'Surface' criteria, such as length, spelling, punctuation, and the more obvious conventions of lay-out and genre (such as fiction/non-fiction) are relatively easy to communicate to pupils, though they certainly do not always apply them correctly. However, there are 'deep' criteria which are much harder to communicate but have more influence on grading. Deep criteria refer to preferred topics and preferred ways of writing about them, including arrangement, emphasis, values, style and tone. The transmission of these criteria becomes more urgent as pupils move into the examination years, whether their work is to be assessed by an examiner or by a moderator from another school. In the latter case it may be more urgent still, since the pupils are to be assessed on the basis of a folder of coursework for which the teacher feels directly responsible.

There are two reasons for finding the transmission of criteria for writing particularly interesting. Deep criteria for writing amount to a set of preferred pictures of the world which gain good examination grades; the teaching of these criteria is potentially the teaching of deep criteria for living. No doubt young people do not always believe — or even listen to — what they are told, yet the pictures of the world which are presented to them in the curriculum are clearly a matter of public importance. The other important aspect of deep criteria is the possibility that they are more available to some pupils than to others: certainly some use them more effectively. One of the many explanations that have been given for differences in school success between children from different social milieux has been Bourdieu's argument that some bring with them from their homes 'cultural capital' in the form of sensitivities and preferences for what amount to little more than differences of style and perspective.[2] Since style in this sense is almost identical with deep criteria, further understanding of what these criteria are and how they are communicated should throw light on some aspects of school failure.

Public and private models of English

In asking 'What view of the world is being communicated to young people?' in the teaching of writing, we shall have to look not only at the *topics* set but also at their *treatment* by teachers and their *interpretation* by pupils. We begin with topics, those set in examination papers for the General Certificate of Education (GCE) Ordinary Level and the Certificate of Secondary Education (CSE) in England and Wales during 1979.[3] Analysing these papers led us to make a general distinction between 'public' and 'private' models of English; here we are applying the distinction only to essays in English Language papers. The public approach tends to detach English from the concerns of everyday life. Essay topics require the writer to stand back from social issues and coolly put arguments from various viewpoints. Some topics recall the *belles lettres* tradition; for others the expected style of composition seems more usually to correspond to middlebrow journalism. Questions tend to be 'open', apparently leaving to the writer the choice of subject matter, form and style, though one senses in the impersonal style of the rubric a whole world of assumptions and values by which those choices will be judged. That is, in the public model what is being tested includes whether the candidate has internalized these assumptions and values enough to judge what topics and perspectives will be preferred, and what kinds of writing will count as well-balanced, rational and inventive. This is a typical public writing task:

> Write, in any way you wish, about ONE of the following titles:
> Peace, Exhaustion, Hatred, Laughter, Hero-worship, Desolation, Memories, Meditation.

The private approach differs from this in two respects: the topics tend to be personal and domestic, chosen to be close to the writers' supposed private concerns; and the tasks often spell out a context and purpose for the writing. It is as if the examiners, wishing to avoid the possibility that the assumptions and values implicit in the public approach do have a social class bias, have made the criteria they will use so explicit that no candidate is disadvantaged by not having access to them. An unfortunate outcome is that in searching for a context and purpose supposed to be relevant to young people, the examiners embed the task in a stereotype of domestic life — the family, the peer group, the club — at worst a parody of urban working-class life. If public issues appear in the private approach, the writer is frequently encouraged to deal with them through their impact on individuals. An example that illustrates the private content is:

> Teenagers are often criticized for not behaving as parents expect. On some occasions, however, teenagers are anxious that their parents' behaviour will not let them down. Describe exactly how you hope your parents would behave if you were to bring your boy or girl friend home specially to meet them, and mention some mistakes that you might fear that they would make.

Some 'private' examinations go to much greater lengths in indicating what content, style and tone is expected.

The public and private approaches to English are idealizations which seldom appear in a pure form. There was some tendency for the (higher status) GCE papers to lean towards the public and for CSE papers to lean towards the private, but many were mixed or even showed the opposite tendency to that expected. The picture we obtained by analysing examination papers has to be severely modified, however. Many pupils in our study are examined in English by the assessment of a selection of coursework, an option which is possible in GCE,

CSE and the Sixteen Plus examinations. To understand what pictures of the world the pupils received, we must turn to other sources, to information about the writing which they actually did and about the lessons in which they were prepared for this.

For those pupils who are to sit an examination in literature as well as in language, this is the major influence on the version of English that they experience. Three out of four such classes which we observed did hardly any extended writing apart from that relevant to the literature examination. During the fifth year they would write no more than two or three general essays, set without previous discussion, and probably completed at home. Several teachers justified this in a similar manner:

> I think that in the top set groups there has been very little specific language work; the language work has come out of studying the literary texts.

This seems to refer to the correction of conventional errors in literature essays, but we did observe that there seemed to be more explicit teaching of how to structure literature essays than there was for language essays.

Mode of examining

The other major influence is the chosen mode of examining in English Language; so we shall present our analysis of pupils' written work separately for classes examined (i) by a once-for-all examination paper, (ii) by the assessment of a folder of coursework, or (iii) by a mixture of the two. (We found only two teachers whose teaching was not consonant with the mode of examination). Most English departments usually choose the same mode for all pupils, this choice reflecting their agreed values and methods.

The effect of examination by coursework, in which pupils were required to write 'assignments' for inclusion in a folder that would be assessed, was most striking. Whatever ability group they belonged to, these pupils would write regularly, completing a lengthy piece every fortnight or so. No writing would be done without time being given for reading, thinking, discussion and notemaking about the topic before the actual writing began. It is in these lessons that the teachers are shaping their pupils' conception of what is appropriate, communicating deep criteria.

Subject matter of assignments

We turn now to the subject matter of the assignments. Pupils in different sets would be presented with very similar titles, but the guidance they received would differ considerably.[4] After introductory discussion the more able pupils would be relatively free to choose the treatment they would give to the topic, and would write without close supervision, whereas the less able would write during lesson time, often with a plan on the blackboard and with the teacher moving round the room encouraging and giving guidance. This reflects in a strange manner a difference observed above in our analysis of examination tasks. It will be remembered that the public tasks were relatively open, and the private tasks closely specified; here in the classroom we have a similar difference in tightness of control, but without any overt contrast in subject matter.

In our first attempt to get an impression of what pupils wrote about we categorized 263 titles which teachers had set, giving these results:

Public topics for discussion etc.	38%
Public topics requiring personal/narrative treatment	14%
Private topics (self, family, friends, school, work)	30%
Subject matter not specific enough to be categorized	18%

Table A: *Analysis of topics set for writing*

This seemed to contradict our impressions by placing too much weight on public topics, so we decided to look instead at our fieldnotes on the 770 pieces of writing by pupils which we had inspected. This allowed us to take into account not merely the titles but how the pupils had interpreted them. In order to describe the results of this second analysis we must first explain the categories we used:

1. *Private/personal* This included autobiographical writing which varied from the anecdotal — purporting to be true but not necessarily so — to the introspective and reflective. The topics were usually private and the treatment always personal. Examples were: *My earliest memories; My grandmother; The pains and pleasures of teenage life.*
(We can illustrate how misleading a title alone can be by taking as example 'The European Cup Final', which we placed in this category because the writer made of it an opportunity to write about the excitement of a trip to London).
2. *Fictional narrative* It was often very difficult to determine

whether a particular first-person narrative — the most common kind — belonged here or in the personal category. The following titles clearly invite a narrative: *The day the lift stuck; Maybe next time*.

However, titles such as *Old Age* or *Prejudice* frequently appeared at the head of fictional narratives, which partly accounts for the over-emphasis on public topics in our analysis of titles. (The former might be a Pinteresque sketch of two old ladies talking in a pub; the latter a sentimental tale of love triumphing over all).

3. *Belles Lettres*   We placed in this category those pieces of writing in which the writer had treated a topic as an invitation to display literary skills, without much personal involvement or serious engagement with public issues. Such writing frequently occurred in the 'examination paper' classes when a teacher set topics from a previous paper, and in classes working from text-books. The mode of writing was often mixed, including passages of anecdote, generalization and description; older teachers would recognize the traditional '0' level essay.

4. *Public issues*   These we subdivided:

(a) *Personal treatment of public issues*   Here the writer, either through choice or following the terms of the set task, dealt with a public topic mainly in terms of its effects on individuals, often himself/herself.

(b) *Impersonal treatment of public issues*   This includes tasks which specify a persuasive or instructional mode, such as: *A speech presenting the facts against smoking* For the most part, however, public topics were open to treatment in either an impersonal or personal manner: *Pop music; 'All young people should learn a language other than their own?' Do you agree?*

5. *Letters*   Letters in general might fall into any category, but all those in our sample were either applications for jobs or complaints about faulty goods or services, so we categorized them separately.

	1. Private/ personal	2. Fictional narrative	3. *Belles Lettres*	4a. Public/ personal	4b. Public/ impersonal	5. Letters
Examination Paper (5 classes)	16	14	30	5	16	18
Coursework Folder (8 classes)	23	50	11	3	10	3
Mixed Mode (4 classes)	34	21	22	11	12	0

Table B: *Pupils' treatment of writing topics in relation to mode of examination (in percentages)*

The analysis of pupils' written work in Table B enables us to compare classes entered for different modes of examination, by examination paper, by folder of coursework, or by a mixed mode combining the two. In interpreting Table B it is useful to keep in mind that the overall amount of writing done by classes preparing for examination papers is considerably less than that done by classes in the other categories. One first notices the high proportion of fictional writing: 50 per cent in the coursework mode. It is less easy to come to conclusions about the relative emphasis on personal and impersonal writing. If we omit Column 4a (public topics but personal treatment) since it is ambiguous, and treat the first two columns as personal and the remaining three as impersonal, we can then say that: 'examination paper' classes' written work divides into 30 per cent personal and 64 per cent impersonal; 'coursework' classes write 73 per cent personal and 24 per cent impersonal pieces — a striking contrast; and 'mixed mode' classes fall between them at 55 per cent personal and 34 per cent impersonal.[5] This is an interesting and unexpected finding in that it predicts a strong relationship between mode of examining and a leaning towards either personal or impersonal writing.

The effect of assessment by coursework

Teachers in England have campaigned for many years to achieve school-based assessment. Were the campaigners those who preferred a personal approach? Or is it that those teachers who have chosen the coursework mode find that the requirements of the coursework folder are most readily satisfied by personal and fictional writing? Ironically, although the campaigners saw school-based assessment as a haven of teacher-autonomy, it has proved for many teachers to be another kind of straitjacket. One teacher felt 'shackled by the syllabus', and another admitted that 'the tendency has been that the assignment has to be over and done with, and move on to the next one'. This was because their work with less able pupils became dominated by the need to persuade them to produce twelve 'assignments' suitable in length and quality for inclusion in a folder. One teacher of a top set, however, helped us to understand the appeal of coursework assessment in a different way. He told us that he disliked the traditional examination paper because it allowed him no contact with what his pupils wrote in the examination room. Assessment by coursework allows teachers to take direct responsibility for what their pupils write, but at the same time makes their work more visible to other teachers. This probably accounts for the elaborate preparation for writing which we have noticed: communicating deep criteria becomes of urgent importance. In sum, the effect of assessment by coursework upon English teaching seems to have been threefold: much more writing is done in class, particularly by less able pupils; teachers take a more direct interest in preparing topics and showing pupils what possibilities there are in writing about them; and the choice of 'private' topics which co-opt pupils' interest has led to a predominance of fiction and what we have called 'personal' treatment.

Individual teachers: the private/personal approach

It is now time to illustrate how the emphases which we have presented in numerical form took shape in the living give-and-take of classroom talk. In selecting an individual teacher to represent a group we unavoidably misrepresent both teacher and group, so the reader is asked to allow for this in reading the section that follows.

In the lesson we have chosen as illustration of a private/personal approach, Mrs Wood of Smalltown was preparing her top set to write about the topic 'Myself'. She began by reading two extracts which exemplified from biographical and fictional works the narration of events from a child s viewpoint; literature often plays an important role in the private/personal approach by setting a tone of reflective self-awareness, or by focusing attention on face-to-face relationships. Then she invited members of the class to tell anecdotes — chosen in advance — from their early childhood: one taken from our fieldnotes can be used as illustration.

> Catherine tells of pulling up flowers thinking they were weeds, getting into trouble so hiding in an old pram for three hours, mother being very angry when she found her.

Mrs Wood responded to Catherine's anecdote with one of her own, and later in the lesson contributed an even more private recollection:

> My mother died when I was very small and I used to snuggle up to my father's back on the sofa . . . I used to sneak into his bed and snuggle up to his back; it stood between me and the world.

Both the subject matter and the style ('snuggle') define a mode of dealing with experience. Mrs Wood, a very experienced and confident teacher, was able to risk intimate anecdotes that might have made her vulnerable to rejection; one remembers Bernstein's suggestion that one implication of what he called 'invisible pedagogy'[6] is to make more of *the pupils'* private lives open to evaluation and influence, which makes it threatening to some young people.[7]

Mrs Wood presents us with a relatively extreme example of personalizing, yet she helps to characterize a view of the world which we have found to be strongly represented in English teaching. Experience centres on personal relationships with family and friends; high value is placed upon self-knowledge and sensitivity to others' perspectives in these relationships. The typical mode of writing derives from late nineteenth and early twentieth century novels and autobiographies with their introspectives concern with protagonists' mental states — how they suffer the world's blows. Experience tends to be decontextualized, or at most located in the family or peer group: when public issues are addressed they are dealt with in terms of the texture of individual experience. It is as if our sole moral responsibility is to those whom we meet face-to-face. The liberal teacher's dilemma of how to cope with controversial and political issues in school is avoided by a concern for private areas of experience. The strategy was incisively characterized by Fred Inglis and by several other writers in an indispensible issue of *English in Education* called 'English and the Social Context':

> Most English teachers, I suppose, teach from a mixture of personal writing, halting talk on tape, improvized drama, and Modern Short Stories, in the interests of a low-key individualism, a deep sense of personal helplessness in a pretty grim world, from which you rescue such meaning as you can from the intimate texture of your private life . . .[8]

He went on to urge that 'cherishing private souls is not enough'; English teaching 'cannot remain pottering in its own backgarden and its private ethic'. English should return to 'the radical tradition', he concluded.

We might now look at Mrs Wood's colleague Mr Austin whose teaching moved some way towards this ideal. He was teaching a bottom set; in a later lesson he was to help them plan a story about an impoverished family, but in this lesson he appeared to be talking about some things that interested him, loosely linking them together by reference to a conversation with a man met in a public house the previous evening. It became clear to the observer that his implicit themes were poverty, and the right of the individual to fight back against the system. In the course of a lengthy narrative-cum-discussion, Mr Austin touched on a remarkable range of topics, including the rock group Steeleye Span, learning Latin, black magic, Airfix models, the names of foreign tanks, the difficulty of getting a rebate on income tax, postal codes and a public swimming bath that was never built. Most of these topics are towards the public end of the continuum, but Mr Austin treated them in a highly personal manner. One underlying theme came through when Mr Austin asked 'How many people tell me what to do?' and made a list on the blackboard. A generalizing analysis was being formed out of the private particularities: being 'forced into a mould' was linked with income tax, postal codes, the numbers on driving licences, and the anonymity of being given a number in the army. It was in part a *tour de force* by a master of talk, yet the pupils joined in with some eagerness. Mr Austin's view of his pupils' world was far from the urban stereotype ('kitchen sink') that we observed some teachers of bottom streams to fall back upon. He actively opposes stereotypes and expects all his pupils to have wide interests; the pupils' enthusiasm shows him to be right. The peroration which concluded this lesson partly sums up this unusual teacher's values. (Here it has to be represented not in Mr Austin's own words but in the cold reduction of our field-notes):

> I like the man in the pub because he was only twenty-one — teachers probably heaved a sigh of relief — but what was he doing? Thinking for himself, following a group no-one had heard, making models, mates probably mocked him but he kept on. Won £20. Looks like a punk rocker and yet sings traditional folk songs. Failure at seventeen, at twenty-one married, looking after wife, saving for baby, interested in all sorts of things. I want to bump into you in the Prince of Wales in six years' time and be as impressed by you.

This remarkable plea to the members of the class to resist the stereotyping that comes from institutional authorities and from the mass media, and to defend their autonomy and self-respect goes further than anything else we have ever met in English lessons. It was a kind of lay sermon, that through its celebration of the individual and its rejection of determinism became the apotheosis of liberal romanticism.

The writing it produced was couched in the domestic fiction of a boy in a poor family kicking against authority. Mr Austin did not demand that his pupils bare their souls in writing; their written work was allowed to remain within the safe limits of fictional stereotypes. By encouraging his pupils to talk freely, however — for example, of what they perceived of as injustice in their own experience — they developed some sense of the interaction of forces in society. The talk of the privations of the fictional family allowed personal anecdotes about the regulations in a local authority home or favouritism in families, but it could also encompass comment on policies about rents and public transport or on sex stereotyping. This heightening of awareness placed the fictional family more firmly in a real world.

The virtue of the fictional and private/personal emphasis is that it can offer to pupils a literary mode — *Cider with Rosie, To Kill a Mockingbird, Joby* — that they can adapt to their own ends, and by accepting these adolescent voices enable their pupils to explore their real or imaginary worlds without the need to adopt a more distant persona. Mrs Brennan — one of the most successful teachers in terms of examination results — taught a top set in a downtown school where the pupils' social backgrounds would not have predicted examination success. A large proportion of the writing done in that class was fictional, and much of it showed admirable sensitivity to people and skill in using words. If Bourdieu's treatment of the knowledge of deep criteria is correct,[9] examination by coursework enables working-class pupils to do themselves justice in fictional and quasi-autobiographical modes of writing when other modes are more inaccessible to them.

Mrs Brennan's colleague, Mrs Williams, however, found that her bottom set was highly resistant to attempts to elicit their private experiences. In one lesson she asked her pupils to suggest occasions when people might be lonely and to provide words to describe each of these 'occasions'. They suggested running away from home, being in hospital, old people without a family and being in gaol, and for each of these Mrs Williams collected words or phrases, writing them on the blackboard. For loneliness 'in gaol', for example, she was offered only single words, 'dark', 'cold' and 'isolated'; the pupils were not willing to commit themselves further. The episodes seemed to function as a way of communicating stereo-typed situations, with words and attitudes to match; the class made it impossible for the discussion to amount to an exploration of personal experience, and the teacher accepted this limitation. This contrasts sharply with Mr Austin's lessons in the other school.

It is a great deal more difficult to illustrate how impersonal kinds of writing were dealt with in lessons, although as Table B shows, this amounted to 64 per cent and 34 per cent of the writing done by 'examination paper' and by 'mixed mode' classes respectively.[10] The difficulty arises partly because much of this writing was done with little or no preparation, and in many cases was written as homework, so that we found that few of the lessons we observed were concerned with impersonal writing. Nevertheless many of the teachers were eager to assert its importance, not only in syllabuses but in conversation. What they referred to, however, was not writing that engages with public issues, but writing with narrowly functional purposes, particularly for less able pupils. One teacher went so far as to suggest that the essay should be replaced by a 'more factual piece of writing where they're asked to communicate a set of instructions, or writing a letter'. Another teacher, Mr Keegan, said:

> I'd like to make the course for those people (less able pupils) more practical, (but) more related to the functional use of language like filling forms, reading telephone directories.

It can be seen from these two remarks that one aspect of this instrumental view of writing is an emphasis on literary skills that can be practised in separation from continuous writing; those departments preparing pupils for examination papers tended to make considerable use of textbooks. This led to the setting of many shorter pieces of writing intended for the practice of particular skills.

In the analysis presented in Table B we separated impersonal writing into three categories: *belles lettres*; impersonal treat-ment of public topics; and letters; and it will be convenient to discuss these in turn. The *belles lettres* category includes those pieces of writing where the writer's intention is to present to the reader a pleasantly entertaining persona without touching upon issues of private urgency or public importance. The model for such writing is middlebrow journalism of a kind more common a generation or more ago, especially in volumes of 'essays'. The genre survives in many English textbooks. Mr Keegan was using a textbook published in 1978,[11] which dealt with writing under a series of headings that included: The Descriptive Paragraph; The Reflective Paragraph; The Imaginative Paragraph; The Introductory Paragraph; The Concluding Paragraph; The Light Humorous Essay; and which provided tasks for writing such paragraphs. The socio-literary values embodied in the approach can be judged from the following sentences which are taken from the paragraph given in the book to exemplify the Descriptive Paragraph:

> This puppy have I called the Lord of Life because I cannot conceive of a more complete embodiment of vitality, curiosity, success and tyranny. Vitality first and foremost. It is incredible that so much pulsating quicksilver . . .

What do pupils make of this verbal posturing? One wrote for another teacher on the topic of 'Fire' (a typical *belles lettres* topic):

> The flames looked like people running after you, shouting death, dressed in falmboyant (sic) clothing. The tips of flames looked like daggers, cutting in to everything. The trees which had been captured by the flames looked like mourners all in black . . .

The girl who wrote this earned high marks; she had admirably picked up some aspects of the manner, and had also learnt that it is possible to manipulate words so as to present oneself elegantly without risking commitment to anything of weight. We might surmise that from the pupil's point of view this offers her partial entry to the manners of an unfamiliar social milieu without threatening any penetration of her private life. *Belles lettres* writing accounted for 30 per cent and 22 per cent of that done in examination paper classes and mixed mode classes respectively.

Public topics suitable for impersonal treatment are undoubtedly set, though Table B shows that they were chosen by a minority of pupils (10-16 per cent of the writing done). Teachers seldom spoke of them, however, and their influence on lessons proved to be strangely oblique. It was noticeable in many lessons — including those, like Mrs Wood's, which were notable for personalizing the topics discussed — that now and again the teacher would adopt a strategy that seemed to be directed to teaching a form of reasoning. We were able to collect and categorize these; the most common forms consisted of: an insistence on pupils giving 'evidence' to support an assertion, and the analysis of a discussion in terms of 'points for and against'. The former probably related primarily to writing about literature, but the latter appeared to exemplify a conception of how to approach impersonal writing. Mr Saxon's strategy is far from typical of what we saw of the teaching of writing to bottom sets, yet he expresses with some clarity a strand occasionally present in English teaching in the fifth year. He said explicitly to his pupils, '. . . I want to teach the principle of having two sides to an argument', and told them to:

> Put a sub-heading 'For and Against the Fifth Year': the columns needn't go more than five lines . . . When we make a point, pop it down either side of the middle line . . .

Later he explained the purpose of this:

> It's a sequence of paragraphs. Each point you make will become a paragraph, because you have a paragraph for each point.

Mr Saxon here seems to take the formal debate as his model of rational discussion. It assumes two opposing sides that can be supported or opposed by arguments which can be conceived of as a sequence of 'points'. It matches perfectly with what English teachers call 'discursive writing', essays in which a detached balancing of points is likely to be valued by an assessor. However, it would be unrealistic to dismiss it as merely the teaching of examination skills. Standing back from one's own thoughts in order to segment them as 'pupils' and to categorize them as 'for' and 'against' is a valuable preliminary to more subtle kinds of analytical thinking, and at the same time acts as a paradigm of liberal rationality, which is free to 'see both sides' of every issue and to engage in cool debate because unthreatened.

Although the third category of impersonal writing was labelled 'letters' it can usefully be taken to represent the instrumental view of English teaching which was noted above in what Mr Keegan and others said about wishing to make English for lower sets more 'practical'. This led, particularly in one school, to the expenditure of a great deal of pupils' time on exercises; our concern in this paper is with continuous writing, however. A surprising amount of letter-writing was done in the classes we observed, rising to 18 per cent in the case of the 'examination paper' groups. (Some of the examinations they were to sit contained an item which sometimes required the writing of a letter). Almost all of these letters were applications for jobs, the exception being an assignment on letters of complaint about faults in goods or services provided. For some reason teachers seemed eager to display to us the lessons in which they taught letter-writing: perhaps they valued the security of transmitting surface rather than deep criteria, though in one interesting lesson a top set pushed an unwilling teacher into some discussion of tone and content. Both teachers and pupils saw this work as relevant to real life; from a different perspective one might relate it to learning how to carry out some aspects of a subordinate role in our economic structure. (In this respect, however, these lessons were a pale and ineffective equivalent of the socializing processes we found in colleges of further education).

We began with the observation that the teaching of content for writing is potentially the teaching of criteria for living, the teaching of values. It remains to assess whether the evidence we have summarized demonstrates that English teachers are transmitting values. Certainly there is nothing to suggest that pupils passively accept the teachers' view of how the world is. It is more exact to say that the various modes of writing offer different opportunities and problems to different pupils, so that each appropriates those modes which can be best exploited, and avoids those which present difficulties. It will be convenient to consider four modes — fiction, *belles lettres*, personal-autobiographical and public-impersonal — in terms of the availability to pupils of appropriate knowledge and a manageable voice or persona. Fiction and *belles lettres*, especially descriptive pieces, are the most available to the largest proportion of pupils. They depend on everyday knowledge, and appropriate personae are easily available, from teenage magazines for example, which do not impinge upon or threaten the writer's self-image. The personal-autobiographical mode is somewhat more threatening. Most English teachers are highly committed to its value: they see personal writing as allowing their pupils to explore their own private worlds and enabling them to take more part in shaping their lives. Personal writing like fiction requires no more than everyday knowledge, but the adoption of an appropriate persona presents problems, which is why so many pupils, particularly from lower streams, do not like writing about themselves. Amongst the young people whom we talked to it was those from professional homes who moved most easily into a persona that allowed them to deal with personal experience without feeling at risk. This is not to ignore the fact that some pupils have good reason to wish to preserve the privacy of their lives, but to note that others are able to engage in successful personal writing without making public any vulnerable areas. Public-impersonal writing on the other hand faces young people with two problems: they may doubt whether they have appropriate knowledge of the topic, and their customary reading is unlikely to provide them with a suitable persona. The minority who read middlebrow Sunday newspapers with the support of family talk about public topics will be provided with both: it is perhaps surprising that as many as a sixth of the boys and girls we interviewed said that they enjoyed writing on topics that enabled them to express their own ideas. (Table B shows that this matches the proportion choosing to write on such topics). The middle-class minority amongst the pupils are thus able to choose and do themselves justice in any of these four modes, whereas the majority are most at ease in writing fiction or descriptive accounts. In the lessons we observed there was little sign of any deliberate attempts to teach pupils to write in the public-impersonal mode.

It will be clear to the reader that in our judgement current approaches to English teaching in the fifth year are too restricted. We want to acknowledge the validity and import-ance of fiction and of personal-autobiographical writing as ways of making sense of experience, while at the same time insisting on the importance of other purposes for language. In the final paragraph we sketch what we have in mind, though in full awareness of the difficulty of carrying out our proposals with those pupils who reject not only school mores but the whole way of life on which they depend.[12] With such pupils a more restricted range of writing may in practice be inevitable, so that the topics and approaches we envisage would have to be rehearsed in speech rather than in writing, since they are convinced that it is talk that matters outside school. We submit, however, that while teaching concentrates on writing we deny young people their rights if we do not attempt to introduce them to wider possibilities.

We suggested earlier that the personalizing approach seems to imply that our sole moral responsibility is to those we meet face-to-face, and that this goes along with a restricted range of topics. English teaching to older pupils should, in our view, expand in four directions: by placing writing in a social context; by grasping controversial issues; by looking for sources of material outside private experience; and by including a wider range of rhetorical functions. English should include attention to the contexts in which particular kinds of writing appear, and how people match what they write to their purposes and audiences. This would include analysis of bias and discussion of ethical issues related to reportage and persuasion, and could be related to simulated writing tasks. Second, there should be no shrinking from controversial public issues: the Third World; weapons, including nuclear ones; the role of the police; relationships between ethnic groups; and the quality of the environment we live in. (Mr Austin provides us with an illustration of one way in which such topics can be approached with lower ability pupils). One of the problems of all schooling is the detachment of what goes on in classrooms from the urgent concerns of the world: this is what justifies the third direction for expansion. Fiction has provided English teaching with both a model of how to write and an implicit definition of acceptable content, and in our view both, for all their strengths, are too narrow. There is much to be said for pupils going out into the world to interview, find documents, record what they observe, in order to engage at first hand in what might be called 'documentary' writing, which presents to a real audience an interpretation of reality that can be documented. This may involve some movement across subject boundaries. Finally, we found too narrow a range of writing from the point of view of rhetorical functions: there was too much narrative and description, not to mention letters of application. Few teachers involve their pupils in writing to persuade, explain, analyse, criticize, plan, or justify; most of the writing done was decontextualized in the sense that one could not conceive of it having been addressed to someone for a purpose other than earning a grade, though a minority of pupils were probably writing for themselves. In sum, English should be giving reality to Friere's dictum that education should be 'the means by which ... men and women deal critically and creatively with reality, and discover how to participate in the transformation of their world'.

4   JOHN DIXON

English Literature — a course in writing

It still comes as a surprise to realise that the standard literature syllabus, while confidently precise about the texts to be 'read', is strangely silent about what is actually assessed: the course in writing, Despite a century of university departments of literature in England, little or nothing has been said about this elementary basis for their work — the discipline of writing in response to literature. What might students as writers need to learn? What new purposes will they be adapting writing to? What range and variety might students and teachers, working together, develop in written response?

Foundations for writing

It's in the senior classes in secondary schools that I take such a writing course to start. But before facing the question of how we set about describing it for, say, sixteen to eighteen-year-olds, let us remind ourselves that *written* response to literature, for all its brilliance, is only the surface show of a mineral vein that must run much deeper. How we talk together in class precedes and guides the writing that comes out, and the way that students and teachers respond to what's written.

In reading literature, there are two main kinds of opportunity for teachers to promote the talk on which writing is built. First, the rehearsal and presentation of literature. A good school makes room for festivals and concerts in which poetry readings, plays and dramatic readings from novels take their place alongside songs and music. And when that happens, it is natural for teachers to work in class in the same way, focusing now not on the product (though that will be enjoyed together), but on the talk that tests alternative readings; explores the implications of phrasing, gesture and intonation; speculates about intentions and the significance of parts in the whole and argues through to the effects to try for. It is that talk which ensures a 'considering attentiveness' to the poet's words, while the acting out is the best way for most people to achieve the 'inner kind of possession' which, as Leavis says, is what we seek in reading literature together.[1]

The second kind of opportunity, especially in senior classes, comes when a talking group learns to explore a poem or a scene. If the teacher can genuinely give a feeling that all's there to be found — that they are open to new expectations from the imaginative richness of the text — there is a chance that a class or group will build an imaginative work together, deepening its felt significance as they share each others' acts of attention, perception and insight. Even here the poem must be 'presented' — read aloud to each other to raise a question, challenge an easy interpretation perhaps, or confirm a new insight, and (as the discussion deepens) simply to promote that kind of contemplation which the miracle of imagination lays us open to. Given this steady presence of the enacted work (if only in a phrase or line), the focus on talk allows for a more reflective awareness in the group of what Knights calls 'movements of sympathy or antipathy, of assent or dissent — in short, of judgement from a personal centre'.[2] We'll come back to this in looking at the writing.

Writing can be seen as a way of internalizing these two kinds of dialogue and carrying them on with oneself. It may be needed as a way of 'getting the poem *by heart*' — of achieving that sense of inner possession. This is the first way, and one of the best in which writing is used in class today. But the very act of writing also offers an opportunity to stand back, to become a spectator of the experience you are enacting, and from that vantage point to realize and articulate more fully those movements of 'sympathy and antipathy' you feel, as human beings act out their lives in your imagination. We shall see both processes — and sometimes the interplay between the two — in the writing that follows.

In order to serve such purposes, writing has to keep the exploratory feeling of dialogue: that is to say, the students need to be used to writing as process, using rough books, doing drafts, reading each other's work, discussing and exchanging ideas, and expecting the teacher's comments to continue the process — not to put a stop to it. Students should also be used to take the initiative in proposing what they write, in discussing the scope, focus and directions they might take, defining their title — and recognizing the pains and revisions this may lead to.

Finally, if they are to write in response to *literature*, they need already to see themselves as writers on a humbler level, to enjoy the attempt to use words for imaginative ends, and increasingly, to recognize and be fascinated by the choices this leads to.

Significant choices

However little we know as yet about a course in written response to literature, it seems likely to begin as often as not with narrative. I say this despite the ironic comments — 'mere narrative' — so frequent in our examiners' reports. Why narrate? Why paraphrase the ineffable? What a sixteen or seventeen-year-old writes is bound to be mere summary, and more clumsy than the original, isn't it?

Let us answer these doubts once and for all. Narrative, as literature itself demonstrates, has a beautifully flexible and rich range. It doesn't rule out philosophic reflection or detailed interpretation of human life; in elementary narratives these may be hinted at in a phrase or a sentence, but the Greek chorus or the nineteenth century novel shows how fully they can be elaborated, too. For any student, a writing course in narrative is full of challenge and opportunity.[3]

But to what purpose? Why re-tell the story? This seems to be the crucial point. 'Paraphrase' to order is a soul-destroying task. The student's narrative has to be impelled by something more personal, a desire to explore, to get oneself into the novel, take over the narration, feel at home with the people — to tell how it is. At the same time, it has to leave room for discoveries, tacit or explicit, in the act of writing: discoveries we are on the alert for as we read what the student has written. They aren't always by any means obvious to the teacher, because many students of sixteen or seventeen are still at very early staging points as narrators. So we may often have to search closely for the moments when the student's imaginative grasp quickens and comes alive. Here is an example from a student still at an early staging point: where can our response as teachers confirm what she is learning, and perhaps take it further in dialogue?

> Paul and Miriam's passion for one another comes to a climax, expecially (sic) during the holiday. The atmosphere is very intense and dramatic. Paul feels very intimate, and is confused over the torture he feels inside.

'The whole of his blood seemed to burst into flames'. Paul fights these passionate outbursts within him, he feels restrained. To me, this signifies the change in their relationship. There seems to be a barrier between them, Paul can't get across to Miriam his agonizing torture. Miriam seems afraid, and deeply moved. She begins to brood and becomes deeply religious. She can't understand him, she ignores Paul's present feelings. Miriam stands there waiting, waiting for Paul to show some religious state. Miriam is troubled, she asks him what's wrong. 'What is it'. But Paul resumes his former state, and Miriam is relieved.

After this incident, Paul feels shame. The first time Paul feels the need for physical contact, Miriam shuns this, and this offends him. The sense of purity prevents Paul from kissing her. Miriam cannot bear physical contact. 'She shrank in her convulsed, coiled torture from the thought of such a thing'. This makes Paul despise himself for thinking such a thing. Paul hates this . . .

When this student began her narrative, earlier in the story, it felt very thin by comparison. She did quote from the text, but her own language didn't seem to catch anything from that contact, and she didn't dwell at all on the experience the words evoked. Here, her language remains simple but catches some of the intensity of the original. 'Passionate outbursts' is a direct response to 'burst into flames', for instance. And the force of 'Paul feels shame' sums up a shift in the relationship, highlighting it.

The second of the two paragraphs follows through with fidelity a sequence of feelings: 'Paul *feels the need* . . . (it) *offends him* . . . *prevents* (him) kissing her . . . makes him *despise himself* . . . Paul *hates* this'. Implicitly, this explains the 'confused torture' of the paragraph before, by enacting it. There is a strong sense of the ebb and flow of his feelings throughout. This is a very important opportunity for imaginative learning. Paul seems caught in a vicious circle of feelings, while Miriam is helpless, cut off from his response: these are perceptions worth taking up, by fellow students and the teacher. They represent a step forward that the writing has made possible and discussion can confirm.

What happens as students develop more powerful narrative possibilities? First, I think they begin to attend more closely to the language of the original and all the purposes it is serving. But also — perhaps surprisingly? — they find more room for asides. You could say that both are a product of greater control *and* awareness of the relationship between language and the thoughts and feelings we are trying to uncover. Here is another younger student, perhaps a step on. What shifts do we notice?

> All dignity is lost, the soldiers are reduced to such a stage of complete exhaustion that they are 'bent double', they see themselves as nothing more than 'old beggars'. The sights and sounds of war are to them so familiar that they do no more than haunt them now. There is a feeling of hopelessness as they begin to 'trudge' towards their 'distant rest'. Marching has become almost an animal instinct to them, they march asleep, they march when they are wounded, they march 'blood-shod'. The rhythm of the lines suggests the slow trudging of the soldiers, cursing through 'sludge' which seems to slow down their pace even more. The soldiers are so 'drunk with fatigue' that they become blind and deaf to the dangers around them, and it seems almost as if the gas shells are taking advantage of this by 'dropping softly' so the soldiers won't hear them.
>
> Suddenly they are woken, an alarm, the rhythm changes, it speeds up, the soldiers are seized by panic they are 'fumbling' to fit 'clumsy helmets just in time', but someone wasn't quick enough and he is left 'yelling out and stumbling, floundering'. The gas is creating 'misty planes' and a 'thick green light' which is compared to a 'green sea' and it is in this sea that the author sees the man drown . . .

This student has added rhythm as an integral effect — a great leap forward in narrating. At the same time, he is fully conscious of the shifts in rhythm and able to comment on them in an aside. He can extend the imaginative effect, sympathetically ('almost as if the gas shells are taking advantage'), and he does struggle with words that are alien to his culture ('flares' and 'panes' — even though this leads to a misreading). Above all, the original language is incorporated naturally and powerfully into his narrative.

Nevertheless, there is an important limitation in the choice he has made. This is a narrative in the present, a choice that lends dramatic immediacy to the events as you struggle to narrate them, and we can see the benefits well enough. But the events we have just enacted are a *memory* in the poem, part of a nightmare past that is afflicting the poet *now* (at the time he writes). We can predict, therefore, that as the student moves on in the poem to the 'present' nightmares, there is going to be an awkward jolt. And there is.[4] But we have grounds for feeling confident that this student writer could well be interested precisely in that problem and the different ways the narrator can cope with it. That is to say, there is a case here, I believe, for teaching something direct about *writing* narrative, and the choices we use for various purposes.[5]

Beyond narrative

Narrative, it seems, offers the writer a way of achieving that sense of inner possession that we feel in a committed 'reading aloud' or presentation. Just as in listening to our students, so when we read we can be alert for signs that the student is alive to the complexity of feeling or thought, and in addition is already beginning to articulate, perhaps, those movements of sympathy and antipathy. At its most subtle, narrative will incorporate both the events and their interpretation. But a young writer needs the chance to explore a number of other simple forms in which reflective commentary has a steady opportunity to emerge without creating structural problems.

I cannot pretend that we know enough about these forms. And perhaps they will always need, like narrative itself, a sense of experiment rather than ready-made moulds. All I can do here is sketch some of the interesting practice John Brown and I came across in a recent investigation prompted by our English 16-19 project.

Perhaps the simplest thing to do is to find some way of inter-weaving the commentary and the text. Younger students often do this unconsciously, for instance in talking about a lyric poem stanza by stanza. Here is an extract of a student following this process with Keith Douglas's poem *Vergissmeinnicht*. What does it leave room for?

> In the fourth stanza, Keith Douglas seems almost to stifle his feelings of sympathy for the german. He tells us that his friends and himself can't quite help feeling happy that this arrogant enemy is humiliated. Then the poet tells us that the german's equipment solid and workable is lying beside him (and) seems almost to mock him by the very fact that it is 'alive' while he, his owner is not. This adds a touch of irony to the stanza and by Keith Douglas informing us that his friends and himself can't help feeling happy at this german's death, it adds a touch of human quality to the poem, as now we can see an almost evil streak in humans. Even though I expect they were a bit ashamed that they were happy at someone else's death, the german was the enemy.

> > 'We see him almost with content,
> > abased, and seeming to have paid
> > and mocked at by his own equipment
> > that's hard and good when he's decayed'.

Keith Douglas then brings home to you that this soldier is really dead. He does this by 'showing' us that flies are moving on his skin, that dust has settled on his eyelids giving them a papery appearance and by using simile he tells us that his stomach has a wide cavernous hole like a cave. Keith Douglas . . . tells us that this man lying dead on the ground has someone to weep for (him) if she could see him as he now was. The degrading way in which this german solider will decay would probably make the girl cry all the more. The use of flies and the fact that dust has settled makes it all the more degrading to me. They suggest hot weather and this again makes it all the more horrid.

> 'But she would weep to see today
> how on his skin the swart flies move;
> the dust upon the paper eye
> and the burst stomach like a cave'.

There is evidence for the teacher that this student is still struggling with language, but to good effect. There is an attentive awareness of the 'poet', who 'seems almost to stifle his feelings' and 'then brings home to you'. There is sympathetic understanding of what he felt ('this arrogant enemy is humiliated') but there is also dissent from it, together with a delicate realization of the possible force of '*almost* with content' — 'although I expect they were a bit ashamed' — giving them the benefit of the doubt, you might say.

It is not easy to bring together how 'he' (the victor) feels, how the girl might feel (he imagines), and how 'I' the reader feel. In much student writing the 'I' doesn't get a look-in. But here the *reader's* sense of the corpse — 'really dead . . . degrading . . . decay . . . horrid' — while still showing signs of a struggle for the right word, does register her revulsion and her unwillingness to acquiesce that a man should become this thing.

I am suggesting, then, that the interwoven form chosen by the student helps her to keep a steady attention to the poet, while finding time also to move towards a 'personal judgement'. Thus, partial (and exact) paraphrase, comments on the poet's intention, and personal movements of sympathy *and* dissent are all given some articulation without the overall structure breaking down.

There is a similar problem when you try to visualise a scene on the stage, following through the lines, and at the same time commenting on the progressive significance. This is how the problem was simplified by another seventeen-year-old.

Movements on stage (Richard II, IV.i.162)	*Reasons for stage directions and interpretations of lines*
. . . Richard stops at stage centre on his way from rear stage left to front stage right, and looks to Bol. for line 162. Richard sighs after receiving no answer and moves slowly to Aumerle at front stage right saying 164 ('I hardly . . . submission'). When Richard arrives at Aumerle's side, Bol. looks to York and after a pause of thought moves to front stage centre.	Richard says 162 questioningly, looking at his oppressors in turn. After '. . . reigned?' there is a pause and silence while he waits in vain for an answer. M. Reese's *The Cease of Majesty* claims 'When Richard is brought in he is by turns theatrical and pathetic'. I disagree that he is pathetic, although I would agree he is theatrical, however I believe the play on the whole to be strikingly theatrical and hence Richard's performance is not over alarming.
After finishing line ending in 'submission' Richard turns sharply and faces Bol. who immediately stops. Richard says 167 'Yet I well . . .' Whilst Richard is saying 167 North. moves slowly towards H. Percy and York, looking at his feet.	167 is said with contempt and a vicious, somewhat disgusted grin crosses Richard's face. Richard's moods and expressions in my opinion change quickly and frequently in this short scene. At times he seems contented and accepts his fate, similarly his mood changes and he becomes very positive of his position as king. I believe he is confused by the abruptness of the swing of power. Northumberland is plainly conscious of his disloyal behaviour and moves for comfort to his fellow oppressors.
Richard looks into space and says 169. Turns sharply and points angrily at Bol. for 170 'So Judas . . .'	'Did they not sometime . . . to me?' Richard asks himself or an imaginary companion a question he knows the answer to. He asks the question sadly but then suddenly becomes angry and turns sharply towards Bol. for 170.
Bol. turns his back on Richard and moves to stage left. At	Bol. shows no emotion at the parallel created between the

same time Bishop of C. moves across to Abbot of West. This means both clergy are on stage rear at right.

present situation and the betrayal of Jesus by Judas. He simply walks away from any connection between religion and the quest for the throne. Both members of the clergy are on the same side of the stage as Richard, symbolizing their alliance with him.

This extract is a healthy reminder to us that in reading lines from a play we are (at best) seeing actions too, realizing their significance moment by moment, generalizing on their significance, possibly accepting or rejecting other people's generalizations as we do so . . . It is a very complex activity to carry forward evenly and to integrate in written form. What we have here is a sensible simplification, satisfactory in its own right, and a valuable basis for discussion. As it happens it is also a useful transition stage towards handling the same issues in continuous prose.

There must be many other ways of interleaving or setting out our annotations in parallel with the text. This is something for students and teacher to explore together. Even to detach the 'comment' from the effective narrative of the play (the left-hand column) is a steady reminder to the student of the value of both sides. It is this kind of helpful, supporting structure that needs open discussion and experimental extension, so that these 'discontinuous' prose forms don't become ossified, as so many essay forms have.[6] The student writer has to maintain a sense of freedom and choice, so that the form is adapted to the particular occasion — a report on improvising and producing a scene, a discussion of how to present a poem, notes for guidance of readers facing a new work, an argument over a producer's interpretation, a comparison with a film version or an account of a personal reading and the stage it has reached.

Unless students know a text extraordinarily well, it is important, too, for the form of writing to leave room for after-thoughts, codas, recapitulations (with extensions) and any other opportunities to revisit the text once more, while it is warmly alive in the imagination.

Progressive articulation
The notion of students revisiting a section of text more than once in the course of their writing may seem rather strange at

first. Too often, it seems, we teachers have had in our minds the model of the published critic who turns after several years' study to a considered statement. On reflection it is very rarely possible or fruitful for students to be encouraged to take up such a stance. This has important implications for what they might be doing as they write.

In the extracts so far the main weight has gone into making the text your own, digesting the experience it offers, finding a committed reading. These mental *actions* imply that we should look at the writing as evidence of process, of gains in understanding, shifts in perspective, movements towards greater (and more faithful) particularity. Such things cannot always be foreseen in the opening paragraph(s). Indeed, the commonest problem for us all in writing about literature that is new to us is to bring the text alive as a start. It is to be expected, then, that the opening of such 'essays' — to recover the original sense — should often show signs of uncertainty or stumbling, rather than confidently prefigure the experience that is to come.

As teachers, then, we learn to read such signs for what they are — an initial struggle to find a way into the text *as experience*. But there are other signs to be looking for as the essay develops well. As the young writers carry themselves more deeply into the experience, what they find to say gains in precision and in its articulate relationship with the original words. It is probably an unconscious acknowledgement of this simple fact that leads so many interesting 'essays' to reformulate and elaborate earlier versions of what they saw in the work. Indeed I have actually come to expect this process when the exploration turns good.

In this short essay I can only suggest what it is like to observe these reformulations.[6] A student writing 'notes' on *A Poison Tree* starts simply by recording that the protagonist 'deliberately nurses his grievance'. He qualifies this briefly after a moment: 'but not with the obvious intention of killing (i.e. it's not to say he went into the situation with that notion in mind'). He goes on with the rest of verse one, before standing back some lines later to agree with Blake that 'there was something humanly compelling about a nurtured and nursed brooding'. Some lines further on, thinking about the apple he adds, almost as an aside, that it is an odd product of 'something as murky and underhand as stored anger'. After thinking more about the man and what he must have been feeling — and his curious detachment — he sees the getting of the apple to grow as an 'obsession', then 'an over-anxious task' and later 'a perverse self-indulgence'.

This process, as you see, is incremental. It starts from a stock phrase, but the student doesn't leave things there. From 'nurse' comes 'nurtured', 'brooding', and 'nursed' again with a fuller context to deepen its force now. 'Stored', 'obsess(ed)', 'over-anxious', 'self-indulgent' follow up two divergent lines from the image of nursing, and the implied judgement is sharpened — from 'murky and underhand' to 'self-indulgent' and, finally, in the last phrase of the notes, 'frighteningly revealing'. It is the movement towards insight and towards a personal judgement of this kind that I am learning to look for.

It is the commentary, I notice, that is being elaborated here. That need not always be the case — think of the possibilities for the *Sons and Lovers* student. And the way elaboration occurs will probably be much less linear than my abstracted phrases have made it appear for *A Poison Tree*. Even here, in spite of the student's articulacy, there is an intriguing movement back and forwards in the 'notes' between this characterization of the action and individual words or phrases that the student wants to probe and digest for himself. The notes are following the mind in action, with a necessary interplay between gaining a sense of inner possession and standing back to reflect on the movements of sympathy and dissent.

Audience and response

What students say — what they reveal and attend to — in writing depends on the reception they anticipate. No point in confessing ignorance, asking questions, puzzling over complex meanings, narrating for yourself, expressing sympathies, discovering new significance, or coming to personal judgements *as you write* if the response is just a mark out of ten, or 'Not bad', or 'Some useful points'. If we have to define a course in writing for the student, we have equally to define a course for ourselves, the teachers, in responding to what's written. What qualities of language, of thought and feeling, may be needed there? Our answers are important simply because their feedback will powerfully influence what comes out in writing anyway.

Finally, among the readers of seventeen to eighteen-year-olds I take it there will be examiners, or moderators of course work. In England, at least, the pre-university examinations have done next to nothing to clarify the kind of writing course they anticipate and hope to reward. The results are very serious. In a sample survey of one of our major boards, an independent panel of thirty teachers and examiners from universities and schools recently found that the majority of scripts offered 'rather thin' or 'very thin and weak' evidence 'of the actual encounter with the text and any appreciation that developed from it'.[7] Yet many of these scripts had been awarded average or well above average grades. One major feedback is obvious: you don't have to appreciate literature to pass the exam.

How can that kind of feedback be transformed and made positive, discriminating and encouraging, for teachers as well as students? One obvious way is already being explored by all the boards involved in the pilot 17 + English exams. Students' writing (from coursework folders or exam papers) is being published together with detailed comments on the positive features and qualities that contributed to the overall achievement in the individual piece, and on the aspects of the 'task' that seem to have assisted the student.[8] What is now needed is a similar series of anthologies of the variety of good practice in English Literature. I earnestly hope that such anthologies will now be produced by teachers and boards throughout England and Wales. If and when they are, a new basis will be laid for the discussion of English Literature as a course in writing. I don't think that will be an easy task. Our joint ignorance is too great. But if that could be accepted, by examiners and teachers, what may now be an annual travesty of literary values could become a harvesting of new ideas for a writing course.

5 NANCY MARTIN

Contexts are more important than we know

Perhaps the contexts for learning are more important than we know. Most people see successful teaching in terms of individual teachers. If they speak of a school as good they usually mean it has a lot of good teachers. Time was when we thought teams of inspectors, or superintendents could go into lessons and assess what was going on as good or less good. In the 1980s this must be regarded as simplistic. Not only have our notions of the nature and role of evaluation changed, but our belief in the independence of teaching and learning from their contexts is changing too. We are now much more aware of all those elements in the school environment which affect teaching, and know that we discount them at our peril. Good teachers are less willing to go on regardless, and are beginning either to move out of the profession, or to abandon the kinds of teaching dictated by their skill and imagination. Lessons are only part of the picture. Evaluators need also to identify those features of the school context which support or inhibit the work that teachers are trying to do. An analysis is needed of the whole environment for learning which a given school provides, and how the various elements in this context affect what goes on in lessons.

In this paper context is taken to mean all that surrounds classroom events including the beliefs and attitudes of the teacher, the way the participants in the lesson see the classroom events, together with those aspects of the school context which impinge on the teacher's intentions: in short, the whole environment for teaching and learning.

No-one in the classroom is neutral
So we have a classroom with a lesson going on, some students, a teacher and a visitor. The visitor may have come to assess the

lesson or just to learn what is going on, but few would now dispute that the observer is part of what he observes. The meanings that each person gives to events relate to his past experience — to the systems of beliefs and attitudes arising from his life history, i.e., we each construe events through our own dark glasses, though, if we grow up within a common culture, many events may look much the same to us. Furthermore, whether the observer has an official assessment to make or not, he or she will be evaluating events for himself — checking what is going on against his or her own experience and trying to see where they lead. He is, in fact, relating local events in, say, an English lesson, to his wider system of beliefs about learning and education. And, of course, this is also true for all the participants in the lesson. Thus, behind the classroom events there is the interaction of all the motivational forces springing from these networks of individual self-systems. And of course, the fact that our notions of objectivity are changing does not mean that an observer's suggestions may not be valuable. We all need listeners, and a good listener can ask questions — real questions — which prompt us to tell the story of what we are doing in a lesson and why. This articulation helps us to uncover behaviour and purposes which we may not have been aware of. Then subsequent suggestions are freed to be acted on.

The different ways in which people perceive the same or similar events are illustrated by the following excerpts from a sample survey of how participants and parents perceived Subject English.[1]

A 12-year-old student said:

> English is to get better at what you already know about the language.

A 13-year-old said:

> English is to make us more interesting people.

Another 13-year-old said:

> You learn about poetry and Shakespeare for the kids in the future. You might not like to learn about them, but the kids in the future might like to.

A 17-year-old said:

> To me English is an art. Nobody can really tell you how to write. We have to go our own way now.

A parent said:

> English is a subject in their school work, isn't it? Or is it the way they are speaking?

Teachers' views showed a similar diversity.

Beyond surface curriculum: personal constructs

The term 'personal construct'[2] has been used to refer to the systems of beliefs and attitudes which underlie behaviour, and are the unseen prompters — perhaps 'determiners' is not too strong a term — of action. And these same 'prompters' are the major influence on each teacher's classroom climate for learning, rather than those surface features of the curriculum — books, resources, programmes etc; they are beliefs about children and how they learn; about authority and the teacher's role in the learning process; about himself, or herself as a person as well as a teacher, and how both roles can be maintained within the structure of the institution which school is. In addition there are the teacher's beliefs about Subject English; his, or her views about what English is; what the terms 'language' and 'literature' represent in classroom events; how children learn to progress in reading, writing and understanding books. These, together with his or her over-riding beliefs about education and his place in it, are likely to be the most powerful elements in the context of the lessons.

Other contextual features affecting lessons: the managerial system

Many elements in school life impinge on what goes on in classrooms. A teacher may or may not be able to carry out the work he wants to do because of what has been called 'the managerial system' of the school.[3] The term refers to those features of school life which are concerned with ongoing arrangements for the continuity and co-ordination of all the diverse activities. It includes such things as time-tabling; allocation of rooms; movements about the building; extent of set programmes; work assessment; departmental allowances and departmental rooms; availability of books; use of the library; out-of-school visits; messages from the school administration, and the way they are transmitted or not transmitted; the availability of staff to be talked to by students; the measure of student responsibility — the list goes on and on, and one begins to perceive its effect on what goes on in classrooms as one enumerates items not always perceived as having anything to do with classroom learning.

It also becomes clear that these managerial aspects of context are partly products of the whole educational system, and partly products of individual schools. The latter would seem to arise from the beliefs and attitudes of the principal and senior staff and must be held to account for a large part of the differences between schools, which after all, operate to a broadly common curriculum and examination system and might, on the face of it, be thought to be very similar places. Yet, if one probes beyond these common, surface features one finds very different things going on in England classrooms, and many different levels of learning occurring. How are these differences to be accounted for? And what is to be learned from understanding them?

I want to suggest that the differences can chiefly be traced to two sources: a teacher's personal constructs, and the extent to which the managerial system in the school allows teaching according to these. The relationship is a complex one; there are so many individual and collective directions to be accommodated, but were the relationship properly understood, its effects on teaching and learning could be less random, and the contextual features could be designed to promote the quality of classroom experience. The difficulty is that we are talking not so much about behaviour as about the springs of behaviour, and we have as yet, few tools of enquiry for arriving at what these really are, and how they change. If a teacher's beliefs and feelings are indeed the prime movers in creating the quality of classroom experience, then these prompters of action and judgment need to be made explicit and open to modification through talk with others. This would carry implications for a focus on mutual communication within a school, and for the responsibility of the managerial system to legislate for it.

Penetrating the quality of classroom experience

The authors of an illuminating study of teachers' understandings of events in their classrooms[4] suggest that we need a paradigm for research which would be as much concerned 'with the quality of experience and the meaning of behaviour as with the occurrence of behaviour' — a shot across the bows at much current educational research — and they suggest a number of strategies 'aimed at eliciting meaning and uncovering various qualities of experience, thought and production'. In the report of their study, and in a subsequent survey of English in government high schools in Western Australia,[5] the following strategies were the chief tools of enquiry; an enquiry which attempted to penetrate beyond surface curriculum, and in the case of the survey, to account for the relation of contextual features to successful and less successful English lessons:

1. Structured in-depth interviews with English teachers willing to explore their work with an interviewer-discussant.
2. The documentation of learning environments, especially lessons, and open discussion with participants of how each perceived the lessons.
3. Analysis of work products.
4. Documentation of how students, parents and teachers perceived the teaching and learning of English.

Space will not allow a full account of what these studies threw up. They are fully described and discussed in the two reports referred to above.

The in-depth interview

The in-depth, structured interview *together with* observation and discussion of particular lessons proved the most effective way of drawing out the beliefs which seemed to underlie the classroom behaviours which the teachers valued most. Yet interviews have special problems, one of which is what status to give the statements made. Even an open and relaxed interview carries its own context, and there is inevitably a gap between the statements and the events observed in the classroom. People say what they intend, or hope should happen, aspiration being a vital aspect of teaching. But the social context of the interview works to cause them to say what they think may be socially or educationally acceptable.

In order to neutralize the social context of the interview we began by asking what teachers had done in a recent lesson that they would like to describe. Given this option, most teachers moved into what was near to their hearts, and almost all then qualified their accounts with reasons. Thus the gap between stated intentions and classroom events was narrowed by locating the statements in the context of actual lessons. The questions about recent classroom events were followed by others of a practical kind derived from issues in the educational scene — the effect of class size, use of groups, arrangements of desks, mixed ability classes, the place of literature, the value of exercises, for example. Discussion of these matters — always in the context of their own lessons — led in turn to a consideration of features in the life of their own schools which impinged, negatively or positively, on the aspects of their work they valued most. If the teachers failed to qualify the stories of their lessons by some reference to general ideas, it was easy for the interviewer to probe for these. What emerged from these interviews of one to one-and-a-half hours was a tissue of practicalities embedded in their contexts of the teachers' educational beliefs.

We thought these interviews yielded two different kinds of information. On the one hand there was the picture of the scope of ongoing activities and of the nature of the students' encounters with books, drama, projects, exercises etc., where at one extreme teachers kept close to provided resources, and at the other tried to develop their own materials and use them in many different ways: On the other hand, there were the organizing ideas or learning priorities which, we thought, lay behind these variations in classroom practice. A study of these interview-discussions enabled us to see that some teachers put more emphasis on what might be called cognitive aspects of the work, and others on personal and social development. Overall, some priorities reflected broad developmental concerns and others rather narrow, conventional ones. What seemed to distinguish the various learning priorities was their measure of comprehensiveness. For instance, some teachers were content if they themselves could distinguish students' progress in language skills, while others were also concerned that students should be aware of the purposes of their work, should reflect on their learning and should inject their own intentions into the classroom activity.

Other tools of enquiry
We looked at our analyses of these interview-discussions alongside transcripts of our interviews with students who had participated in the lessons, and found the variations in the ways students perceived their classroom activities seemed to correspond to the learning priorities of the teachers. For instance, students in some classes took part in what was going on for better or for worse; they liked some things and disliked others, and judged what they did primarily by this criterion. Other students in different classes reflected on their learning

experiences in a much broader way. Apart from individual rebels and thinkers, an understanding of the educational directions of their work was mostly present among students taught by teachers with comprehensive learning priorities. Compare, for instance, familiar comments by students about which parts of English are boring or interesting with the following conversation between three 12-year-old students and an interviewer in a school where the English staff discuss their work a great deal amongst themselves and with their students:

Bevan: I find it easier to talk on, write and explain things that I know about and have experienced and have heard about or read than something you are making up out of your own mind and you don't know anything about.

Interviewer: If we've each only done a certain number of things, where would the new things come from?

David: I think it's when you read books you find out things ... different things ... Well, visiting different places, speaking to different people, you find out different things.

Interviewer: Are you thinking about excursions — or drama?

David: Yeah, it makes you aware that you've got to ... It's not always things in the classroom ... We do a lot of work and then Mrs S. knows when we are getting worn out and takes us outside — for drama like that — for a couple of days.

Peter: That's more or less Mrs S. She is trying to teach us ... This is how I think that English is more ... of a way of life. That it's not just bookwork and studying a lot.

Here we have not only the children's perceptions about English lessons, but their awareness of their teacher's purposes for them.

Our third source of enquiry, the observation of lessons and the subsequent discussion of what we had observed, reinforced what we had derived from the interviews, and also revealed the pressures from the managerial system. The three sets of data gave us some evidence for our hypotheses about the underlying forces in the classroom, and the effects of external arrangements upon these. Outstanding in what emerged from our interviews was the teachers' desire for freedom to teach as they thought best, and different teachers identified different features in the context of the school as preventing or assisting their work. It seemed that those with the most comprehensive learning priorities suffered most. For example, prescribed programmes of set texts, chapter by chapter, linked to weekly assessments, made long assignments, *ad hoc* events, drama and projects very difficult, if not impossible. Again, while constraints on moving out of classrooms were happily accepted by some, for others they represented a very real conflict with their educational beliefs. One teacher said:

> The chief constraint is the classroom. We've had public edicts here about taking classes outside the classroom, which is a constraint on me. The desks are in rows; there's nothing on the walls: they're remarkably sterile . . . If I had my way, what I would like to do is take forty students on a world tour for two years! I took forty-odd away in the holidays and we learnt an awful amount. That's what I saw as education.

An extreme case perhaps, but it well illustrates the nature of the conflict.

From another school an experienced teacher said:

> As an English teacher I value most the freedom of choice. Definitely I want freedom of choice of material and the way I would like to use it and the areas I would like to cover. I would not like to have, as we did in the past, one period of this, one period of grammar, one of written expression, one of comprehension . . . Even my poems and stories were chosen for me. I hated that.

How can such freedoms for the diverse learning priorities of teachers and students — and increasingly of parents — be reconciled with the managerial systems of a big institution? It was clear from our survey, that in most schools, teachers and students played little part in the framing of the external features of school life, so it was not surprising that the teachers in the survey saw the educational philosophy of the principal as a major element in the context affecting their work. A teacher in a small country high school said about the principal:

> It seems easier to leave school and take trips to expand the students' background mainly because the principal is so very co-operative . . . He encourages anything we want to try.

The principal himself said:

> I enjoy finding out what teachers are doing and I enjoy working to make the climate in the school beneficial to everybody. I want my

teachers to enjoy teaching; I want my students to enjoy learning and therefore I'll do everything I can to help that.

In a different school two comments by the same teacher point a contrast. She said:

Yes, we are told here what course we must cover, and we are told, in quite some detail, what sections of grammar, what sections of literature, whatever, we must do. We are told what topics we must cover each term, and we are told how the term's marking system will be organized in great detail.

and:

I don't think I've ever had any writing worth a pinch of salt on anything that's my subject and not the students' . . . I am finding it very hard to get them to value their experiences.

Clearly, school administrations and teachers in classrooms have to compromise. It would seem worthwhile to attempt to go beyond the surface of expediency and uncover the nature of the conflicting demands. Then it should be possible for administrators to plan the the managerial systems of schools to support rather than constrain the teachers in their purposes.

The nature of the conflicting demands: multiplicity of intentions

Each of us teaches, or learns, against a background of intentions, our own and other people's. These are often unrecognized and inexplicit. Teachers are sometimes called boring, and students apathetic; their various intentions have not matched. Take also the fact that teachers of the same subject have diverse personal constructs about it and about education — as do their pupils — and one can begin to see how a multiplicity of intentions is behind the differences in classroom events and classroom climates. Almost no-one gets a clear run. The intentionality of school administrations is more difficult to assess. Broadly, they seem to belong to tradition, expediency and the educational philosophy of the principal and senior staff. Add to these the demands arising from the intentions of parents, and of the generally non-educational purposes of the media, and it is easy to see how school administrations get caught in the crossfire.

Nevertheless it is now becoming clear that the pursuit of individual intentions is a major element in learning — and in teaching. The problem is to find ways of making more of the varying intentions match, or at least accommodate, each other. It is probably true to say that student intentions play little part in most classrooms, except in as far as some students make the teacher's purposes their own; similarly, most staff other than department heads have little influence on organizational features which profoundly affect their work. Yet, the managerial system is the means by which the accommodation of diverse intentions could be deliberately planned for, could be built into the institutional framework. There are attempts to do this here and there, but largely, the power of intentionality in its widest sense is neither understood nor catered for. The most that most teachers can do at present is to get round the obstructing features in their environments as best they can. Some of their attempts are illustrated in the following examples which show both the strength of shared learning priorities, and the frustrating effects of certain features in the contexts. The final example describes briefly a school whose structure was designed to provide scope for many intentions.

Some resolutions

The principal of a country high school believed that a school should be an active community institution. He set about creating a community school by extending operations beyond the usual age levels and by involving members of the community in as many aspects of school life as possible. He well understood that institutional features would have to be created to do this. Among these was a school council with standing committees for education, finance, grounds and buildings, canteen, agriculture etc. There was student and community representation, and the school buildings and resources were available from early morning to late at night. There were many other innovative features, so the school was, as far as it went, an example of a deliberate attempt to create a managerial system which would assist in all sorts of ways the policy of community involvement in the school. It was curious, therefore, to find no set of corresponding features designed to enable the large staff to understand the innovations, and to discuss their individual work as part of the broad picture. Department heads and staff engaging in special operations such as Work Experience knew what was afoot, but most staff did not. Meetings were few and never for discussion. The existence of two small staff rooms which had to serve all purposes of a large staff in effect divided teachers into opposing camps; there were no features in the school context which would provide for discussion and resolution of the hostilities. Let us see how the intentions of some of the staff and students fared in this school.

As part of the community school approach parents were invited to join senior classes to prepare, alongside school students, for qualifying tertiary examinations. The scheme was negotiated in discussion with all parties. The following brief excerpts from interviews with the teachers, the parent-students and the school students seem to show that the intentions of all concerned were known to all and mutually pursued:

Interviewer: (to teachers) Will you tell me something about how the mature students fit into your classes?

Teacher 1: I find they fit remarkably well. You will see when you come into the class. They're not considered by the others as anything different.

Teacher 2: And I think it helps them with their own kids. It's amazing the insight one of mine now has just by sitting back and listening to her own boy joining in.

Interviewer: Do you think, perhaps, a case could be made for this happening more generally?

Teacher 3: I would be all in favour of it . . . It makes me myself look much more closely at my behaviour and my teaching. It opens my eyes. They can see through me far more easily than young students can . . .

Interviewer: (to mature students) Do you think your presence has had any noticeable effect on the class?

Parent 1: Well, I think so, because we are quite enthusiastic, and I think that helps, you know.

Parent 2: You feel nervous the first couple of times but after a while . . . Everybody is here to learn, and that's the thing about coming to class.

Interviewer: (to school students) Does having mature students in your class make any difference?

James: I see a maturing influence actually. With the mature students in there it seems to keep down a lot of the school romantics. I think we'd probably be a bit rougher and wilder if it wasn't for the mature students.

Roy: They know exactly what they're after — they know what they want to do.

James: I enjoy talking to these people on not necessarily school-related subjects, but it's still quite an education just taking to people. We're rejuvenating them and they are maturing us.

These lessons seemed very successful. Work was serious and enjoyed, and examinations were passed. We noted the following features of the context:

1. Students and teachers worked within the expectations that belong to established examination classes which provided overt purposes.
2. There had been full discussions with staff, students and parents before the scheme began and in student and parent councils.
3. The teachers were a small group of experienced staff who were accustomed to discussing and planning their work together; moreover they — observably — agreed about their subject and how to teach it.
4. Discussion of course content and of educational issues was a feature of the classes; both kinds of student trusted their teachers; the teachers felt free to pursue their own particular interests and styles of teaching within the limits of the examination syllabus.

In effect, these classes and their teachers constituted a well-defined sub-group within the school with specific contexts which supported the intentions of all the participants. The contexts for other English lessons were very different. For instance, a young English teacher working with younger classes in this same school said:

What I really miss in this school which we had in my other school was all the staff got together in lots of staff meetings . . . Anybody who had anything they wanted to air could bring it up and it was thrashed out . . . and everything that was going to be innovated the headmaster brought up in front of us and we could argue about it . . . but here I just get the feeling that I am a sort of teacher who teaches, and things get passed down to me, and that's it.

What began to emerge from this case study, and others, was, first, the frustration of teachers working in relative isolation, and second, the ways in which teachers created sub-groups in schools where they felt the environment was hostile or indifferent to their educational aims. We found Science departments particularly tended to form coherent sub-groups and seemed able to pursue their intentions almost as if they were independent kingdoms. It seemed that it was the existence of the labs as the centre of their work that gave them their strength. Labs are a physical centre where the work is located, where teachers have their resources, and where they can exchange ideas, plan, and even relax. We observed that Science teachers tended to work in independent groups, and that there was little attempt by school authorities to extrapolate the advantages of Science departments into other parts of the school.

Given this lead we looked at English in a school where there was an English staff room and time set aside for meetings, and compared what went on there with the school described above where there was no English staff room — only two small general staff rooms.

In the first case the English staff room had become a centre for work in English for teachers and students. Meetings took place there; plans were made and exchanged; conversations took place between lessons; ideas were discussed, both specific to English and more general, and students came for consultations and joint meetings. Thus the level of understanding of mutual intentions was high.

In the other school with only two small general staff rooms, and where classes were peripatetic and there was no centre for English, the English department was split down the middle according to divergent views about the subject. Protagonists frequented different staff rooms, and their differing educational aims resulted in two syllabuses for English with two different sets of text books. Time and a place to meet were not among the arrangements from the school administration because they were not perceived as affecting teaching in any significant way. It seemed unlikely that the situation would be improved without some deliberate channel for communication being created.

We found the schools bewildering in the ways in which items in the context of lessons affected what the teachers wanted to do. Senior staff, on the whole, managed to get what they wanted; younger staff suffered most from what happened to be the random origins of the managerial systems; but one school, from its inception, set out to take account of intentionality at the level of the whole school. In the first instance this meant the creation of flexible school structures designed to allow teachers to work according to their lights, and secondly to provide for communication between them. Specific concepts of flexible use of space and time and of people determined the physical and psychological features of this school environment for learning. About people the principal said:

I mentioned about the use of space and time. The third part of the triangle is people ... I'm convinced that typically, in a hierarchical, authoritarian structure, good staff members work only at a percentage of their potential — about 70 per cent to 80 per cent perhaps. I feel the environment we have managed to develop here where they're released professionally (as you know we share decision making and that kind of thing) — in this kind of environment they explode into action.

'Explode into action' — a powerful image expressing the principal's belief in the power of intentions in learning and teaching. The corollary of this view was a recognition of the need for opportunities for staff and students to communicate with each other. This meant time, and places to meet and talk. Both were provided. Every department had a small seminar room close to its teaching area. Lessons were timetabled with large blocks of time which department heads could juggle with to suit teaching, meetings or private study. Through their respective councils students and parents could enter the dialogue.

Thus, in this school, the managerial system was designed to be the means through which many different intentions might be realized. Channels were created through which things could be discussed, and, by agreement, modified. The contexts of work in classrooms were recognized as influential and were designed for support. The central notion of flexibility was an attempt to realize in the structure of an institution the widest scope for the multiplicity of intentions of its members.

It would be a pity if this consideration of some of the contexts of English lessons, and, more generally of learning and teaching in school were to be interpreted as of more importance than the imagination and skill of teaching. Enough focus has been given in this paper to the beliefs and attitudes of teachers to suggest that these are the most powerful of all the features in the context of learning; but in school, as in nature, human beings have a habitat which may be favourable or unfavourable, and can affect what goes on in lessons more than we have, perhaps, realized. Given knowledge of what items in the context most affect what teachers want to do in classrooms, we should be able to develop school structures which support teachers instead of inhibiting them.

6 MARGARET GILL

Three teachers: defining English in the classroom

When English teachers write about teaching English they often seem to move a long way from the classroom:

> English teaching is a question of drawing out from each child his own voice, his own dynamic engagement with the world, and his existential search for his own sense of identity and his life-role.
>
> Holbrook, 1977[1]
>
> The English teacher is now committed to both liberating and refining the child's powers of thinking, feeling, imagining, perceiving, sensing, relating, through the medium of words and gesture.
>
> Abbs, 1972[2]
>
> To learn English is a way of becoming humanized. On the one hand it is a way of finding out about one's commonality with others ... On the other hand it is a way of discovering one's own uniqueness, by trying out one's identity, by exploring one's own nature.
>
> National Association for the Teaching of English,
> United Kingdom, 1973[3]

The level of abstraction in such descriptions of English makes them hard to disagree with. At the same time such generalized definitions do not tell the outsider what English teachers actually 'do', nor do they throw light on the choices English teachers make: why they teach the different 'Englishes' they teach.

In this article I want to try and look closely at three different 'Englishes' as illustrated by the courses of three experienced English teachers. I want to find some answers to the questions: How do English teachers construct their definitions of English? What influences lead them to adopt new curriculum ideas or change their teaching practice, to define English one way, rather than another.[4]

The three teachers whose courses are described all hold certain views and experiences in common. All teach senior English. All have found reasons to be dissatisfied with past syllabuses and have devised new courses to meet the needs (as they perceived them) of the students they teach. Yet each response is different.

Mike teaches English to groups of apprentices in a technical (or further education) college. He calls his course Communications, and integrates much of the syllabus with the work his students are doing in their 'trade' subjects. Anne, with other members of her English department, designed a core English syllabus for all the sixth formers at the large private girls' school where she is head of department. It is a 'language awareness' course and is compulsory because, she says, 'all pupils need the opportunity to become familiar with other ways in which language may be used (beyond the literary): to observe, record, speculate, judge, generalize, reason, to marshall, summarize, organize ideas in the interests of clarity and precision'. Tom's Year 12 pupils have stayed on at their inner urban high (or comprehensive) school, because, in their view, the alternative to school was the dole. Tom is preparing them for an external English Literature examination, and, in his spare time, is a member of a working group designing a new English Literature syllabus which he hopes the examination board will accredit. He feels the present English Literature course is 'too narrow': 'We wanted a combination of prose, poetry and drama so that we could give the kids a much wider impression of what English Literature was all about'.

Three English courses: each different from the other; all recognizably 'English'.

Teaching 'vocational' English

Mike, like Anne and Tom, qualified as a secondary English teacher with a university arts degree and a one-year postgraduate teacher training course. He began his teaching career in an 'ordinary' high school and did not like it.

> It seemed to me that English existed as something that was on the timetable, and you went along and there was a set book, *The Art of English*, and it was expected that you would go through the exercises in that book with a class. And that on another day you would do a piece of literature. And if you had *Pride and Prejudice* with the Third Year Remedials — who were really not up to it — it was a waste of time . . .

> Nobody clearly stated what the aim of the whole thing was . . .
> so I was just told 'Well, start on Monday, and this is what we do
> with this class. Just follow on. This is what we do with the second
> class'. And so on. And I found it very limiting indeed.

Mike chose to solve the problem by moving into the technical
education system. It would not be every teacher's choice. In a
highly instrumental technical school curriculum, the value of
non-vocational subjects such as English is not immediately self-
evident to the clients. Indeed many of the students will have
chosen a technical school precisely because their earlier
encounters with subjects like English have been unfavourable
or unsuccessful: 'So many of them come to us with a history of
failure'. Even the value of basic literacy skills may not be
apparent: they judge English to be their least relevant subject.
They say 'I'm going to be a panel beater. What's English got to
do with that?'

It is often for these settings that the most reductive and arid
'basic skills' English courses are devised. One general syllabus
which Mike inherited included prescriptions such as the
following:

Unit (e) Libraries and Information Retrieval
At the end of the unit the student should be able to:
1. demonstrate a knowledge of such information retrieval systems
as indexes, abstracts and library catalogues;
2. perform an exercise in collecting information and collating it
into logical form;
3. appreciate the possibilities of using other informal retrieval
systems as interviews and questionnaires;
4. demonstrate that he has established the habit of presenting
information thus retrieved in oral as well as in the written form.

The view of English suggested by such tightly prescribed
activities or 'behaviours' is a utilitarian one, light years away
from the humanistic values of Holbrook or Abbs. The 'content'
of the syllabus appears as a set of decontextualized communication skills expressed in the voice of Benjamin Bloom. It looks
even more limiting than the high school English Mike left
behind. In practice he does not find that to be so. For him the
lists of 'skills' are viewed as guidelines, and he has complete
freedom in deciding how to translate them into a course of
study. With his photography apprentices, for example, Mike
used Unit (e) as the basis for a term assignment which

integrated work in English with the students' vocational interests:

> Your task is to choose a particular aspect of the city environment, to carry out research upon it, and to produce a report of your findings in the form of a display for an exhibition or conference, or an illustrated article for publication in a magazine.

The students were invited to choose from a list of topics, such as housing, shopping centres and entertainment facilities. A public audience (consisting of students, staff, parents, local employers, industrial training officers) was to be invited to a presentation of the completed assignments, and Mike saw his role as that of advisor, offering help on how to go about the business of collecting information; helping groups of students sort out and select material; and advising on presentation problems related to the production of the final reports. Lessons appeared to be haphazard affairs with students disappearing for an afternoon's interviewing, photographing or library research, and reappearing to talk over their activities and plan their next task.

Sometimes Mike would intervene with systematic guidance in particular areas such as information gathering or report writing. He prepared the following flow-chart because, he said, 'I felt I should be able to present information to the students as systematically and graphically as we expected them to':

But he did not see himself as teaching a set of isolated skills:

> I see Communications as being, really, a set of interrelated skills which the student would need at college and in his working life . . . and thus as a member of society. In other words communication skills would enable him to function on all those levels.

In interviewing the students it was clear that they too, while concentrating on the short-term task of producing an assignment, were aware that they were using skills that had wider applications in their personal lives. One group of three boys prepared a tape-slide sequence on urban housing. The finished product was an impressive presentation consisting of 130 slides showing contrasting housing areas, accompanied by a linking commentary, interspersed with interview material and carefully-chosen background music ('We used a sonata by Beethoven for some of the posh scenes').

The students' progress was interesting to watch. For the first

Make sure you *understand* your brief (your task) Your *aims* should be clear Terms of reference	**Check objectives with project supervisor**
Consider all possible sources of information	**Libraries Technical, commercial, reference books, journals, reports, maps, charts, films**
Experts in the field of your enquiry	**Personal investigation**

Gathering information.   Library research, letters, interviews, discussion, on-site fact-finding

Evaluate the material you have gathered	**Reject irrelevant material**
Arrange remaining material into main categories. Use logical sequence. Layout	**Most important points**
Subsidiary points	**Notes Appendices**

Write the report. Present the information in an orderly fashion. Use paragraphs. Construct sentences to make meaning clear. Use clear, accurate English. Explain any technical terms you use.

Illustrate with photographs, drawings, graphs, charts, tables etc.

Make your conclusions. Make recommendations (if specified in your brief)

1   2   3   4   5   6

Table A: Undertaking a research exercise and preparing a report

four weeks they devised questionnaires and conducted interviews with varying degrees of success. Their account:

> First of all we were very, almost, frightened at the idea of knocking
> at people's door and then asking questions. We didn't know
> people's reactions. But sooner or later you — you get used to it.
> You know what people are gonna say ... I mean, if someone
> opened the door there was three people there: a bloke with a
> camera, a bloke with a — with a microphone stuck up, almost up
> their noses, and a massive great tape recorder, and a guy with a
> clip-board babbling away, then, obviously, they're not gonna
> answer anything. They're just gonna shut the door and run off. So
> it's a matter of being very careful, and assessing the situation
> immediately they open the door.
>
> Interviewing is just a matter of ... progressive assessment of
> people's reaction to questions and the situation — and to situa-
> tions. That's what it is. You learn to assess a situation in terms of
> communication, that's what you learn from interviewing. You
> learn that what you're getting from the person has got to be
> moulded into an end result. Interviewing isn't a chit-chatty thing;
> it's a formal way of extracting information.

In the course of the assignment the students have extended
their understanding (and grasp) of interviewing beyond the
mastery of its social demands, to a recognition of its function as
discourse, 'a formal way of extracting information' for a
particular purpose. This is a vastly more complex 'skill' than
the stark requirement of Unit (e): to 'appreciate the possibilities of using other information retrieval systems as interviews
and questionnaires'.

Similarly, Unit (e) 'perform an exercise in collecting information and collating it into logical form' is transformed in the
students' account of the process:

> We got all the information together in the bottom room of my
> house. We put it all on the floor all over the place, and sorted it
> out into Council information and tenant information. We got all
> this information together and made notes on that information —
> each of us — David did Leake Street. I did Quarry Hill — and so
> on.
>
> Then we put all those notes together, and we had them — sort
> of — almost like a filing system — it was the only way of doing it.
> Then we wrote out a sort of 'score' system [i.e., for the musical
> background] and we got it into an order, and we kept up that
> order all the way through. We got all the information, edited it all
> down and got it together. Then I spoke it into the tape recorder,
> and we put in the commentary from the interviews ...

Implicit in this narrative is the practice of a variety of inter-related language skills, ranging from the cognitive skills associated with the sorting and categorizing of data, to the necessary social skills involved in co-operating and reaching agreed conclusions. In fact, when the group was asked the general question what had they 'learnt' from the assignment, they included an unprompted account of 'learning to work together':

> Obviously we didn't agree on everything. I mean, it wasn't all plain sailing . . . If the three of you don't get on, then you've had it. You just can't do it. It simply doesn't work. You just spend your time arguing. Simon got shouted down a few times, incidentally.
>
> We learnt that you have to listen to someone else. You can't — kind of — go battling on with your own ideas, and not listening to anyone else's ideas . . . If you start going off into bits — and trying to enforce your own ideas on to the other partners, then you just finish up spending half your time arguing, and it just doesn't work. You've got to keep in a team situation.

It is the students' commitment to their task which encourages them to draw on broader social skills, as well as on the technical skills which appear so narrow in the written syllabus. Looking again at the technical skills it is now possible to see that they make more subtle and complex demands on the student's language abilities than might at first appear. For example, Unit (e) 'presenting information' is contextualized in the students' decision to present their tape-slide production to a particular audience.

Once the question of an audience is taken into considera-tion, the process of 'presenting information' becomes much more complex. The material now has to be appropriately adapted in content and style to take account of the knowledge, experience, purposes and expectations of the particular audience intended. The boys' reply to the question 'Who did you envisage as your audience?' reveals these multiple dimensions:

> It [the tape-slide production] was produced for someone who didn't really know much about housing, but wanted to know more. We wanted it so that if someone went into the room where the tape-slide sequence was being shown, they weren't forced to listen to anything. They could wander round and listen to what-ever they wanted. When they'd had enough they could get out. Because there's nothing worse than boring someone. If you bore

someone they never — they don't — retain the information you've given them anyway.

So we started off with a basic tape-slide sequence . . . This tape-slide sequence was geared to people who didn't know much about council-housing, were interested in knowing something about it, but didn't want to know too much.

The sense of audience is indeed finely tuned, blurring the boundaries between 'personal' and 'vocational' language uses, and raising the question whether such a distinction is even useful. The students' final summing up presents a graphic picture of a complex learning process in which direct experiences have been documented, evaluated and interpreted, and new knowledge has been mastered and communicated to new audiences with resourcefulness and confidence.

But when you start getting going you get interested in it, and you keep on going. It's starting which is difficult. When you go into a room and it's just a — the floor's completely covered with bits of paper, and there's empty cassettes and tape recorders all over the place, and everything. It's not — you know — it's a *daunting* thought. But once you get moving you're all right. As it starts to shape, it becomes really interesting. It becomes great fun. We smoke a lot, and we get very up-tight at certain times. But it's good fun. The whole thing. The most important project we did.

It is a far cry from the exercise of isolated language skills.

Mike is pleased with the way this course has developed. He believes it suits his particular groups of students, and that, in their crowded timetable, it represents the best use of their time. What about literature? His reply is practical and personal. It reveals how, in his case, past experience combines with a present teaching context to confirm a curriculum choice about what he will 'leave out':

I've got to decide what I can do with my time to most effect . . . I do talk to them about books as well. Sometimes at the beginning of a lesson for a quarter of an hour I might take in a book and read them an extract. Or just talk about a book, or a film, or an exhibition. And out of their own interest they might follow it up. But I certainly don't have the time to try to develop a love of literature. A true appreciation of literature depends on the private reading habit, and I'm not sure I could teach that . . . I could teach them facts about the characters, the language, the author. But I would be very doubtful whether they would come out of it having a greater understanding of English Literature . . .

I remember when I did English Literature I was bored stiff, and it was only when I got to the university and started reading on my own account that I began to enjoy it. I went through a period when I didn't go to a lecture, I just read on my own. If I was a student I suppose I was a very bad one, because I was the one who wasn't there . . .

A picture begins to emerge of one teacher's view of what teaching English is about. Mike's operational definition of English is shaped by his personal history, his view of his students and how he conceives his responsibility towards them. It is further modified by the ethos of the institution in which he has chosen to teach, and by his interpretations of the conflicting educational values and pressures which community and society exert.

Teaching a language awareness course

Anne's definition of English is shaped by similar influences, but the picture that emerges is quite different. For Anne's sixth formers at a private girls' school, the 'private reading habit' presents few problems. All students are pursuing academic Year 12 courses and over three-quarters of them will go on to university or other tertiary institutions.

English is not a compulsory subject at Year 12. However, Anne and a group of staff have designed a school-based English course which is taught in mixed-ability, cross-discipline groups to all Year 12 students. It does not replace English Literature but exists alongside it. Anne's justification is interesting:

I was longing, really, to get people [her staff] to want a bigger spectrum of language use for their students. It seemed to me that this is what we could do with great advantage for all our sixth form students.

Anne's implicit aims appear to be congruent with the 'language for life' recommendations of the Bullock Report:[5] 'In the course of the child's life in school there should be a gradual and growing extension of his powers of language to meet new demands and new situations'. This is equally what Mike is encouraging, and in his hands, as we have seen, a narrowly job-related activity becomes a rich learning experience. But Anne is not bound by job constraints. In the context of a private grammar school, 'vocational English' can have a different meaning. For the predominantly middle-class clientele, academic achievement is one of the main goals of the school, and schooling is described in terms of 'giving the children a broad education', a phrase much used by the principal. (The students' views were more pedestrian: they were unanimous that the chief goal was 'passing the exams').

Thus when Anne talks about wanting 'a bigger spectrum of language use' for her students, the scope of her choice is greater than Mike's. In the uncomfortable language of Bourdieu and Passeron[6] this is so because of the greater 'linguistic and cultural capital' her students possess; capital which schooling and examinations are designed to endorse, and society rewards.[7]

The scope is apparent in the working paper Anne drafted, based on her staff's responses to the question 'What are the language needs of our pupils?'

> All pupils need encouragement to use language for a variety of purposes — both emotional and intellectual. For example, many students at this age are still thinking out their careers, and need to assess themselves in a fairly searching way. The opportunity to talk and write about themselves can be an essential clarifying activity.
>
> All pupils need the opportunity to become familiar with other ways in which language may be used (beyond the literary): to observe, record, speculate, judge, generalize, reason, to marshall, summarize, organize ideas in the interests of clarity and precision . . .
>
> Many students regret the termination of English studies after the fifth form and welcome the chance to continue with reading and writing which they have enjoyed. Often they lack opportunities (both oral and written) for extended expression . . .

This document provided the blueprint for the syllabus. Initially it proved difficult to decide what content to choose. The staff began with firm ideas about what the course should *not* be: it should not be a watered-down version of a literature course; it should not be a language course 'in the old restricted sense'; it should not be General Studies. The final course was designed as three term units, each taught by one teacher and repeated each term to a different group of students.[8]

Unit 1. Language and the Development of the Individual
   a. early language development of the child
   b. development through adolescence
   c. the individual in communication with his (sic) world

Unit 2. Language and the Techniques of Communication
    a. barriers to communication: emotional, educational, cultural, political
    b. communication in commerce, industry and entertainment

Unit 3. Language and the Imagination in Literature
    a. the creative process: inspiration and craftsmanship
    b. the power of language in literature
    c. style and individuality

Certain parts of the course are well within the traditional concerns of the English teacher. Unit 2 inclines towards a 'functional English' approach not too far removed from Mike's Communications course. Unit 3 does not appear to offer work significantly different from that which might be found in English Literature classes.

It is in following the course in the classroom that differences emerge. Each unit places a heavy emphasis on the student's own active role as a language user. This was apparent in the style of personal, reflective classroom discussion which was encouraged, and in the students' coursework folders which contained their year's work. Behind the varied projects undertaken in each of the three units there is a coherence which can be traced back to the earliest aims of the course and the shared values of the teachers. The 'bigger spectrum of language use' is discernable.

The most striking feature is the quality and range of work. The students may have had the external examinations as their main end in view, but this does not appear to have prevented them from undertaking extremely ambitious tasks. For one project the students studied the development of language in children of different ages. This involved visits to primary schools and pre-schools to record different speech samples. One such study, undertaken by a group of students, asked different children their 'ideas about God', and interpreted the replies by drawing on simplified accounts of Piaget's and Bruner's developmental theories which they had discussed in class lessons. They presented their findings authoritatively:

> We found that the best way to encourage the young children to talk and not to mind the tape recorder was to ask them to sing. They were not shy or self-conscious but were delighted by the prospect of hearing their own voice on tape . . .
> We found that children in the lower age group tended to string

everything together with 'ands' when they had a lot to say, whereas the eight-year-olds formed more sentences and used more varied methods and phrases . . .

Not all the work involved investigations of language. Some studies were reflective and autobiographical: 'My development as a language user'; 'My personal anthology of favourite writing' (ranging from Kenneth Grahame to Solzehnitsyn); or 'My view of the world', built around a study of one child's paintings. These examples are selected from all three units of the course. The coherence of the overall rationale is demonstrated by the fact that it is not immediately obvious which example came from which unit. Even in Unit 3 which, in appearance, is closest to an English Literature course, the approach to 'the language of literature' invites a personal bias. For example, in one study of 'language of power and beauty' the student attempts to explain what it means to 'enjoy reading'.

Class lessons continually encouraged such reflective awareness of language and language processes. The students were continually urged to draw on their own memories and their own experiences of different language contexts in order to explore the particular aspects of language under discussion. Such a speculative and personal approach was not always wholeheartedly approved by the students, as their evaluations of the course sometimes revealed:

> Everything we were discussing was already quite obvious to most people, and I did not learn anything new.
> I cannot really say that any part of the course was really all that valuable, personally, as we talked about things I knew about anyway.

Or, on a kinder note:

> I don't mean to criticize you as teachers. I think, in fact I know, you did your best to make the lessons interesting, but I feel you were given such a free hand that you didn't know quite what you were aiming at.

The students regularly grumbled that their time would have been better employed 'studying for the exams'. However, when the students reviewed the course after the exams were over they were more magnanimous: 'I don't think we realized its use at the time'.

This student's final evaluation is illuminating:

> I think the main benefit I derived is to a certain extent indefin-able. To look at something to which we have become deeply accustomed, like the language we encounter every day of our lives, from new standpoints has been very valuable. This applies not only to a completely different understanding of the purpose of English, and all languages, but a general awakening in me that other everyday things merit new objective re-examination. Here I found the part of the course dealing with the building up of a mental picture of the world particularly valuable. At the time it seemed to me to be putting the obvious into words and fancy phrases, but the idea of a continually reforming outlook (and inlook) has influenced a lot of my general thinking.

This student recognizes value in the study of language, without anchoring the study to more instrumental ends (or even to the 'But it's good fun' criterion which Mike's student used). Her freedom to do this tells us something about her socio-cultural security; she can afford a privileged long-term perspective which allows her to recognize benefits that are 'to a certain extent indefinable'.

Anne has reason to be satisfied with the way her course can satisfy the 'broad spectrum of language use' she desires, and which her pupils can capitalize on.

Modifying an English Literature course

Tom has twelve students in the English Literature class at his 'disadvantaged' school.[9] All of them have stayed on at school to 'get more qualifications'. But for what? Seven of the twelve have no career plans at all:

> It's a matter of leaving and going on the dole. I'm wasting my time looking for a job. So I might as well get more qualifications.
>
> I want more qualifications. I don't know what I want to do, but my cousins stayed on into the sixth form. They urged me to.

For these students, HSC (or 'A' level) is seen, at best, as a step towards employment, and, at worst, an alternative to the dole. The students are vague about the purpose of schooling — other than 'to get more qualifications', and the term 'qualifi-cations' appears to be used to describe a diffuse, job-catching attribute.

Tom's school follows a traditional externally-prescribed Year 12 curriculum, governed by the requirements of the regional examination board. The English Literature syllabus is, in fact, the same one which Anne's students follow, but its meaning for the students is quite different. Anne's sixth-formers regarded the external examinations as the final hurdle before moving into tertiary education or career training. Although they were critical of exam pressures they accepted examinations as part of the structure of schooling, the necessary link with the post-school world of higher education and a career. Tom's students lack that certainty, and their uncertainty is largely a direct product of their socio-economic backgrounds and the expectations they and their parents share about schooling and its relationship to the world to work.[10]

When Tom was asked to describe his English Literature course, he described the structure of the examination paper, and the unsuitability of the prescribed texts for his particular pupils:

> We are dealing here with kids who have opted to do English Literature but hardly ever read anything . . . My job is to build up confidence in the kids as discriminating readers with worthwhile opinions . . . I am trying to build up confidence in very unconfident children.

Tom sees the existence of the examination system as an insuperable constraint in this context:

> We've become accustomed to an approach which is to give you a poem and ask you questions and test you and assess you on the basis of your answers. But how *do* people read? And how does the method of examining and the manner of syllabus construction relate to the way people read? And again and again we felt that syllabus construction and exam paper construction were perverting the normal reading process. If you're reading a Jane Austen novel you have to read it over and over again and milk it for marks. Who reads like that? We are asking students to do with a book what we would never do ourselves.
>
> Similarly, who reads a poem and then sits down and answers a question? How do we relate to poems as readers of poetry? All right, a good academic justification can be made for setting that kind of question [referring to an examination paper]. But we ought not to be concerned with good academic justifications; we're concerned with our kids, and whether they will leave our school and like poetry and want to read it. If we can find some new method of examining which will not pervert the normal process, then fine. Let the universities find out what they want to in their own way. In other words, we must not tailor-make our own courses to help them select for university courses.

The conflict between 'teaching a course' and 'teaching an

exam' is a familiar theme for many Year 12 teachers. In the classroom Tom continually struggles to reconcile the two. He does this firstly by introducing the students to texts which he judges to be more accessible than those prescribed for study. The students are encouraged to discuss themes and issues raised by the text, and to examine their own experiences and values in relation to these. Their opinions, rather than the text, are the subject of the lesson. For example, during a play reading of a contemporary play on the subject of student protest, the students stopped to explore their response to the main character, Malcolm, who has been expelled from his college:

Tom: Do you feel sympathy for Malcolm?

Brian: No, it's his own fault. It's people like him who are dragging the country down.

Kathy: I agree.

Tom: Do you think the college treats him fairly?

John: Yes, the college knows what's best for him.

Tom: Does this school know what's best for you?
[Pause] Yes.
[Pause]

Tom: What about D.H. Lawrence? [referring to their expressed disinclination for Lawrence's poetry].

Sue: Well you don't have to stay if you don't like it.

[They digress to discuss friends who have left school and their own reactions to last year's English course].

Kathy: We had too much to study. Five poets was too many.

Tom: What about the poems and the way we taught them, did that turn you off poetry?

Kathy: Yes.

Tom: How should it be changed?

Brian: The only people who could change it are the boards, the people who control it.

John: You've got to have set texts so that the examiner can set questions. If you could pick your books they'd take ages to mark them, wouldn't they?

Brian: Everybody puts too much on examinations. You could go to night school and work your way up. My dad did. Everyone puts too much on it.

John: I don't think doing exams is being educated, really. I think experience is what educates you.

Tom: Well can we come back to Malcolm now, in the light of what you've just been saying, because he doesn't think exams is education either; he thinks *experience* is — just as you've said . . .

Two points are worth making. Firstly, in the students' reading of this play, and in discussion such as that demonstrated in this extract, they achieve a degree of confidence which is lacking in their studies of Shakespeare and Eliot. Secondly, in these classroom discussions the children are observably, though perhaps indirectly, deepening their understanding of literary texts: the journey from 'it's his own fault' to the discovery that the students themselves share something of Malcolm's values is not a haphazard one. In Inglis' words, the students are learning to 'evaluate and adjust an individual scheme of values in relation to personal literary experience'.[11]

But the prescribed texts prove difficult. In a lesson on Hughes' poem 'View of a Pig' the students struggle:

Tom: Why does he keep all feeling out of the poem?
Sue: Because he doesn't want us to feel about the pig.
Tom: Why doesn't he want us to feel about the pig?
　　　[Pause]
Sue: [as a question] Because he wants us to feel how he feels?
Tom: Let's look at the use of language in the poem.
　　　[Pause] Is there anything that sounds like music in the poem?
　　　[Pause] What's the commonest feature shared by music and poetry?
　　　[Pause]
Brian: [as a question] It's something you hear?
Tom: What do you hear?
　　　[Pause] Rhythm, isn't it? Let's look at the rhythm.

After the lesson the students talked about whether they enjoyed studying poetry.

John: Last year I started to enjoy it. I don't know why. I liked listening to Mr C. [Tom] I wasn't bored by it. And when you start going into it, and you read it through again, and you think 'Oh yeah'. It all comes out more clearly.
Brian: I don't like poetry. I can't stand poetry. Mind you, John Betjeman's stuff, I could read that all day!

Why study poetry at all? There were no high claims: 'You have to. For the exam'.

The Bullock Report[12] observed 'There is no doubt that many secondary school pupils develop unsympathetic attitudes to literature as a result of their experiences in preparing for an examination'. (Mike and Tom both remembered such experiences in their own education). Brian's firm distinction here between 'poetry' (which he 'can't stand') and 'John Betjeman's stuff' (which he 'can read all day') illustrates this danger.

A critic might question whether Tom should be able to achieve more. Would a more skilful or imaginative teaching methodology achieve greater success with the prescribed texts? Are there ways in which the students' real progress can be registered as examination success? Tom's answer is no. His solution is to design a new English Literature syllabus, in which the responsibility for the choice of texts, and for the students' assessment, is located with teachers, and not with external examination boards. The story of Tom's attempt to have his syllabus accredited lies outside the scope of this article[13] but the implications are particularly relevant in Australia, as the movement to school-based curriculum responsibility at Year 12 gathers momentum.

Tom's action raises two key questions: Who owns the curriculum? Who has the right to choose? Two final points are worth making. Firstly, there is a real danger that these questions are never fully addressed, and that the rhetoric of 'school-based curriculum responsibility' may encourage little more than cosmetic tinkering with a system still geared to serve the interests of particular power groups in society, at the expense of the real clients: what *ought* the phrase 'equal educational opportunity' mean for Tom's students?

I do not wish to diminish the work of Tom, or Mike, by suggesting that their real achievements with their students amount to 'cosmetic tinkering', token gestures by which economically and culturally disadvantaged children are conned into docile acceptance of capitalist inequities. The danger with much of this kind of critique of schooling and capitalism[14] is that it overlooks the actual events of everyday classroom practice, and the quality of professional thinking and practice which teachers such as Anne, Tom and Mike offer their students as they seek to improve the curriculum for them. But the large questions remain to be addressed, particularly by the new state secondary education boards who, in recent years, have begun to rethink the nature and function of Year 12 curricula.

Secondly, this study raises questions about who should define English, especially in the school context. English teachers are often accused of lacking a clear understanding of the content of their subject. The existence of an extensive, and frequently contradictory, literature on the theme 'What is

English?', and the recurrence of that question as a popular conference topic, support this image. But one way or another English teachers in their classrooms answer that question every day. The nature of their choices will not always be of the kind or quality of the three teachers described in this study, but choices they are, and they are informed by the teacher's knowledge of the students, and by the socio-cultural (or multi-cultural) settings in which they and their students work.

Mike, Anne and Tom all possessed a reflective, self-evaluative stance towards their role as teacher, and a genuine intellectual curiosity about both the nature of their subject and the way children learn. These qualities enabled them, though in very different ways, to reflect on past experience, take up new ideas, and build new curricula for their students. The real work for curriculum, or subject, committees lies, not in prescribing better booklists or newer courses of study, but in helping teachers develop sufficient professional confidence to do these things for themselves.

7   C.T. PATRICK DIAMOND

How to succeed in composition: 'Large as life, and twice as natural'

Hunt has argued that, if every person is a psychologist[1] as Kelly[2] hypothesizes, then certainly every teacher is a psychologist, too. To view teachers as psychologists is to emphasize the importance of their personal conceptions of teaching; that is, their ideas about their goals, their teaching and their students. To accept that teachers are psychologists, however, is to admit that their students are as well, since they also seek to make sense of themselves and their social worlds. In this present study, the writing development of students is explained in terms of the Kellyian view of role and the students' construing of their teachers' personal construct systems is seen as providing a jumping-off ground for the growth of their own construing systems.[3]

Theoretical background
While Kelly's 1955 psychology of personal constructs is theory pre-eminently about the individual and the fact that people differ in their construction of events, no-one is uniquely alone. Everything people do, say and even think is a product not only of their individual processes but also of their interaction with other people.[4] People tend to affect the constructions of others in a number of ways: they may change the way reality is seen; they themselves enter into reality as objects in the others' phenomenal fields; they too have constructions that must be considered in interacting with them; and finally they have their

own constructions of the others. The whole notion of the construction of social reality becomes more complex once the possibility is considered that more than one such system exists. Many students' statements, such as 'I think I know what you mean', are indicative of the cog-wheeling of construing in classrooms.

Kelly's 1955 commonality corollary states that to the extent that a person uses a construction of experience which is similar to that employed by another, his or her psychological processes are similar to those of the other; that is, as birds of a feather they construe together. Triandis[5] writes that similarity of subjective culture is fostered by factors such as similarity of occupation, proximity of location and frequency of interaction. Thus, two classes of students might have what seem to an observer to be very different teaching-learning experiences and yet they may behave almost alike; that is, if they have construed the events in similar ways.

Within a given classroom commonality alone is still not sufficient for interpersonal understanding or for the process of social interaction. For this the construct system of the other (in this instance, the teacher) has to be subsumed by the students. According to Kelly's sociality corollary, to the extent that one person construes the construction processes of another he or she may play a role in a social process involving the other person. This does not imply that there is agreement with the other person's views (for example, 'You mean you want a two-page essay for homework?'), but rather that the act of seeking to understand how another sees things defines a role relationship and is linked to behaviour. Kelly regards this social aspect of his theory as of considerable importance. The construing of individuals and groups is negotiated with those with whom they live and work — even with those whom they must obey. Conversely, if teachers do not understand their students, if they do not construe their developing constructions, they may do things to them, but they cannot relate to them.

Teachers and students both contribute to the social organization of classroom events, with teaching being a constant process of decision-making and trade-off. The teacher and his or her students negotiate and bargain together in order to construct shared meanings, to organize rules, to live in a joint world and to engage in joint actions[6] but, because of his or her power, it is the teacher's constructs that are usually imposed as the defining elements in the classroom encounter. To construe their teacher's construction processes so that they can play a social role in classroom processes, the pupils place themselves in the shoes of the teacher; that is, they take the 'attitude of the other'.[7] They are then better able to understand and predict their present and subsequent bahaviour. Interpreting teaching as a joint act does not mean that the protagonists can interact only when they have similar constructs of, for example, written composition. It implies rather than the pupils' construct systems give them a meaningful picture of their teacher's constructions. The pupils may subsequently wish to help, hinder or remain neutral toward their teacher.

Rosie[8] has found that students are particularly alert to the constructions of others such as teachers. Salmon[9] also argues for a phenomenological conception of students' relations with others. To take this view seriously in the way the social lives of children are regarded, means that not only have they inside stories to tell, but they are also uniquely authoritative, having ownership of their personal domains. Students are not merely the passive recipients of the socializing influences of teachers. They are experts in knowing the sorts of behaviours that are expected of them, as well as the kinds of social negotiation that goes on in classrooms. Despite such theoretical acknowledgement, Leigh and Leigh in 1981 reported that the pupil perspective is not nearly as well understood as their teachers' and that much work remains to be done. Accordingly[9], I set about construing pupils' constructions of their teachers in the following way.

Method: subjects

Fifteen teachers (five men and ten women) from nine large state high schools in south-east Queensland volunteered the co-operation of their Year 10 English classes. These teachers represented seven demonstrably salient perspectives on the teaching of composition derived from an original sample of ninety-three teachers.[10] All fifteen teachers had received some pre-service teacher education. Although three had only one year of preparation, seven had four years. Since eleven of the teachers had been teaching in high school for only one to five years, they probably represent a relatively young, inexperienced but recently trained group of specialists. Only one teacher had taught in primary school. Four of the teachers had been promoted to head their English departments.

The student sample of fifteen classes consisted of 372 pupils

(195 boys and 177 girls) as in Table A. The teachers are grouped in clusters from I to VII and also individually from 1 to 15. The students' mean age of 15.4 years at the end of the academic year shows that they were very representative of the Year 10 population from which they were drawn. When the breadwinners' occupations were classified, a large group of middle-class parents was indicated. A wide range of academic ability was suggested by the kinds of classes that were represented. Teachers 4, 6, 7, 11 and 14 taught top level academic classes, while teachers 5, 9, 10 and 15 worked with lower stream classes. Teacher 15 had a single sex (boys') class and teacher 1 had a composite class that existed only for English. Teacher 9's class was following a specifically modified programme.

Teacher Group	Teacher	Boys	Girls	Total
I	1	16	13	29
	2	12	11	23
II	3	14	17	31
	4	3	16	19
III	5	12	10	22
	6	5	19	24
IV	7	24	6	30
	8	7	15	22
V	9	14	5	19
	10	10	16	26
VI	11	15	8	23
	12	10	16	26
	13	10	17	27
VII	14	15	8	23
	15	28	0	28
	Total	195	177	372

Table A: Student sample

Procedure
The Repertory grid technique is Kelly's (1955) best-known suggestion for eliciting constructs. However, the traditional

triadic or 'three-card trick' method of elicitation has been found to be far too complex for children under twelve years or for those who do not have a substantial command of the language of the test.[11] A much wider range of constructs emerges when children are asked to write short essays; for example, about children and adults they like or dislike.[12] In the present study, the domain to be investigated was pedagogy; that is, the teaching of composition, rather than that of inter-personal relations.

Twenty minutes were allowed for the students' responses. The topic chosen to elicit them was:

> A FRIEND of yours is planning to complete Grade 10 at your school next year. He or she has just written to you asking what they will have to do in order to succeed in WRITING for Grade 10 next year. EXPLAIN how your friend could gain the highest possible grades or marks for writing and also OUTLINE some of the things he or she is likely to ENJOY or find DIFFICULT in being taught how to write.

Analysis

The student responses were coded by an experienced researcher who was otherwise not involved in the study. The categories were left to arise empirically out of the data. First, 178 protocols from seven of the fifteen classes were coded by this researcher and the present writer, with re-consideration and discussion of responses on which they disagreed. After thus establishing an acceptable coding procedure, the more experienced analyst coded all the 372 protocols.

The students' responses were not analysed according to sex since Davies[13] has found that girls' views of schooling do not differ from boys' in most respects. Analysis by sex would be rather like highlighting the lion's view of captivity: it implies that it is demonstrably different from the tiger's view, and thus draws attention away from the central fact of captivity.

Results

The coding first revealed that, while the students made direct statements about how their teachers instructed them, many more suggestions were made about what needed to be done by students in order to succeed. While advice usually can be regarded as a response to having experienced a particular teacher's pedagogy of writing, it may also represent the accumulation of folk wisdom relating rather more generally to all teachers of writing. The direct statements were classified into ten categories, eight of which had negative as well as positive poles. The bi-polar categories were 1, 2, 3, 4, 7, 8, 9 and 10. The components were as follows:

1. *Basic skills*: Parts of speech, clauses and phrases, length, margins, grammar, spelling and punctuation. 'Get it right!'

2. *Teacher relationship with students*: 'Our teacher is very understanding' versus 'They nag a lot' or 'They like to make a fool of you in class'. Supportive or not.

3. *Interest, motivation*: 'They try to make everything as interesting as possible' versus 'We don't learn anything' or 'The teacher doesn't make it interesting'.

4. *Workload*: 'It's hard work with a lot of writing' versus 'It's easy' with very few restrictions.

5. *Personal development*: 'We are encouraged to write about personal experiences' or 'We are free to write as we like'.

6. *Discussion*: Oral work, debates and 'Your own opinion can be given'.

7. *Deductive*: 'We are encouraged to plan our essays and to develop better essay skills' versus 'We're not taught about writing essays'.

8. *Topics on set books*: 'The choice is good and interesting' versus lack of choice, too artificial and 'The subjects are not good to write about'.

9. *Marking*: 'We're marked for originality and quality rather than quantity' or 'for participation in class' versus 'He's a hard marker' or 'There are no helpful comments'.

10. *Time*: 'There's plenty of time' versus pressure of insufficient time.

When the complementary suggestions were coded, twelve categories emerged with the following components. Only two of these categories (2 and 11) had negative as well as positive characteristics.

1. *Basic skills*: Neatness, margins, spelling and punctuation.

2. *Teacher-student relationships*: The importance of a good teacher and a sound relationship versus the need to 'crawl' to teachers and to write what they want.

3. *Self-expression*: 'Be honest, write what you think, be natural' and 'Enjoy writing'.

Teacher Group	Teacher	1 Basic skills		2 Teacher-pupil relationship		3 Interest		4 Work		5 Growth	6 Discussion	7 Deductive		8 Topics		9 Marking		10 Time		Total
		21	921	22	922	23	923	24	924	25	27	28	928	32	932	33	933	34	934	
I	1	7	1	1								3		1					1	14
II	2	2										3			1		1			7
	3	2		1	3	2						4		1			1	1	3	16
	4							1	1	1	1	1		3			1		1	11
III	5	1		2		2	1		1	1		1		1			1			9
	6		1	1		1						5		1		1	1	2		15
IV	7		3	3		2	2	1	1	2	1	3	3	1	1		1			21
	8			1				1	1			2		1	1		1		2	11
V	9	1						1				1								2
	10		1						1			3		1				3		8
VI	11	2			2	2		7		4		4	1	1	1		1	3	2	24
	12				2									2						6
VII	13	4	2	2	2	1		1		1		2		3	3	2				17
	14	1	1	1				1	1	1		2	1	1	1		1			11
	15	6			5			1				10		3	1		3			25
		6		5								10								197

Table B: Direct statements

Teacher Group	1 Teacher Basic skills	2 Teacher-pet student	Teacher-pet crawl	3 & 5 Self-expression growth	4 Attitudes	6 Read	7 Deductive	8 Organization	9 Transition	Feedback	10 Upset	11 Tutor	12 Don't overdo	Total
	01	02	92	03-05	04	06	08	10	11	12	912	13	14	
I	23	3	7	16	46	11	23		3			1		133
	9	3	7	5	28	2	23	1	2			2		82
II	18		7	4	27	5	37	3	6	1		1	1	110
	8	1	2	5	8	10	25	1	8					68
III	8	2	2	5	10	4	12	1				1		45
	9	2	6	8	11	16	44	3	5	1				105
IV	7	9	5	37	45	2	13		1	1		1		121
	7	1	8	18	18	2	16	2	5		2	2	1	82
V	26			4	21	1	2							54
	23		2	10	18	4	18	1	2					78
	11		6	19	24	5	18		3		1			87
VI	22	11		15	35	4	20		7	1		1		116
	20		5	4	17	6	36	1		2		1		92
VII	9	2	2	8	32	7	26	2	2	1				91
	16	2	1	2	16	7	14	3	1	1		1	1	65
														1329

Table C: Student suggestions

4. *Student attitudes*: 'Try hard, study a lot, listen to your teacher' and 'Hand your work in on time'.

5. *Growth*: 'Write about your own, personal experiences' and 'Use your imagination'.

6. *Read a lot*: To get knowledge, to increase your vocabulary and to see other people's styles.

7. *Deductive*: 'Plan your work, do rough copies first, capture the reader's attention' and 'Use a mature style'.

8. *Programme organization*: 'Make sure you use time to your best advantage, plan your study' and 'Allow time for revision'.

9. *Transition*: 'Write in your own way but experiment with different techniques' or 'Be descriptive but don't sacrifice narrative qualities' or 'Use your imagination as a mechanical skill'.

10. *Feedback from marking*: 'Learn from your mistakes' versus 'Don't let comments upset you' or 'Don't be discouraged by the hard marking'.

11. *Teacher or friend as tutor*: 'See your teacher when you have problems' or 'Get a friend to help you'.

12. *Don't overdo Your studies*: 'Don't study too much as it may get you nowhere'.

The results relating to direct statements about the teachers are presented in Table B. The negative poles of the categories are indicated by an initial '9'. The student suggestions as to how to succeed in writing for their respective teachers are revealed in Table C. Categories 03 and 05 were collapsed to form a single growth category in Table C because they were so alike. The 197 direct statements were found to place the 1329 suggestions in perspective and to confirm their interpretation. Teacher 7, for example, is seen in Tables B and C not to stress the basic skills.

Table C was examined in order to reveal the larger clusters of categories which together accounted for over 75 per cent of the total number of responses made about each teacher. Using teacher 1 as an example, Table C reveals that 133 suggestions were made by his students. The four largest clusters of the responses they made were coded as relating to the mechanical skills, student attitudes, deductive teaching and teaching for personal growth. This combination suggests a mixed or transitional approach to the teaching of writing. It also accounts for 81.2 per cent of their total number of responses. The skills-based component of this teacher's approach is evident again in the students' direct statements in Table B. The results for all the teachers are summarized in Table D.

According to their students, teachers 1, 5, 8, 11, 12 and 14 communicated what can also be described as a transitional cluster of constructs; that is, deductive teaching, student attitudes, teaching the skills and teaching for growth. Teachers 2 and 3 are construed as traditional, with an emphasis on the first three of these categories. They replace teaching for growth with poor teacher-student relationships to produce a skills-based version of teaching writing. Teachers 4 and 6 employ the four-fold transitional or mixed cluster, together with an emphasis on the importance of reading. Teachers 10, 13 and 15 are perceived by their students as skills-based, communicating the first three categories of deductive teaching, student attitudes and teaching the skills, while teacher 9 stresses only student attitudes and skills. Teacher 7 is unique in that he is reported to be teaching in such a way that can be classified as teaching for personal growth. Only teachers 7, 8, and 11 are reported to insist on teaching for growth in any way more than the skills. However, even teachers 8 and 11 are strongly deductive in their construed overall emphasis and poor relationships are also reported of the former. At least eight of the teachers are seen as traditional or skills-based in their teaching of composition.

Discussion

Table B reveals that 89 responses, or 45 per cent of the direct statements, related to the basic skills, deductive teaching and to the need to flatter or to 'crawl' to teachers. In order to succeed in composition, students were advised to:

> Get it right! Watch parts of speech, clauses, phrases, length, margins, grammar, spelling and punctuation. Plan your essays. Crawl! Become teacher's pet.

When lack of student interest, boring set topics and poor reactions by teachers to student writing are also included, 52 per cent of all the responses are accounted for.

This negative conclusion is confirmed by another 601 responses, or 45 per cent of the student suggestions, which similarly related to the basic skills, deductive teaching and poor teacher-student rapport. If only those clusters of categories which implicate over 75 per cent of the total suggestions made about each teacher are considered, 54 per cent of the responses again accentuate the basic skills, deductive teaching and hostile teacher-student contact.

In contrast, when direct statements about not teaching the skills, positive teacher-student relations, interest and teaching for personal growth are examined, they explain only 19 responses or 10 per cent of the total. When student suggestions about good teacher-student relations, teaching for growth and self-expression are located, they amount to only 195 responses or 15 per cent overall. Twenty-four per cent of these favourable suggestions refer to only one teacher — teacher 7. Apart from conscious pre-planning and a rejection of 'shaping at the point of utterance'[14] the single other overwhelming suggestion for success (356 responses or 27 per cent) was for students to be positive, to try hard, study a lot, listen to their teachers and to hand in their work on time. This category recalls the English morning assembly prayer, 'Teach us, O Lord, to labour and not to ask for any reward, save that of doing Thy will'. One of the main purposes of school may still be to make students work and to keep them busy. If this call to industry is included with the basic skills, deductive teaching and poor interpersonal contact, 957 responses (72 per cent) are explained. Table D confirms that, while eight of the fifteen teachers could be construed to organize their pedagogy mainly in terms of teaching the mechanical skills, only one could be characterized in terms of the development of personal resources.

The students have depicted their experiences of being taught composition in the last year of compulsory schooling as fairly bleak and often conflicted. If teachers see themselves as reflected back in the eyes of their students, these data are disappointing and even disturbing.

Though there are some exceptions, with teachers 1, 5, 7 and 14 being less formal and beginning to develop a growth-centred model of teaching writing, the majority of the reported classroom experiences seemed to be surprisingly alike in reflecting the traditional, didactic pedagogy. Despite the cries that continue to go up, the 'basics' model was all but universally put into practice. Though the construct systems of only six teachers were described in Table D as transitional, most of the teachers had never abandoned teaching the skills or so-called 'basics' in the classroom. Students recognized the cluster featuring the mechanical skills as their teachers' main concern. Many teachers of English are still in the forefront of keeping the 'back to basics' movement alive.

Teacher Group	Teacher	Deductive	Positive attitude	Skills	Growth	Poor Teacher-student	Reading	Good relationship	Pedagogy
I	1	23	46	23	16				Transitional
	2	23	28	9		7			Skills
II	3	37	27	18		7			Skills
	4	25	8	8	8		10		Transitional
III	5	12	10	8	5				Transitional
	6	44	11	9	8		16		Transitional
IV	7	13	45	7	37			9	Growth
	8	16	18	7	18	8			Skills
V	9		21	26					Skills
	10	18	18	23					Skills
VI	11	18	24	11	19				Skills
	12	20	35	11	15				Transitional
	13	36	17	20					Skills
VII	14	26	32	9	8				Transitional
	15	14	16	16					Skills

Table D: Largest clusters: teachers' pedagogies

The students referred overwhelmingly to their teachers' insistence on 'good spelling, grammar and punctuation'. The emphasis was clearly on form and the mechanics. Contrary to the clichéd assertion, there was no 'trendy' approach using pop materials. Similarly, neither the Bullock Report[15] nor Bennett *et. at.*[16] could find any evidence of a wholesale move towards informality of teaching methods in British schools. Certainly, these present teachers were not dabbling in permissive, 'soft' or progressive practices.

So great was their expressed fear of error-making and subsequent reprisals that pupils alleged they did not feel free to express themselves. They complained about having to 'stick to one topic' which was often described as 'boring' and also about having to do precisely what was set, even down to completing the exact number of words — a curious carry-over from the public examinations now defunct, at least in Queensland. The students felt that they were somehow being cheated and diminished as young people. No matter what they wrote about or how they wrote about it, they believed it would be 'looked down upon'. However, 'you'll do well if you crawl'.

Though some scope was afforded for the imagination, the form of writing that was most prized by the teachers was expository and persuasive. Writing was taught through its transactional mode and was not prepared for by extensive and continuing, personal writing. The students complained that the essay was still the standard by which their writing was judged:

> The thing you might hate in English as I do is writing essays and getting marks for them.

> The worst thing is having to do essays.

> All you can do is make certain that your essay is neat and try to make as little mistakes as possible.

As Martin[17] has suggested, the writing demanded of students most often resembles 'a raid into alien territory'. Flower comments in support:

> What started out as a TEST has become an end in itself. To test writing ability we used an essay; to prepare for the test of essay writing we study essay writing and we write essays. The final step is when essay writing becomes the main form of our written work.[18]

Conclusion

Pupils practise classroom observation every day. While their aims, criteria of significance and contexts of concern are perhaps different from an investigator's, to a considerable extent the pupils are dependent upon their skill as observers in formulating their next steps in the joint act of the classroom. This 'natural practice of classroom research'[19] is taken as providing valid evidence as to the ways in which teachers present composition. In support for this position, Ehman[20] and Remmers[21] have indicated that students' observations provide an accurate picture of classroom practices. Goldberg[22] too has pointed out the validity of this approach since pupils observe more of the typical behaviour of the teacher than is usually available to the outside observer and since, additionally, students are directly participating in the classroom activities. Finally, Glass[23] agrees that students are responsive to and can provide measures of, classroom events. The use of such student ratings of teachers has yielded slightly stronger results than has the use of observer ratings.[24]

Underlying the present study there is a set of fundamentally Kellyian notions about the ways in which students relate to their teachers, the classroom and the world. The most important of these is the idea that this relation is active on their part. They do not just sit and wait for the world to impringe upon them. They try actively to interpret and make sense of it. They grapple with it, they represent it to themselves, they construe it. Donaldson[25] also argues that children are questioners by nature. They approach the world wondering about it, entertaining hypotheses which they are eager to check — at least initially! By directing their questions to other people and to themselves they build up a model of their world, including one of pedagogy. These personal construct systems or inner representations help them to anticipate events and to be ready to deal with them.

In the present study, how 372 students or fifteen classes in Year 10 construe their English teachers' constructs of writing was revealed by asking them to advise a friend who was wanting to succeed in being taught composition by that teacher. These suggestions highlight the meanings imposed on the teaching as the students experienced it. They were constantly seeking to discover the patterns and regularities in how they were being taught to write. Because students are in a single class, they share encounters with the same teacher and they can form common understandings of these events. These constructions parallel those of the teachers' since some form of classroom order must be negotiated. Such shared viewpoints represent significant, psychological facts.

In the main, the students provided a grim definition of their culminating experiences of being taught composition, one that was couched largely in terms of the basic mechanical skills and obedience. The students themselves felt stigmatized as linguistic vandals. As one student states in his own way:

> Some of the things my teacher wants are just too much for example, A marchin, paragraphs, perfect punctuation, etc. You would have to write in a sentence form and know the adverbs and adjectives etc. You will probably find most of this boring.

Writing came across to the students as rigidly rule-governed and the rules were often picayune in character.

To view students alternatively, for example as psychologists, is to remind teachers of the need to take their ideas and intentions into account. For any change to occur, it is necessary that students be construed as like their teachers; that is, constantly engaged in theorizing and experimenting. According to how one person reconstrues others, he or she will moderate his or her own thinking and action in relation to them. Ultimately, education needs to be seen as arising from a specific and caring relationship between teacher and students which can be augmented by writing and sharing. It is then one of the chief means by which young people can develop the capacity to realize themselves as human beings. As Lewis Carroll wrote,

> 'What — is — this?' he said at last.
> 'This is a child!' Haigha replied eagerly, coming in front of Alice to introduce her . . . 'We only found it today. It's as large as life, and twice as natural!'
> 'I always thought they were fabulous monsters! . . . Talk, child'.
> Alice could not help her lips curling up into a smile as she began: 'Do you know, I always thought Unicorns were fabulous monsters, too! I never saw one alive before!'
> 'Well, now that we *have* seen each other', said the Unicorn, 'if you'll believe in me, I'll believe in you. Is that a bargain?'
> 'Yes, if you like', said Alice.

Perhaps if teachers can believe in students as psychologists, they in turn will be believed in as people.

8 JAMES MOFFETT

Excerpts from an educator's notebook

I keep notebooks on ideas that occur to me about language, learning, and other matters that to me seem related. Some notes may end as a talk or article; some may remain isolated and undeveloped, for now. Topics vary as much as the three here. The first came off the wall, the second in response to an assignment commissioned me, the third as part of long-range ruminations about a subject I constantly refer to. These are not un-edited inner speech but elaborations to be shared with other educators, who may keep and value similar notebooks.

Tally me a story
Have you ever noticed a connection between telling stories and counting? The root of the word *tell* means to calculate or reckon, based on the idea of number, series, and list. In 'The Eve of St. Agnes' Keats writes, 'Numb were the beadsman's fingers, while he told/His rosary . . .', that is, while he counted the beads to tally the repetitions of his prayer. A tale is a kind of tally. A raconteur recounts stories. Corresponding to the idea of counting *over* again in the French verb *raconter*, the German *zahlen* means to count and *erzahlen* to recount or narrate. The Spanish *contar* means both to count and to tell.

The chief connection seems to be the idea of a series. Like numbers, events have a fixed order, chronology. Thus in telling a story we enumerate events. But since reckoning or calculating goes beyond mere seriating to the idea of permuting or recombining numbers, does telling imply more than listing over the sequence of actions? In addition to 'keeping track', does a narrator perform other arithmetical operations? Is he a manipulator or creator?

We also *relate* stories. Perhaps the most fundamental comparison makes of counting and narrating two ways to make sense, to relate elements (quantities and events). At any rate, the parallel between counting and narrating becomes amplified on a grand scale when we look at the roots of such words as *reason, ratio, rite, arithmetic, read, art*, and *rhythm*, which all derive ultimately, it seems, from the Greek *arariskein*, to fit or measure, and they share the idea of proportion and number.

Consider accounting as the practice of relating sets of figures so that they mesh, match, and mean something. We give an account of what happened when we relate events. Thus, 'rendering an account' could result in a fiscal balance sheet or a narrative report. Both relate elements to make meaning and to explain.

The idea of repetition in *recount* may stem from the pre-literate practice of telling a story over and over from memory — *reciting* tales in lieu of reading books — as well as from the idea that the counting of events corresponds to the original noting of their sequence as one experienced or heard about it and that, therefore, any narrating of events has to be a re-counting.

Then, of course, some of the very first writing was simply symbolizing quantities of goods that had been tallied or was the tallying itself, as in the Sumerian cuneiform tablets or ledgers recording business transactions. The ultimate connection between counting and telling may lie in gematria, the ancient practice, so central to caballistic traditions, of identifying letters with numerals so that the spelling of words corresponded to the summing of numbers. Hence numbers meant not just quantities as applied to objects, but constituted a kind of code for a subterranean message under-riding that of the letters.

The terrible twos of junior high

Grades seven and eight make up a unique and strongly characterized stage of children's growth and hence of curriculum development. Whenever in talking with teachers I compare this stage to the 'terrible twos' of pre-school life, I get smiles and nods of recognition. Around age two children are feeling their oats because they are experiencing a surge of power from learning to walk and talk and gain other control over their body and their environment. They declare their independence, say no to adults as a matter of principle, and yet still depend desperately on adults. At age 12-14 children get another huge surge of power from discovering through the change of puberty that they can now do what seems to make adults adults. And yet they don't feel nearly ready to take on the world alone, and are in fact bewildered and intimidated about both it and their own feelings. So again they go through an independence/ dependence syndrome, spiralling at a higher level over a place they went through about ten or twelve years before. One moment they will be barking off adults, or defying them outright, but the next they may be all child again, asking for help and stroking. This erratic and turbulent behaviour drives many adults wild. Teachers tend to abhor or adore this age, reacting extremely to the extremity of the age itself.

Junior high youngsters turn toward peers more than do any other age group. Primary children still orient very much to adults. Upper elementary children begin creating and obeying a peer code and behaviour system, but split their allegiance because they need adults very much, are still undergoing massive inculcation and acculturation in and out of school, and devote much energy to building individual skills and competencies in a variety of areas. Whereas pre-school children are naturally non-conformist, and primary children not yet thoroughly acculturated, children of grades three or four to six tend to conform considerably to the adult world, at least in their conscious thought and voluntary behaviour. Senior high students, on the other hand, identify increasingly with the adult world. They take their sexual power more for granted, start to look for jobs and mates, and enter the stage of more abstract and formal logical operations. They too orient very much to their peer group, but this peer group more nearly resembles the general older membership of the society. Comparatively, then, junior high youngsters represent the peak of peer orientation when peers still constitute a non-adult sub-culture. They represent also the resurgence of non-conformist experimentation. To some extent, this exploratory spirit arises from a state of being at sixes and sevens — unsure of identity, role, and ability; half child, half adult; thoroughly acculturated by adults but impelled to use peers as a bridge toward independence from adults.

A third development for practical consideration may actually be more induced by school and society than programmed by nature. The fact is, as many parents and teachers know very well, around third and fourth grades a great slump occurs in school children that often lasts through upper elementary and affects junior high considerably. Children lose enthusiasm and seem not to know any longer things they knew before, even including how to read. Many get on a negative track, building up a deficit of school defeats that leads to dropping out. Entering junior high, these students are so shaky academically (as well as otherwise too perhaps) that they become super-sensitive and capable of freaking out at any moment. The heavy conformist acculturation of the elementary years, the formalization of schooling into specialized 'subjects' that occurs during upper elementary, and the further specializing, during junior high, into separate classes, rooms, and teachers generates considerable anxiety and feelings of remoteness and conflict. So several negative potentialities of growing up in our society may culminate in junior high, compared with which senior high represents a land of survivors, of self-selected students who made it through the worst of these negative possibilities.

In my experience consulting with schools and putting together curricula, I find that Grades 7 and 8 are the hottest spot in the whole school curriculum, the area educators feel they know least what to do about. Primary goes all out for initial literacy, elementary fills in introductory knowledge of content areas, and senior high prepares for college or vocations. These teachers at least *feel* they know what they are doing and that their mission is clear, even if results often do not fit what they have in mind. Consequently, I find, the greatest exertion toward curricular innovation occurs in junior high, where, closer to desperation, teachers reach out and try out more readily than anywhere else. They *know* they need help, and they feel they have little to lose in making changes. It follows that media producers can expect the kind of receptivity that goes with a feeling that conventional stuff doesn't really work, and special measures have to be taken.

What about thought and language itself at this age? Although Piaget's theory that formal logical operations become possible only after puberty has been recently questioned as underestimating younger children, still it is safe to say at least that the fullest maturation of logical powers will occur only after puberty. The best policy is to assume the best and offer *opportunities* for higher thinking by proposing a choice of projects for students that entail, or *can* entail, such thinking, and by organizing them into working parties that facilitate pooling of their resources and cross-stimulation of minds.

In accordance with the general transitional unevenness of this stage, thinking capacity may run a wide gamut among individuals of Grades 7 and 8 and across the same individual on different occasions and for different subjects and situations. Group projects calling for mixed sorts of thinking — categorizing, serializing, assigning causes, analyzing, synthesizing, summarizing, syllogizing — will allow students to try out different thinking roles, witness peers' thinking, and eventually exercise or explore whatever kinds they are capable of. Serious introspection begins after puberty as the complexity of inner-outer relations requires more self-knowledge, and as drastic physical and psychological changes within call attention to themselves. So inner life becomes more the subject itself of inner speech or thought.

In language, students of this age will want very much to follow peer codes and fashions in what they talk about and which words and structures they express themselves in. So they could do collaborative projects about topics they consider important but that force them, in effect, to enlarge their language expression beyond the peer group. Uncertainty, the tentative quality of feelings and ideas, inchoate identity, conflicts with tradition — all of these make thought and language less distinct and coherent, more groping and inconsistent. For such a strongly transitional stage of growth, it makes sense to afford much practice in thinking, talking, and writing that is *dilatory* and *exploratory*, not always neatly definitive, and to afford working-up phases before a final closure or polished product. Junior high students need a lot of scope and time to find out what they think, and to formulate what they perceive.

Their thought and language derive strongly from models they identify with, from heroes and heroines or other significant figures in their immediate environment or media-relayed worlds. Seventh- and eighth-graders are constantly *acting*, consciously or not, as they try out different roles and relationships, and this 'casting' about or seeking identities influences much of their thought and language. In reading, they look for figures representing a kind of person, they think tentatively, they might like to become. Many still use animals and fantasy actions as symbols through which to look on feelings or issues they are not ready to treat explicitly.

In summary, the learning needs of seventh- and eighth-graders centre around peer interaction balanced by adult direction; exploratory thought and language permitting much trying out of roles and ideas; exercise of the new capacity for introspection; new kinds of activities different from grade school; personal and integrative approaches offsetting the traditional impersonality and fragmentation of secondary school; and the learning of ways to deal independently with their own problems and those of the environment.

The wordless world
Language is not entirely a good thing. However useful and beautiful it may seem at times, it is also very dangerous. It is divisive and dualistic, stereotyped, partial, and far too crude to be any match for reality itself. As the general semanticists say, it is only a map to the territory, not the territory itself, which remains forever unspeakable. Now, we can recite that semantic credo to ourselves as much as we wish, but mostly we limit ourselves and our world because we seldom really believe it. Most of the time we go on assuming that statements can be made about the world that are true. But statements are never true; they are only useful or beautiful. The reason that we persist in believing our maps, and having faith, is that we learned language as infants and were hypnotized by it at our most susceptible moment without knowing what happened. So we have never in our maturity known reality directly, unabstracted by language. We don't even know what it is we don't know. The thoughts, feelings, perceptions, and behaviour of our maturity are essentially post-hynotic sugges- tions, verbal/conceptual commands absorbed during the trance of early childhood and carried out somnambulistically in childhood. This is no doubt why mystical literature refers to the ultimate enlightenment as an awakening.

So we share a great linguistic dream, much as the original Balinese are said to have hallucinated together. This sharing enables us to communicate, because communication is based on convention and agreement, but *what* we can say is limited to those consensuses we have agreed on, that is, that others agreed on before we were born. So strongly does concept dominate percept, in symbolically-organized creatures, that we end by being limited in what we can see to what we can say. To gain a management of reality through symbols we trade off some of reality itself. It is a law of the abstracting process that the more abstract the map the less it resembles the territory, and the more it resembles some inner structure of our own, the neural networks of our nervous system, our webs of intent, and so on.

But it would not be nearly enough anyway to understand the general semanticists' dictum that map and territory are different, that utility is one thing, truth another. To grasp our situation as symbol-making animal we would have to realize that normally we never know the territory *any other way* than through some map. We cannot even compare map with territory to check for distortion and omission. We can only compare map with map. We can put aside the realtor's description and go look at the land parcel described, but what we see will only be a less abstract abstraction that our visual perception makes as it peers through the mesh of our verbal/conceptual cage. Ironically, the cage itself is invisible, because we have been seeing *through* it too long to be able to *see* it. Our so-called facts are social artifacts. Language fixes and transmits these illusions.

By its very nature language is divisive. The Biblical story of the tower of Babel probably refers not just to the nationalistic divisions within a polyglot world but to the fundamentally fragmenting effect of any lexicon. To name things is to cut up the indivisible unity of the world into man-made 'objects', to segment the continuous movement of the world into man-made entities like time and space, and, falsest of all, to reify, to make *things* out of vibrations, to convert energy to matter. Thus broken down, these named objects must be related to each other with other words that make statements — certain verbs of mental action, including *to be*, adverbs and pre-positions of time, place, manner, etc., and conjunctions of time, space, causality, conditionality, etc. Behind language lies the man-made analysis and classification of a god-made world. Mathematician Norbert Weiner said, 'Scientific discovery consists in the interpretation for our own convenience of a system of existence which has been made with no eye to our convenience at all'.[1] By means of grammar and connector words we try to put back together our own pieces of this world we never made but feel compelled to dissect and re-make to suit ourselves. God composes and man decomposes.

It was Adam, not God, who gave names to the creatures of the earth, according to Genesis; and when Adam and Eve ate of the tree of knowledge of good and evil what they partook of was conceptualization with all its mortal dualities and break-downs and assumptions. That the knowledge of this tree is very limited and social is shown both by the necessity of the fig-leaf and by the very strong contrast the Bible draws between the tree of knowledge and the tree of life, which is also located in the centre of the garden. It is very clear that Adam was not expelled merely as punishment, but to bar him from the tree of life, 'lest he put forth his hand and take also of the tree of life, and eat, and live forever'. (This was not unkind of God; expulsion insured they would develop spiritually). After the expulsion, God places cherubim at the east of Eden 'and a flaming sword which turned every way, to keep the way of the tree of life'. Very ambiguous indeed. A flaming sword is both a defence and a beacon, and 'keep the way' means both to guard the gate and to maintain the roadway. The home fires are burning, but expect an ordeal regaining paradise. The way of life is not the way of mundane knowledge, the kind embodied in language.

Language not only divides the indivisible, it stereotypes the unique. Existentially, nothing every recurs, and nothing belongs to a class. These are fancies. But language can operate only by rough-shod generalizing and by suppressing parti-cularly, constantly forcing us to favor similarity over dif-ference. This sameness may make the world more manageable but it also makes it seem more boring and remote. To begin to match its territory less grossly, language would have to forsake common nouns for proper nouns and even to date the proper nouns, since things change. Or, like the characters in a novel of Jean Giraudoux, make up new words for 'indescribable' moments of experience — let's say, glimpsing a shiny frog at the same time as hearing a train whistle while mulling over a business problem in a wooded Montana valley. What's the word for *that* experience? But how can I complain one moment about language being divisive, then complain the next about its not being particular enough? Neither is a complaint. Both, rather, define language for what it really is — a kind of bourgeois compromise between the unity and the uniqueness of things of this world, what seems like a contradiction when put into language. Blake had to say it as a paradox, the universe in a grain of sand. A compromise that touches neither the truth of wholeness nor of particularity is all right . . . so long as we know every minute what this can and cannot do. But can we really know this in our normal state? Can a person under a spell dispel the spell from within?

Verbal stereotyping fulfils itself: we perceive in the way language habits structure perception, then our consequently gross and standardized perception seems to corroborate the structure of language. Benjamin Lee Whorf's hypothesis about thought and speech has been disputed, resulting in a strong version that language *determines* thought and a weak version that language only *influences* thought. One example from his cultural comparisons is a Hopi word that stands for any object having a *Gestalt* or silhouette like that of a mushroom, including disparate things, or what seem from our functional point of view to be disparate things, such as a hammer, a mushroom itself, and presumably an atomic explosion. Classifying by shape rather than by purpose is certainly a different way of cutting up the pie of reality and indeed could hardly fail to influence thought.

An example from our own culture will illustrate not just how languages may vary in their influence on thought but how language locks in outright mistakes and prevents their exposure. In Western medicine the concept 'involuntary' has been used to designate body functions thought to be beyond the control of the conscious self — heart beat, respiration, electrical brain activity, skin temperature, glandular secretion, etc. — but which yogis and swamis have been learning to control for centuries, as Western monitoring devices are now proving, and as Westerners themselves are learning to do. We will never know how much this miseducation of generations of doctors has set back man's development in our culture. It is a truism in science that half of making a discovery is knowing that it can be done at all. If the scientific community says certain functions cannot be controlled, this creates a mental set few colleagues or laymen are likely ever to break. The basic problem here, of course, was the duality, built into the language, about voluntary and involuntary, one term implying the other.

Why tolerate such blinders? Well, doesn't language just as often remove blinders by allowing us to think new thoughts? Yes, but if you examine closely a case of a new concept 'liberating' our minds, you will almost certainly find that the 'new' concept would not have been necessary had we not previously believed some other concept that was false or limited. In other words, most so-called breakthroughs in thinking are really cases of *un*thinking something that was not so. Language never appears so effective as when undoing its own mischief — naturally — for it speaks truest about itself, which is precisely its basic limitation . . . and the limitation actually of any symbols.

But in a sense none of us really wants an open mind: the economy would burst overnight. Ours is a society that *needs* all its problems, in order to generate jobs, markets, and votes, so we all have an investment in believing that the solutions to grave problems of commerce, government, law, medicine and education, require perpetual conceptualizing and verbalizing — more research, more negotiation, more legislation, more administration. The more our problems are man-made — and which of them isn't? — the more they involve replacing old concepts with new concepts, that is, one mental limit with a perhaps less narrow one, but one almost certain to spawn other problems that will sustain jobs, markets, and votes. The art of living in our society is the art of converting worthless states of nature into valuable problems calling for expensive treatment — and I for one am tired of brilliant solutions to stupid problems.

So far I've said that language does not tell 'the truth' because symbols constitute only a facsimile of the reality they point to. It does not give us 'nothing but the truth' because it speaks as much about itself as medium as it does about its message. Now, last, it does not tell the 'whole truth' because the editing that goes on as a medium simulates reality omits much of the reality it tries to capture. Language is partial, partial in two senses: it's not the 'whole truth', and it's biased. But a biased truth is a half-truth. The underlying difficulty of all verbal concepts is that, by their very analytical and categorical nature, they cannot ever get beyond the relative knowledge of which Adam and Eve partook with the apple to the total, instantaneous knowledge that constitutes 'the whole truth', the tree of life. Part of the difficulty with language is that it is linear, not simultaneous, and no amount of stringing language can build up a whole, because the linearity is only a surface reflection of the analytic nature of language. The partiality comes not just from the analytic breakdown, however, but from the impossibility of putting the pieces back together again, which requires an instantaneous fusion, not merely an additive or linear linking. Humpty Dumpty's egg reappears in some oriental philosophy, as indeed in other Western lore, as a symbol of original unity. Once you've shattered that unity by conceptualizing, you can never put the pieces back together, even if you're a king, and you stand, like Adam and Eve, barred from the tree of life.

The original sin is not anything as frivolous as sex, which was enjoyed before the fall, but the sin of objectivication, of losing primal oneness with the world. This oneness carries with it the insider's truth, which is the whole truth. Once you're outside, you can spend all your life rattling different gates trying to get back in. There is another meaning of objectivity, however, that does fit unity. They come together in the word 'impartiality', which means freed of local or relative viewpoints by virtue of being integral, whole. So the hunger for a transcendent perspective seems better fulfilled by oneness of man with world than by analysis by man of world. And if language is only a worldly tool for getting the day's work done — the tree of knowledge, not the tree of life — then we are caught in the big metaphysical catch, namely, that our worldly problems require, precisely, a holistic and holy understanding well beyond anything we will ever get from verbal concepts.

The good news is that techniques have been evolved over the centuries in all cultures for liberating the mind from language after the initial language acquisition. These techniques suspend inner speech, the internal carrier of acculturation, and thereby spring the mind from its verbal conceptual cage. Certain activities in sports, martial arts, and crafts can suspend inner speech through the sheer intensity of attention focused outward when errors are very costly and success depends on getting outside of oneself. (Ego arises with acculturation, and so both are suspended if inner speech dissolves, since skull chatter maintains them both). Intensely demanding physical action, then, requiring considerable self-discipline, supplies some of the techniques for altering consciousness beyond the ordinary, limited state.

Other techniques are entirely perceptual or inner — gazing, visualizing, meditating — some way of holding the mind in one place such as on a single image, thought, or sound. (Chemical and electrical means work too, but are not recommended). The purpose of all the arts — music, dance, drama, painting — was originally to offset the strictures imposed by verbal thought and to restore attunement to inner and outer forces of nature, unmediated by local culture. The arts are among the techniques developed to suspend inner speech.

But isn't literature art, and isn't it also verbal? Yes. In fact, it may well be the highest function of literature to undo language with language. Poetry represents this function in purest form, and that is the real meaning of 'poetic licence'. It has the culture's blessing to go counter-cultural in the sense of presenting, through imagination, alternative realities that expand consciousness beyond those very limits set by ordinary verbalizing. Although readers expand their minds from the best literature, the writer benefits more. It follows that students should create as well as consume literature. To become steeped in imaginative modes of writing as both reader and author is to become rich enough to afford the price of verbal conceptualization.

As the thief to catch a thief, literature may be a key technique of liberation, but schools could and should teach youngsters the other techniques also — the other arts, crafts, sports, and survival activities — from the viewpoint of their relation to attentional self-control and mental balance, so that people can benefit from the abstracting power of language without being permanently distracted from the greater, silent knowledge from which it draws.[2]

9   ROSLYN ARNOLD

How to make the audience clap: children's writing and self-esteem

Teachers looking for insights into writing development from theory and research over the past twenty years might well be baffled by the plethora of ideas about teaching writing, some-times held together very loosely by notions of what constitutes and promotes development. Although theory and research are still in a fledgling state, some concepts do have both practical and theoretical value because they seek to identify core influences upon the writer in the act of writing. For example, Moffett's concept of authentic discourse (1968, 1981a-1981b) and the complementary concepts of audience and purpose (Britton, *et. al.*, 1975) have helped move writing theory and practice towards an integrated study of the thoughts and feelings of the writer at work. More than ever the work of scholars like Britton (1970, 1975), Emig (1971, 1980), Graves (1975, 1979), Martin (1976, 1980), Moffett (1968, 1976, 1981a, 1981b)[1] is receiving wide and favourable attention because it is recognized, even intuitively, as coming close to, and elaborating, the truth of the writing process.

Teachers with a feel for that process through their own writing and their involvement with students' writing will be drawn to the theories and practices which confirm their own intuitions and beliefs. The attunement we recognize between theory and practice matches the attunement students recognize when writing accords with their own needs and develop-ment. This suggests that we are programmed to seek and recognize what we need for language development. That is, aware students and reflective teachers (or very small children and parents) often know intuitively what is necessary for survival and growth at a biological, linguistic and cognitive level. But how does writing fit in? Surely we don't need it to survive and grow? The anatomist J.Z. Young cites evidence that human beings are programmed to write. He describes individual mammalian life as following a programme written in four main languages in man:

> ... these programmes find their physical expressions and codes not only in human habits and speech sounds but also in writing and other forms of *recorded* speech. These provide a fourth level of coding, also peculiar to man enabling some of the information for living to be recorded outside of any living creature.[2]

This places writing beside speech as a primary form of human expression. Because it develops after speech we tend to think of it as a secondary form of expression and therefore less significant. It is timely to rethink that. As Moffett[3] reminds us, the 'prehistoric' form of writing was building, where ancient monuments *embodied* information. Writing was not singled out as a specialized activity but was integrated with the curriculum for living. These reminders that writing can have both personal and collective significance for humans highlight the need to retain a sense of continuity between expressive and transactional writing, personal and public writing. There will be no split if there is a consistent sense of the self at the core of the writing experience. Then writing will be authentic, no matter what the mode or the audience addressed.

Authentic discourse

The concept of authentic discourse rests on a deceptively simple natural foundation. Because schooling often thwarts the natural flow of development we often mistakenly believe we have to do more for students than is really necessary. We lose sight of what they can do, naturally. Authentic discourse harnesses the innate expressive energies of the writer involved in creating personal meanings. This process is essentially the same, though more or less complex, whether the writing involves spontaneous, free association thought or speculative theorizing. An aspect of personal experience is expressed and explored through language and thought.

One of the significant outcomes of writing research in the past decade has been an increased awareness of the self at the centre of the writing experience, anchoring the disparate influences upon the writer in a secure and liberating way (anchor chains can be infinitely long in the mind's sea). The security comes from feeling self-involved, and the liberation comes from discovering that the self can be reflected and shaped by genuine symbolizing experiences such as writing, talking, making. In a sense, as we centre experience where it can only ever truly belong, in the mind and heart of the individual, we can then re-embody experience by the process of symbolizing it. We write it out to take it in. In this essential interplay between the individual and society, each knows what it owns and contributes and each gains in the exchange. Artists, writers and students are usually prepared to share their work when they are satisfied with the process they have engaged in, although the product may be imperfect and indicative of work in progress. That is, we are confident about our creative, expressive experiences when we are centred in them. Negative responses, however unwelcome, are not intolerable in such contexts.

Students produce perfunctory writing when they have had insufficient time and experience to write otherwise, or when they recognize that judgements will be made about them from their writing. This is not to argue that self-indulgence or egocentricity is all. Rather that the capacity to decentre, to move beyond the self, the present and the immediate, depends on the realistic confidence that the self is still the core of that ever-spiralling experience of human development.

Moffett's elaboration of the process by which the writer abstracts from experience, selects from inner speech and organizes thought and feeling in writing, simultaneously creating data for further abstracting, points to a continuity in the human experience of symbolizing, if nature has its way.[1] As we write and compose the mind, that composition provides further raw material for the continuation of the process. In authentic discourse the writer's intentions are engaged, motivation is stimulated by the possibility of genuine feedback and a real purpose and audience is perceived.

It sometimes happens that theoretical concepts divorced from context become confused as precepts. Authentic writing cannot be an externally imposed demand. It arises from within when writers have experienced their own expressive written language. The process of decentring to reach audiences beyond the self is really a process of reaching out and internalizing a sense of that audience. The audience is found within, through the process of reading, listening, experimenting with writing and internalizing audience responses.

Sound theory recognizes the complexity of the writing act, and recognizes also its own shortcomings in accounting for that complexity. We know that personal constructs, past experiences, future expectations, a sense of audience and purpose may help or hinder the scanning, remembering, selecting, creating processes involved in putting real pens to real papers. We separate these influences for our cognitive convenience, sometimes creating the impression that they are perceived separately by writers. In fact we don't know the relative strengths of the influences. We often analyse features of writing separately, yet we know that the real experience of writing, reading, thinking and symbolizing is very much larger than the sum of the parts, or the sum of the concepts. As we move closer to knowing some of the universals of the writing act we cannot expect anything less than multidimensional answers. That is, the factors influencing writing development are legion, but we don't have to wait for further research to tell us what to do. In natural, real communicative contexts students reveal their capacities to write authentically.

How then do we find writing experiences which students see as authentic? What is a real audience and purpose? What is development and how is it promoted?

David Dirlam points to a contemporary source for the answers:

> Advances in writing research over the last decade and a half have provided significant knowledge of the natural design underlying the development of writing ability. James Moffett provided a comprehensive theory of discourse development which analyses discourse into levels of audience, subject, viewpoint, logical sequence, literary form, continuity, word selection, and syntax. This theory has received extraordinary empirical support from the studies of James Britton in England and from my own work.[5]

However Moffett cautions that this correspondence to growth 'is not fine enough to warrant a claim for any span of time so small as a year or even two'.[6]

One research project

In an attempt to better understand writers' processes and the nature of authentic discourse, I am engaged in a four-year longitudinal study of children's writing development, Years 6-9 inclusive (ages eleven to fourteen). Thirty-five case study students (25 girls, 10 boys) drawn from a private girls' school and a state co-educational school are involved in a writing programme with me. This involves working in groups for one period each fortnight. Originally the intention was to explore students' attitudes to writing and to track their development over a four-year period. By the middle of the first year of the study it became apparent that an intervention programme involving the researcher as a teacher might be more valuable all round. For a start, it takes time to develop in students a self-concept as writers. From interviews and observation it was clear that several case study students equated writing with handwriting and thought that to be a good writer meant to be neat and correct. Students do not naturally see themselves as writers unless they have had experiences enhancing their self-concepts as such. Authentic discourage suggests an exchange between writer and reader, especially in the early stages of development where writing concepts are being nurtured. It became important to build such exchanges into the programme.

Towards the end of the first year of the study the students began some concentration work and free association writing in order to free them from some of the constraining notions inhibiting their writing. In a drama-type exercise students sat quietly with their eyes closed concentrating on the images in their mind. In their own time they wrote down what they saw, thought or felt. This developed later into an exercise where they wrote down 'I am thinking about . . .' and kept writing as long as possible. Even when blocked, they were encouraged to write about their difficulties with writing. This helped them use a potentially negative experience as further writing data. These exercises produced some interesting comments:

> Now I'm thinking if this is the longest writing I have ever done in my whole life of school. I think it is
>
> Lynne

> The last thing I am thinking about is what the others wrote on their papers because I don't know whether mine is right or not.
>
> Justine

> The easy part about it was that you had a picture in your head and that was all the help you needed.
>
> Aldo

my writing is slower than my thinking and while I write I think ahead trying to see what I'm thinking of next ... I'm writing in the present tense when things are in past tense ... This is an interesting thing to do because you have to really think to see what you are really thinking.

Julia

It was all easy because I could just think of it in my mind. At the beginning I couldn't think of anythink but when I closed my eyes, and I wrote that down on the sheet of paper.

Lino

here you write for pleasure and at school you have to write one certain thing.

Edwina

when we write here it is just our minds and more ourselves it is all totally free and easy.

Julia

Students *can* write when they get in touch with their own thoughts and feelings. It needs nothing more than a teacher who believes that deeply, and students willing to concentrate for a few minutes. Unfortunately, school 'busy work' often hinders natural expression. As one student put it after her second experience of free association writing 'Now I know what writing's about'. All that had happened was she had discovered her own resources.

At the end of the first year of the study the following writing task was set across Grade 6 in five schools, including the two schools and classes of the case study students, in an attempt to distinguish any differences between the case study students and their peers:

Imagine a friendly visitor from outer space comes to your school. He is very interested to see that children write in school.

Could you write him a letter explaining why you write in school? You could tell him what you find easy or hard about it and what you like doing most. Try to help him as much as you can.

It was not possible to distinguish differences in development between the case study students and their peers but other useful data emerged. Most noticeable was the writers' engagement with the task. All 199 writers created a name for their space man thereby establishing rapport with him, and all satisfactorily completed the letter writing task. Engagement with the task was revealed in the sense of a real audience addressed (even though the audience was both imaginary, the space man, and shadowy, the researcher). The degree of empathy with the space man was expressed in the writers' goodwill and anticipation of his problems. Even where the writer expressed negative attitudes towards writing, helpful advice was offered to the space man:

Put your whole mind and imagination into it
You don't have to tell the truth
A story is like a picture in your head and then it is printed on paper

Even though the task was set in a context potentially seen as a testing one, it seemed to stimulate the students' imagination. They extended the context for the letter in their own ways and could be self-revealing without fear of retaliation. They knew the writing would not be returned, but a measure of their involvement in the task was the often-expressed wish that the space man would write back. Real letters, of course, should be replied to. The writers' capacity to respond to the demands of this task was impressive. They saw themselves helping an uninitiated peer in an aspect of school work which obviously determines success or failure in the system.

Their ideas about the place of writing in school showed their attempts to make sense of their school experiences:

people know you have a good education if you are good at wrighting

(we write) to help our brain to grow and be more powerful

(pupils write) because they learn more and that's why they have to have a pen in there hand every second

The 199 Grade 6 writers showed a capacity to write with commitment to the space man possibly because the task invited them to make sense of an important aspect of school life: written discourse with an interested other. The fact that the space man was ignorant about writing and needed information gave added impetus to what was really a self-exploration. As is most authentic writing.

Letter writing is one of the most realistic writing tasks we do. The writer often has a clear sense of purpose which might be articulated in the letter. An appropriate image of the self as a writer, a point of view or an expressed need might be required in order to receive a reply to the letter. Few other writing tasks so clearly demand a response, often a written one, from the reader. The reciprocal nature of this writer/reader relationship is usually well understood by early school age. Fully extended, letter writing can provide contexts for a wide range of language functions, from personal, exploratory writing to the speculative and theoretical. The space man letters offered evidence that when writers have sufficient prompts to imagine a task as authentic, they will attempt to find language suitable for the task. If they are able to remain at the centre of the experience, drawing on personal knowledge and feelings to share with another, their search for meaning and expression in language is often surprisingly successful.

When this case study began in 1980, the students in the two schools were to be studied as separate groups. However, as they became more attuned to their work in the group they became curious about their counterparts in the other school and expressed the hope that they could meet one day. My reluctance to encourage this for the sake of the research design prompted a creative solution from one of the students: to instead exchange letters with a case study partner in the other school. While this also posed problems for the research design, the students' enthusiasm persuaded me to rethink the priorities of the research and to hope that whatever arose from such enthusiasm would be valuable. The exchange of letters was set up by a fairly random matching of writing partners (a couple of girls said definitely they did or did not want boy partners) and I became teacher, researcher and postman. Seven letters were exchanged between the writing partners over a four-month period towards the end of the second year of the study.

The first letter in the exchange was probably the most difficult because it required a presentation of the writer to the reader in a way likely to encourage a reply. The initiative for the exchange came from a girl in the more able case study group and that group wrote the first letters. That may have provided a model for some of the writers in the other group. Several writers in both groups found the initial letter difficult but they were encouraged to write in the letters whatever they felt about the task. This was in keeping with previous writing that they had done, where they were asked to write down whatever they were thinking, including negative thoughts about the free association writing process. Knowing they could start where they were at, and their anxiety, keenness and curiosity, helped break the ice:

This is the first time I have beening writing to someone I have never seen before. I am wondering what you look like.

Tell me about yourself and your family when you write, Hopefully someday I'll meet you.

I think this is a bit strange writing to someone I don't know but it might be interesting as well . . . I hope you will right back because if you do I will.

I feel really funny writing this letter to you because I don't know who you are or what school you come from . . . I'm looking forward to your letter.

Most of the initial letters contained biographical information, questions, and an expectation of a reply. The particular tension of letter writing is to write in a way which will elicit the reader's reply. In this situation where the writers have never met, the relationship is created and maintained solely by letter writing. Inevitably these writers have to draw on their prior knowledge of relationships and their tacit understanding of how language (usually spoken) creates and maintains them.

In subsequent letters the tension centred on developing the new relationship, while striking a balance between self-revelation and boring egocentricity. Writers are often very conscious of this tension. Here the students expressed it as a shared problem to be faced:

I've liked your letter very much and your letter never bored me a bit. I just hope I never bored you.

Lino — letter 2

I don't think you are a show off because talking about yourself is the way you find out about others.

Robyn — letter 2

I hope I haven't bored you. Your letter was very entertaining.

Claire — letter 2

Sorry my writing is messy but I am very interested in you and have so many questions.

Judy — letter 2

By the way my writing is off its to big. By the way I don't blame you for liking some boys.

Catherine — letter 2

I'm very pleased that you have sent a letter. I enjoyed reading your letter.

Shane — letter 2

In the early stages of a relationship, tension about one's accept-ability to the other is often dealt with by politeness and the mutual maintaining of self-esteem. The writers recognize that from prior social experience. At first they see the reader as very like themselves, and they do share their task in common, so their mutual identification is a helpful starting point for the negotiation of their relationship. What they continue to share in common is the wish to continue exchanging letters because the feedback is self-endorsing. When one partner seemed to falter, the other encouraged with positive comments or advice. Stephanie, however, was exasperated with Aldo's repetitive letters and wrote:

> Please keep off the soccer for awhile (it) is getting a bit boring since I'm not a soccer fan. Please write something interesting next time you write. What other dreams do (you) have besides soccer.

She then wrote a lengthy fantasy about being a ballet dancer, finishing with a promise to 'fill you in on more ballet, next week, because I know you find it interesting'. Aldo replied:

> Please keep off the ballet for awhile because everyone loves Soccer (He then asked her for a photo of herself) I think your (story) wasnt true ... I think we should be honest with each other.

Balancing egocentricity with the demands of relationships can be a lifelong struggle. Aldo's wish to maintain the relationship may help him to find ways to make his soccer sagas interesting, or he may give up.

These students engage in the struggle to decentre because arguably, they like the relationships offered and because they see their letters as close to social reality. It is not that authentic discourse here necessarily promotes unique kinds of cognitive or emotional development but that it allows writers to use their tacit understanding of human interaction in new ways. They can explore relationships and reality through their expression in the written language of perceptions, feelings and fantasies. In expressing one's self and world view in writing, many pressures have to be resolved. Not the least of these is the need to maintain a sense of self-esteem, while recognizing one's shortcomings and the risks in the situation. For several students matters of tidiness, punctuation, spelling and format became important because their partner modelled a particular standard.

In the 245 letters written by the thirty-five case students, there are ninety examples of self-esteem comments. There is at least one example from each student and a maximum of six from three writers. These comments were classified as those which functioned to make either the writer or reader feel good about themselves. They included apologies for handwriting or the content of the letter or its length, and the writer clearly sought acceptance for shortcomings and forestalled criticism by acknowledging them: other comments expressed interest in the other, enthusiasm for a reply or congratulations; exchanges of confidences or the giving or taking of advice. For example, Julia asked Anne Maree how to deal with the problem of being chosen for a solo part in a musical — 'I know I can't do it . . . Another problem is none of my friends got in!!!' Anne Maree shared her experiences:

> If they sort of disliked you cause you made it don't worry they'll get over it. And once its over they'll be even better friends than before. But if it isn't that way don't let me put ideas in your head. (I hope I don't sound bossy). When I first did a play Hansel and Gretal my friends were jealous. But eventually they were there when I had trouble. If they have a fight. Talk to them and prove that it wasn't your fault you made it and they didn't.

While this extract was counted as one example of a self-esteem comment, it is more extended and complex than most. Julia and Anne Maree, though randomly matched, are fairly alike in personality type, interests and writing style. Their letters, like their conversations, are lengthy and self-revealing.

In a different kind of relationship where Sean had greater difficulty than Jane starting his letters, he used as a model her 21-point format until he became concerned that he could not match the length of her letters. In his second letter he wrote:

> I repeat please do not write more next letter unless it's imperitive.

In the same letter he responded to her comment 'By the way I am a shrimp' with the encouraging note, 'Size doesn't mean a thing'. In his fifth letter he wrote:

> please don't write 4 pages until we've written about 10 letters and we get to know each other a bit better. I can't keep up.

In his next letter he complimented her on her handwriting:

> Compared to your friends writing your's is very neat. I can read it at least.

In the next line he admits he 'got badly busted at school for stealing starter units out of the heaters'. It seems from the context that this provocative disclosure is just part of his sharing experiences with Jane. He acknowledges the help her letters are to him and how much he enjoys them:

> These classes probably help me to write better but most of the magic is in the brain. I think I'm fairly good at writing.

Given a suitable context and a few prompts these writers ranged over a number of topics, some predictable such as sport, school, teachers, hobbies and holidays, but often unexpected issues of personal significance would emerge. When this happened, the writers took calculated risks for the sake of exploring their experiences and responses with another.

Isabella had some difficulty writing her letters, though she could write well when motivated — and when her partner was encouraging. She seemed blocked by a lack of confidence and her early letters to Caroline were perfunctory and apologetic. In her sixth letter she wrote:

> I got many feelings. Every single thing I do is wrong bad, awful.

She had been expressing some of this in the group throughout the year. She was encouraged consistently to write about the difficulties she had in any way she liked. At the end of the year she wrote a story, *The new adventures of Fluffles*. In part she wrote:

> Fluffles is a girl 'flurry'. She is five years old and she desperately wants a friend.
>
> Although she had problems in her life, she thought her biggest and everlasting problem was 'herself'.

Fluffles meets 'one of her own kind', thereby fulfilling Isabella's wish for self-acceptance by another. She then wrote a Christmas story to be given to Caroline. It was about a paralysed girl who was granted three wishes by an angel. Her first wish was to be able to walk, her second was to have presents for all the children in the home for the disabled, and the third to have presents to give her parents. All the wishes were granted and her parents 'were delighted'. Without analysing intrusively Isabella's Christmas gift of her story, it is clear she was discovering for herself a way of dealing with her inner world, and she was willing to share it. Her demeanour when she handed in the story indicated sufficient pleasure in her achievement to be almost independent of feedback. She had endorsed herself by her writing and found her own writing voice after a year of incubation.

The issue of maintaining self-esteem through writing was not intentionally a research focus in this letter writing experiment. It arose from observing what writers do naturally in a school-based context freed from marking or other constraints. After writing for self alone, which can lack feedback, writing for an attentive peer audience is a powerful motivation for twelve-year-olds. One measure of development in writing is the ability to move across a continuum of audiences and purposes, increasingly distanced from the self in time and space. These twelve-year-olds were moving towards an audience they knew little about, except through the exchange of letters. The primary purpose for authentic writing is to express the self, then reflect and shape it through a long-term process of varied discourse experiences. Given a context close to their naturally-developing sense of others with similar or different points of view and needs, the young writers in both the space man letters and the extended letter exchanges, start with their prior knowledge of relationships and their self-knowledge, working tentatively out from there. With confidence the writers take risks in sharing their fears, hopes and successes. Achilles wrote in his sixth letter:

> Well what I like about being a writer is writing to someone else. I hate being a writer when I get bad marks for my writing. I think of my writing good when I feel like writing and bad when I don't. My best writing experience is writing these letters. I like writing in letters.

And this was after Sally had admonished him:

> Your letters are about Soccer so if you don't mind would (you) write about something else like your other interests.

Possibly he had begun to see writing as one of his other 'interests'.

What is consistently remarkable, though it shouldn't be, is the amount of effort students will exert in self-exploration and in maintaining or increasing their sense of worth. Examples proliferate in schools of students who will use negative behaviour to this end, but given a genuine opportunity to gain self-esteem, most students will at least attempt the task. Where the context involves a mutual support system they know how to endorse the other, to seek self-endorsement and to tolerate mistakes in the relationship. They also know how to use to good effect in written language their intuitive knowledge that language can function to establish and maintain relationships.

What does this offer writing development theory and classroom practice? It offers support for the belief that students can be at the centre of their learning experiences, drawing on past learning experiences and experimenting with new ones, provided there is a possibility of genuine feedback, self-endorsement and discovery. How this best links with using writing to develop formal operations and the internalization of 'school' knowledge depends very much on the continuity of authentic discourse experiences with built-in variety. As Moffett points out:

> We would do well also to regard any sequence of writing assignments as an *accumulating repertory* from which nothing is ever really dropped. Growth means being able to do more things and to do old things better, not merely hopping from one stepping stone to the other.[7]

The challenge is to find writing experiences which students see as genuine, rewarding and self-developing. It helps to recognize that the potential for language development is there, then we can organize experiences which ensure that students are in touch with their own innate resources. When they are, we as teachers may have the humbling experience of discovering they have abilities too rarely tapped in much school curricula.

Students know how to develop and maintain relationships, using spoken and written language for that purpose. They like writing and will persevere with the search for appropriate language when there is an intrinsic reward in sight, such as an increase in self-esteem. When they begin to see themselves as successful writers in one mode they will take up the challenge to write in different modes and for more distant audiences. The timing of the transition can be difficult for a teacher to anticipate but the more involved students become in their own writing processes the readier they are to acknowledge their strengths and difficulties, and work on both. Then the teacher becomes a resource for ideas and another interested reader/ writer in the working group. Changes in students' attitudes to writing are more easily monitored, and contexts productive to growth recognized, when the teacher becomes an alert observer and responsive audience rather than sole motivator and final arbiter. Students pick up very accurately their teachers' beliefs about them. Often we forget what they are capable of doing in natural learning situations such as learning to talk. Remember that every parent expects that their child will learn to talk, and rarely doubts their ability to do so. It can be liberating for both teachers and students to discover that classrooms can gainfully exploit the natural learning abilities we all have. The need to maintain and promote self-esteem is an intrinsic part of the learning process, as the student-writers show here.

This argument should be self-evident, but I don't think it is. Sometimes it takes both a long time and a ruthless belief in students' capacities before we discover that in the right contexts they can become self-motivated, self-editing writers. They know how to gain and hold the attention of the audience, initially in reciprocal writing contexts, then later in more distant ones. When they are encouraged to do what comes naturally, they can make the audience clap because they can put on a real performance.

10   MARGARET MEEK

How do they know it's worth it? The untaught reading lessons

I am sure I became a teacher of English for a number of reasons that appointing committees found acceptable, but deep down I know I realized that it meant I could earn my living by reading poems and stories, writing some, despite my lack of creative talent, and encouraging the young to do all of these things better than I did. Like most English teachers I studied literary criticism, as I had done when an undergraduate (in the Scottish tradition) and practised with my ablest students, thereby ensuring the supply of new undergraduates. For the rest, I enthusiastically promoted the enjoyment of books and plays and wondered, increasingly, about the mysteries of 'response' and 'comprehension'. As for reading, I took it for granted as a fairly general ability and assumed that only perversity, ill-fortune, or an addiction to football or pin-ball kept some pupils from enjoying this natural extension of experience. I do not excuse this ignorance and naiveté. My academic and professional history is common to others of my generation, although I have long since realized how eccentric it now seems, just as I understand how few of my contemporary colleagues are women.

When I began teaching in England, it was assumed that the sensibilities of the rising generation were refined by reading works of acknowledged literary value and discussing them in terms borrowed from Arnoldian mandarins and Leavisite elitists.[1] I was brought up short, I think not when I read *Mansfield Park* with boys in Leeds who accused me of 'speaking Lunnon' (London). They felt kindly towards 'that Fanny'. The

shock came when I failed to communicate my enthusiasm for
Lycidas to a class of girls in a leafy London suburb. Then post-
war inner-city schools and post-Dartmouth constructs enlarged
the scope of English lessons and 'response' grew to include the
normative adjectives of psychology and sociology. Where once
there was I.A. Richards teaching us to read a page, there came
Walter Benjamin, and so on, to post-structuralism and the
rest. Now that I have some responsibility for the continuing
education of teachers, I find that the excitement of English
studies lies in the scope for meddling — for me an important
operation if it is done seriously enough to rebuff the charges of
dilettantism and amateurishness — in every activity related to
language and story-telling.

Story-telling is still at the heart of it all; everyone is now 'into'
narrative, from free-shop monologues to children's literature;
from the revival of oral story-telling to the further reaches of
narratology and literary theory. One significant difference. No
English teacher, whether or not her background is in literary
studies, takes for granted, in any group of pupils or students, a
common experience of learning to read and a background of
shared textual experience. Nor can we ignore those for whom
reading is an alien school-based activity with none of the
pleasures and excitement that we fancy we have always known.

Teaching reading in secondary school

Secondary school teachers of English in Britain have, traditionally, little experience in the teaching of reading which, in
our training institutions, has been the purview of educational
psychologists and primary school teachers. A great deal of the
research has passed unnoticed by those who could profit from
it. But after the publication of the Bullock Report in 1975 no
teacher was exempt from the concerns that cling to the promo-
tion of universal literacy and the extension to all pupils of the
type of literacy that was once the privilege of the few.[2]
Research reports continue to insist, although I believe that
pragmatic evidence is against them, that too many children do
not read and write well enough to participate in the life of a
literate community. For teachers of English (as mother tongue
or as second or other language) this is a special kind of
challenge. As our awareness of children's language development grows, as literature written for children becomes more
and more the material by which they can learn to read, as we
see the growth of understanding that, despite the proliferation

of information retrieval systems and 'non-paper' materials in libraries, there will still be a kind of reading one must do for oneself,[3] so we need to enter more fully into the business of how children learn to make prose mean. This is central in any coherent rationale for English studies in the context of our changing culture.

The reader and the text

Our responsibilities situate us between two reservoirs of perceptions with access to both. On the one hand are the literary theorists, notably those concerned with the inter-disciplinary relationships of structuralism, whose writings promote the idea that 'a theory of literature is a theory of reading'.[4] By opening up the questions related to interactions between the reader and the text, critics have shown how reading as an activity has none of the literary or ideological innocence that is still generally assumed in the teaching of it, whatever the age of the learner. Questions as to the extent individuals perform the same operations or how far these operations are confined to a tiny community of professional critics cannot really be answered until we are rather better at describing the operations in question, says Culler.[5] I want to ask: who can best describe the operations in question? Must they be 'only a tiny community of critics'? Agreed, they read more, but is it not possible that in teaching children to read, to re-learning to look at reading, or in helping those for whom the operation is still stubbornly a mystery, teachers might uncover what could count as evidence of the development of literary competences? Have not teachers in school promoted much of the data on which studies in children's language development have been founded?

If we enter this field we need our second reservoir of insights, drawn this time from the reading experts, notably those, like Smith and Goodman, in the psycholinguistic tradition.[6] By moving the model of reading away from behaviourist hierar-chies of learned skills to the interpretative understanding of written language they emphasize the reader's role in the *production* of a text. Their central pivot in articulating the reading process is the learner's proven ability to make text mean, so they investigate the relationship of language and thought. Psycholinguists are less concerned, however, to make distinctions within the process itself as the reader responds to different kinds of texts. For all that Goodman assumes that a story is the appropriate text for a young reader he does not differentiate kinds of narratives, or the relationship of the surface of text to the deeper structures of meanings, or the ways by which one is transformed into the other.

We who sit in classrooms read in Iser's theory of aesthetic response statements about the reader's communication with the text. He sees this as a dynamic process of self-correction where the reader formulates signifiers which must be continually modified,[7] and we think it could easily be Goodman's 'psycholinguistic guessing game'.[8] We see with pleasure the *rapprochement* of studies in language and literature. We know that as children 'learn how to mean' by taking part in conversations, they are also learning their culture.[9] So we might guess that they develop literary competences by adding to their natural inclination to narrate[10] and to the inherited folklore of childhood the story-telling proclivities of their clan.[11] Learning to read introduces them to the bond with the author[12] and the conventions of narrative discourse in archetypal forms such as the fairy-tale. The earliest experiences of stories in books come to children who hear enough of them as a special kind of play, a game with rules, codes and language conventions on the one hand, and the culture code of everyday life on the other. These lessons, like speech, are learned, but rarely, in the pedagogic sense, are they *taught*.

We are apt to glide over our ignorance of what kinds of literary experience generates and nourishes reading competences and how development proceeds. Individual case studies of how readers (and, for that matter, writers) are made are rare. My guess, not yet dignified as a hypothesis but in the process of investigation, is that children develop literary competences by interaction with what they find to be significant texts and literacy develops as they learn to *produce* texts, by reading and writing. The teacher's role — whatever the experts say it should also include — is to help the writing to happen and the texts to be read, not just as classroom exercises, but so that the young become independently responsive to both what they read and how they write.

It is fashionable now to talk of teaching as 'facilitating', in which lurks an implied meaning, 'to make easy' (but they may learn more easily without us). I don't think helping children to learn to read is easy, but when it is explorative and collaborative it is exciting. Long before they can write critical essays for examinations good readers practise reading, as James

Britton says, as doctors practise medicine.[13] Unlike violin playing, the practice passes unnoticed in the ordinariness of our print-soaked environment and the reading no-one else can do for you can begin from the first encounter with a picture book. Readers are made when they discover the activity is 'worth it'. Poor, inadequate, inexperienced readers lack literary competence because they have too little idea of what is 'in' reading for them. We, their teachers, are to blame not because we didn't give them reading lessons, but, as I hope to show, because too often we kept the essential reading secrets to ourselves in the mistaken belief that they are common knowledge.

Three learning situations
I propose to take you into three learning situations and to adopt the narrative mode.

First, a large group of post-graduates in training, most of whom have no background in literary criticism, are having their introductory lesson in the teaching of reading. Of the sixty or so, only three can remember their own childhood reading lessons and they are the ones who experienced difficulty, chiefly in understanding their teachers' instructions (e.g. 'sound it out'). The rest are mildly surprised by the suggestion that the very fact that they take their reading skills so much for granted may prove a hindrance to their teaching. The tutor's concern is to make ordinary reading anthropo-logically strange so that practised readers can inspect what they do without thinking.

The class is to read the first page of a novel without knowing where it comes from[14] (Those who guess or recognize the writer's style are asked not to say). This situation is common in school when children are given similar typed sheets to work from 'new text'.[15]

> Behind the smokehouse *that* summer, Ringo and I had a *living* map. Although Vicksburg was just a handful of chips from the woodpile and the River a trench scraped into the packed earth with the point of a hoe, it (river, city, and terrain) lived, possessing even in miniature that ponderable though passive recalcitrance of topography which outweighs artillery against which the most brilliant of victories and the most tragic of defeats are but the loud noises of a moment. To Ringo and me it lived, *if only because* of the fact that the sunimpacted ground drank water faster than we could fetch it from the well, the very setting of the stage for

conflict a prolonged and wellnigh hopeless ordeal in which we ran, panting and interminable, with the leaking bucket between wellhouse and battlefield, the two of us needing first to join forces and spend ourselves against a common enemy, time, before we could engender between us and hold intact the pattern of *recapitulant* mimic furious victory like a cloth, a shield between ourselves and reality, *between us and fact and doom*. This afternoon it seemed as if we would never get it filled, wet enough, since there had not even been dew in three weeks. But at last it was damp enough, damp-coloured enough at least, and we could begin. We were just about to begin. Then suddenly Loosh was standing there, watching us. He was Joby's son and Ringo's uncle; he stood there (we did not know where he had come from; we had not seen him appear, emerge) in the fierce full early afternoon sunlight, bareheaded, his head slanted a little, tilted a little yet firm and not askew, like a cannonball (which it resembled) bedded hurriedly and carelessly in concrete, his eyes a little red at the inner corners as Negroes' eyes get when they have been drinking, looking down at what Ringo and I called *Vicksburg*. Then I saw Philadelphy his wife, over at the woodpile, stooped, with an armful of wood already gathered into the crook of her elbow, watching Loosh's back.

'What's that?' Loosh said.

'Vicksburg' I said.

Loosh laughed. He stood there laughing, not loud, looking at the chips.

'Come on here, Loosh', Philadelphy said from the woodpile. There was something curious in her voice too — urgent, perhaps frightened. 'If you wants any supper, you better tote me some wood'. But I didn't know which, urgency or fright; I didn't know because suddenly Loosh stooped before Ringo or I could have moved, and with his hand he swept the chips flat.

'There's your Vicksburg', he said.

'Loosh!' Philadelphy said. But Loosh squatted, looking at me with that expression on his face. I was just twelve then: I didn't know triumph; I didn't even know the word.

Without the support of the rest of the book, the cover, blurb, author, the readers have to rely on their experience of how first pages work. Most of them tackle the reading as if it were a test — interesting in itself. On being asked if anything impedes their understanding all agree that they can 'work it out'. Sometimes the form of 'recapitulant' is queried and the difficulty of knowing exactly why the reading is not straightforward is pointed out. All are confident that they can 'guess' their way through the passage. With this agreement it is not difficult to establish 'guessing' as acceptable reading behaviour.

Next, they read it again. According to Barthes, this is the habit of the young, the old and professors.[16] Rather, it is read to them by someone who knows the text well and who treats it as a score, tuning it with subtleties of intonation in response to speech marks, commas and paragraph separations and giving it the dynamics of a coherent interpretation. By virtue of inserting a voice into the text, the readers now separate the author from the narrator and the narrator from the child he once was. With no more explanation, the page becomes 'known text' for the readers who thereafter set about their own *readings*, discussing in groups what is happening *as an actuality*, treating the characters as new acquaintances and 'reading between the lines'.[17]

Some of the outcomes are the predictable result of a *prise de conscience*, but as the discussion proceeds the students are surprised that what first seemed obvious in the narrative was no longer so. There is uncertainty about who was involved in and who won the Battle of Vicksburg, whether it matters or not, and whether the author was counting on the reader's knowledge. Assumptions are made and changed about the age and colour, relationships, political stance and affiliations of the characters. The gaps in the text are filled in. There is a fairly general assumption that the author has made this account of a children's game unnecessarily complicated, and on the whole the students are not disposed to do more on their own than draw narrative inferences about 'what is happening'. A secondary school English teacher might recognize this as fairly characteristic behaviour of fifteen-year-olds in response to an examination 'set book' — the last time most of the class engaged in this kind of activity. Everyone agreed however that collaborative discussion had been helpful, and they were tolerant of divergent interpretations.

Even at this stage, however, their view of 'being able to read' is changing. At the start of the class they had expected to be instructed in a 'method' or 'approach' to teaching reading that bypassed this systematic investigation of their underlying assumption of what reading is. They have now to see how speech and written language differ by being asked about the way dialogue is written. They realize that events are ordered by the author in a significant sequence that is not necessarily chronological and somehow the reader sorts this out (or doesn't). That 'narrative events have not only a logic of connection but a logic of hierarchy'[18] is the reason they eventually adduce for the clarification of this particular page. Everyone agreed that before the passage seemed complicated it had appeared straightforward, so clearly being able to read was connected with expecting to understand.

Two further questions were asked: What does Loosh *know*? Vicksburg is again the problem. If only we *knew* what *actually* happened! Why a *living* map? Ah, metaphor. They invent the answers and neglect the phrase beginning 'if only . . .' so that they miss the secret of the omitted 'but also'. Then another look at these unlikely sentences, ending with 'between us and fact and doom'. Is that how you expect an adult narrator to remember an ordinary day, or an extraordinary one? So we go back to the beginning, to the fourth word that we scarcely noticed even at each re-reading, '*that* summer'. What was so special about it?

By now the students have realized that a writer takes infinite trouble with an opening paragraph while a reader, with a whole novel to sort things out in, rushes ahead. Then they can understand that the author is making them read *against* the text. (It is very difficult, in fact, to read it aloud). So the next possibility unfolds. So used are they to the past tense of narrative that they sacrifice the symbolic for the sequential (as Genette explains, they do not recognize *seeds* and *snares*).[19] Very few students propose, even after several readings, that the boys are playing their game at the same time as the battle is being fought. Once this is suggested, the page can be read again, quite differently, and with the additional element of *surprise*, another aspect of reading that we take for granted.

As a reading lesson this discussion dispels the idea that reading is 'decoding' words to speech. Guessing, anticipating, predicting, drawing on life experience, reading experiences are readerly activities and collaborative moves are helpful. How did we learn that? Were we ever taught that:

> Fiction can hold together within a single space a variety of languages, levels of focus, points of view, which would be contradictory in other kinds of discourse organized towards a particular empirical end. Barthes says that the reader learns to cope with these contradictions and becomes the hero in the adventures of culture.[20]

The problem is still, how does the reader learn? Yet many, many novel readers clearly do, without the benefit of literature lessons, or even in spite of them. More certainly, children are now learning from texts most of us haven't read. At one point, when the class was marvelling at how easily they did something as complicated as reading, a student suddenly asked about children: how do they know it's worth it? — the critical question.

The insights of 'untaught' lessons

The second lesson involves a group of teachers who are caught up in what they see as the problem of 'to have read'. They 'have read' a significant proportion of touchstone texts in English and are persuaded that children who are not initiated into the high literary culture are somehow 'deprived'. The children's cry of 'Oh, miss it's *boring*' in response to *The Wind in the Willows, David Copperfield, Alice*, to say nothing of poems and the Carnegie prize-winning novels of the sixties, cuts them like a knife because they really believe that what Barthes calls 'les desinvoltures de lire' in their pupils are somehow their fault.[21]

So we agreed to work at what the difficulties are for a young 1980s reader of reasonable disposition and moderate skill to tackle a 'classic' text. I confessed an ulterior motive. Given that English is a world-wide literary language, that our educational tradition has been, until recently, insular, I wondered if the lessons to be learned in reading a text of non-English provenance, of earlier age, would apply to reading, say, Caribbean, African and Australian writing in English. So we chose *Huckleberry Finn* as the classic book 'to have read', and concentrated on the problems of 'getting into' the story up to end of the third chapter:

Hucklebrry Finn

We played robbers now and then about a month, and then I resigned. All the boys did. We hadn't robbed nobody, we hadn't killed any people, but only just pretended. We used to hop out of the woods and go charging down on hog-drovers and women in carts taking garden stuff to market, but we never hived any of them. Tom Sawyer called the hogs 'ingots', and he called the turnips and stuff 'julery', and we would go to the cave and pow-wow over what we had done and how many people we had killed and marked. But I couldn't see no profit in it. One time Tom sent a boy to run about town with a blazing stick, which he called a slogan (which was the sign for the Gang to get together), and then he said he had got secret news by his spies that next day a whole parcel of Spanish merchants and rich A-rabs was going to camp in Cave Hollow with two hundred elephants, and six hundred camels, and over a thousand 'sumter' mules, all loaded down with di'monds, and they didn't have only a guard of four hundred soldiers, and so we would lay in ambuscade, as he called it, and kill the lot and scoop the things. He said we must slick up our swords and guns, and get ready. He never could go after even a turnip-cart but he must have the swords and guns all scoured up for it; though they was only lath and broom-sticks, and you might scour at them till you rotted, and then they warn't worth a mouthful of ashes more than what they was before. I didn't believe we could lick such a crowd of Spaniards and A-rabs, but I wanted to see the camels and elephants, so I was on hand next day, Saturday, in the ambuscade; and when we got the word, we rushed out of the woods and down the hill. But there warn't no Spaniards and A-rabs, and there warn't no camels nor no elephants. It warn't anything but a Sunday-school picnic, and only a primer-class at that. We busted it up, and chased the children up the hollow: but we never got anything but some doughnuts and jam, though Ben Rogers got a rag doll, and Jo Harper got a hymn-book and a tract; and then the teacher charged in and made up drop everything and cut. I didn't see no di'monds, and I told Tom Sawyer so. He said there was loads of them there, anyway; and he said there was A-rabs there, too, and elephants and things. I said, why couldn't we see them, then? We said if I warn't so ignorant, but had read a book called *Don Quixote*, I would know without asking. He said it was all done by enchantment. He said there was hundreds of soldiers there, and elephants and treasure, and so on, but we had enemies which he called magicians, and they had turned the whole thing into an infant Sunday-school, just out of spite. I said all right, then the thing for us to do was to go for the magicians. Tom Sawyer said I was a numskull.

You know, of course, what emerges; another series of untaught lessons. Again the problem: how do children learn to 'tune' the voice on the page? A child I knew well once asked me to read the first paragraph aloud for her ('and no more') as she 'couldn't make it come right'. After I had added a nasal note to my reading voice she said, 'That's it' and went on. Understanding, it seems, in the sense of taking on the world the author has made, is linked to the creation of the illusion which is, again, an act of collaborative communion. My young reader tuned into Mark Twain by means of cowboy films she'd seen on television. Lesson one: Don't assume ignorance, find connections.

Potentially successful readers tolerate uncertainty because at some time someone has made the narrative connections come quickly enough to make the story 'interesting'. Dialogue keeps action moving, or seems to. In Chapter 3 of *Huckleberry Finn* are two pages of close type that proved a stumbling block for the pupils in our experiment. Here the readers' tolerance of Huck, sympathetically extended to his spelling problems with Miss Watson, and the formation of Tom Sawyer's gang with its bloodthirsty proposals, falters on the game of robbers. This passage is written as a report. We looked at it in detail, for it is on just such text that the teacher's most frequent, authoritative interpolations and commentaries occur. This is school reading of the classics, with yawning accompaniment. The teacher wants enjoyment of what is, for her, clearly humour; the class announces boredom.

Culler again shows exactly what we take for granted. In asserting that 'a criticism based on a theory of reading ought at least to have the virtue of being ready to ask, for whatever work it is studying, which operations of reading will be most appropriate to minimize boredom and to awaken the drama latent in every text', he says we should 'move in if the reading goes astray or founders'. What a cover-up there is in 'move in'. We all act as if we know, and no-one would suggest a universal model for our operations, but do we really know what we do and what happens? Have we watched ourselves or each other? I have not even gathered from my colleagues or on my own account how thirteen-year-olds who can be persuaded to try sort out the fantasy world Tom Sawyer derived from his 'pirate books' from the pragmatic-seeming realism of the narrator 'who claims to be naturally wicked while the author praises his virtues behind his back'.[22]

It is not difficult for experienced readers to list what can here be learned: how Huck Finn needs a shared sense of humour between reader and author and an agreed tolerance and sympathy. Wandering *inside* the text to see both Huck's and Tom's view of the game,[23] we see the camel train and the Sunday-school class in a kind of double vision by means of the interconnecting narrative perspectives; we are both in the game and out of it. When Tom says that Huck would have seen the A-rabs if he read *Don Quixote* we know the rules that let an author refer to the whole pantheon of literature in the way that football experts cite teams and games and chess players read classic moves.

We are wont to say that these questions are answered by the close reading experience. But what, exactly, constitutes this experience? At first my student colleagues thought that only books of a certain 'density' offered this kind of textual awareness, but when we came to list them, the problem came back in a different form. (Did the 'pirate books' include *Treasure Island*? Is popular fiction ever 'dense'?). A more honest inspection of our own reading habits and a closer look at our pupils brought other notions. First, we realized exactly how little we re-read the books we were so pleased to have read until we shared them with out pupils. We were revisiting memories; they were reading new text. Our concern to let nothing of the resavouring escape the young often blocked what they could have done for themselves. Successful readers 'press on regardless' leaving the gaps in the text (*Don Quixote*, for example) as adult's business. They grasp, apparently without effort, that Sam's freedom was jeopardized by Tom's pedantry, an idea that I knew escaped me when I first read the book. But our thirteen-year-olds read *Huckleberry Finn* with sensibilities refined not by books but by events in the streets of the inner city. So we, the teachers, learned that what we really had to look at is not what young readers don't understand, but how they ignore what does not make the story work for them. This is literary competence of a kind we are too practised to recognize.

In traditional reading lessons, literature teachers tend to be the leaders. But group work, collaborative learning, children choosing texts all offer opportunities for understanding what our very experience may shut out. This is in no way to undervalue the teacher's competences, but simply to say that we must guard against living on a diminishing capital. We shall not discover the growth of literary competences in children if we invite them into literature only on our terms. As has always happened, they will simply behave well (or not) in class, and read other books under the desk.

We still have to understand more about the ideological hinterland of 'to have read' (Raymond Williams: *The Country and the City* was a good starting point for us).[24] Our most pressing current reading problem with regard to adolescents is not to make the classics readable but to deepen and extend reading skills developed on a range of narrative texts we know nothing or too little about — new comic strips, films, video images and the mental images that go with them. The young who read as we do have only us to talk to, which may guarantee that the circle of readers remains tiny, but can hardly be what we want — or is it? If we make the terms of entry to the inner ring of readership too exclusive, our pupils will decide the game is not worth the entrance fee of the effort to an esoteric cult. We shall always have the books we are glad to have read, but the young will eventually write their own. We cannot transfer the desire to read and train their competences only on *our* known texts. The wisdom of age lies in knowing how these things are recreated. I'm not sure I know a good book about it.

Helping inexperienced readers

The third learning situation involved five London teachers and the same number of adolescent pupils whose reading was too unpractised to let them function adequately in ordinary lessons. In these cases it is usual for 'remedial' action to be taken. These teachers decided to offer the pupils the chance to become readers by inviting them to take on that role in as normal a situation as could be devised: to learn to read by reading real texts instead of specially constructed materials. The experiment lasted for years and has been fully documented in order to present a different kind of experience from that usually contained in books on the teaching of reading.

Our concern was to help our inexperienced readers to read a book with confidence and pleasure and to see what was involved in the teaching and learning of this process. What, we asked, could the competent readers do that the less successful do not know they had to learn?

Our ignorance proved more than a little shaming. Videotape recordings of lessons showed us how even the most caring, insightful, well-read teachers can unwittingly take from a pupil what little competence he has. In sharing a book, for instance, who turns the pages, smooths them down, looks back at the pictures? As a colleague said: 'Some lessons you do not even know you teach. When I turn these pages over I'm really saying 'you are such a poor reader I even have to find the place for you' when he could certainly do it on his own. In one such recording we saw the same colleague reading Roald Dahl's *The Magic Finger* with her pupil. In casual conversation at the end of an episode she asked, 'What kind of people lived next door?' The pupil was bewildered, not because he didn't know they were game hunters, but because he had no idea what relevance the question had to his oral reading of the text.

No-one who has taught or seen 'remedial' lessons given to inexperienced readers can fail to be struck by the apparent distance between the halting, word-by-word deciphering of those whose concern is 'to get it right' and the rhythmic patterning and apparently effortless command of narrative conventions of the practised readers of the same age. The poor reader is seen as the victim of his background and experience, despite the fact that there is plenty of evidence that middle-class children have the same problems. The pupils we taught were content to go through any motions as long as we would collude with their belief that they would never really be able to master this puzzle. They could not understand why we persistently refused to do so.[25]

From the significant lessons these pupils taught us I offer two for inspection. The first concerns the way the learner's view of the task maintains or inhibits real reading competence.

Trevor certainly had no idea that he was a natural disciple of Toderov in the way he dismantled the system of texts.[26] When his teacher read to him he would demand: 'Why does it say that . . .? 'Doesn't this stupid writer know that . . .?' and proceed with systematic commentary on the words and the plot. The teaching problem was to keep this activity intact in the face of Trevor's insistence that reading was 'saying the words right', a lesson that had been fiercely driven home in his first years in school. When he was finally aware that he could read, three-and-a-half years later, the elusive joy of his earlier approach was gone.[27] He learned to read by means of a compromise between his desire, the excitement stories awoke in him, and what he mistakenly believed, against all evidence, was what a teacher wanted. Trevor taught us how high the wall is for inexperienced readers to climb into the enchanted garden, a wall, I feel, we build.

Throughout this, often painful, learning time with these pupils we discovered more about why they didn't think reading was 'worth it'. We strove to help them to predict and guess their way through narrative texts outside the remedial reading schemes, we discovered how 'readability', the measurement of text, vocabulary and sentence length, is not what makes text difficult. Instead, we studied the significance of what the author doesn't say, about the world inside the story and the world outside it, with the scores of unexplained textual conventions that the reader has to learn. That they *can* learn them is evident; they have little trouble with comics which are equally rule-governed and which they read out without difficulty.

Gradually our pupils discovered that there was more to be gained than reading skill. We *did* invite them into the circle of readers without the demands that they imagined would be attendant on their acceptance. We simply argued that if there was no text they could enjoy and make sense of, then they must help to produce one. Thus we became the scribes of their stories. They dictated to us and we wrote and in so doing we discovered they already had the competences we imagined were lacking as the result of their inexperience. They related one incident to another; they tagged dialogue or not as the occasion demanded. One boy dictated 4000 words in narrative chunks and in prose rhetoric. They needed our educational skills when the gaps in the text were too wide for another reader and in sorting out the cohesion within the sentences, but the narrative conventions were generally firm. We learned what we had always known: you don't teach children to tell stories; you let them, and then help them to know that's how other authors — the ones who write books — do it too. Their stories were both fantastic and everyday, informed by both poetic and common sense. They were drawing on a storehouse of narrative structure that psychoanalysts have long since known to be common property.[28]

Children's deep responses
We learned most from these pupils where we expected to learn least from their interaction with narrative texts. The slow oral production that they believe is reading is a kind of gripping grief to the well-practised listener. As we had laid on each other the obligation to inspect all the evidence we collected we listened, painfully, to many hours of this. Gradually we listened differently as we learned the techniques of chronological strangeness. We learned again, as in literary criticism, to *over-read* what we so usually under-read — books written for children. We discovered what Frank Kermode calls 'secrets' which resist 'all but abnormally attentive scrutiny, reading so minute, so intense, and slow that it seems to run counter to one's 'natural' sense of what a novel is'.[29] Kermode is describing hermeneutic criticism; it applies perfectly to what our pupils made us do.

We discovered the deep structures of some children's novelists, the construct of childhood latent in the writings of Dahl and Philippa Pearce, and the way 'popular' texts transform the motivations of authors. Our most successful book was *The Iron Man* about which its author, Ted Hughes has written a persuasive analysis of myth in education.[30] As we read it again and again we saw how our inexperienced readers had more than enough of the common understanding of the clash of technology and nature to match the workings of the poet's imagination with their own. They had learned the conventions from Batman and Superman. They could make the story work as a metaphor of their own convention. They were the little boy who befriended the Iron man, and the Iron man who saved the world. As for us, we had to learn again the history of literature, the creation myths, St George and the Dragon, *Pilgrims Progress*, the reconciliation of man and nature. Unlikely? Reading as slowly as our pupils did, we discover with them how we moved inside a literary text and gained 'the moving viewpoint which travels along *inside* that which it has to apprehend'. As our pupils learned, so we came to understand what they were learning. 'This mode of grasping', says Iser, 'is unique to literature'.[31] That was the lesson for us all.

These are some of the untaught lessons. But my opening question — my students' insight — still stands. How *do* they know it's worth it? What gets in the way is, I believe, our view of the task. We are so keen to make our readers competent, lettered, skilled, that we foreground what is *not* our joy in reading and background the fact that we have been secretly playing games. Story-telling can be a kind of lifelong play. As Vygotsky tells us, play can give the child a new form of desire and teach him to relate this 'to a fictitious 'I' — to his role in the game and its rules. Therefore, a child's greatest achievements are possible in play-achievements which tomorrow will become his average level of real action and morality'.[32] We have to be more hospitable to new texts and new conventions of writing, and must nurture the latent competences of story-telling that children learn without our teaching, if we are to enlarge the 'tiny' community of those who read with desire.

11 ROBERT E. SHAFER

Pushing the pendulum: new perspectives for teacher education in the eighties

This ideas in this chapter have come about from my own thirty-year involvement as a teacher and teacher of teachers in various parts of the United States. In addition to that experience I have also had the opportunity to study developments in education and in teacher education for prolonged periods in the United Kingdom, Canada, Australia, New Zealand and the Federal Republic of Germany. From the time spent with colleagues both within the United States and these other countries, I have concluded that the problems discussed in this chapter, represent for the most part 'universals' in teacher education. Although there are distinct differences in the 'mechanics' of teacher education within the various national systems referred to in this chapter, it is my view that teacher education reflects the various public attitudes towards education pervasive among opinion leaders in a society at any particular time. Over the past several decades these public attitudes in most Western industralized countries have tended to insist that education be conservative with a distinct focus on teaching the 'basic skills'. Education and teacher education are not seen as producing dramatic changes in the society, and the focus has been, as far as most members of the public are concerned, on the production of an educational product in the most economic terms and those most subject to accountability. Teacher education has clearly reflected these public attitudes and has tended to become increasingly conservative. Teacher education in English has been affected significantly by these trends.

In England, despite the work of the National Association of Teachers of English, which developed proposals for a variety of innovative schemes for both pre-service and in-service teacher education in English, many teacher education institutions have been closed in wide-sweeping government cutbacks of teacher education. During the mid-1970s many of the most innovative and prominent teacher educators in English found themselves unemployed and have been given 'the golden handshake' by the government and their own institutions. During the spring and summer of 1981, similar developments began to occur in Australia, where the government has begun to merge previously independent teacher training colleges into single institutions, ostensibly for economic reasons. Such activity has thrown the faculties of long established teacher education programmes such as the one at Melbourne State College, for example, into turmoil, with considerable damage to the morale of many people working in teacher education.

In the United States, long-established centres of teaching and research and teacher education may be going out of business. The University of California at Berkeley, for example has proposed to close its School of Education and transfer persons in teacher education to various other parts of the University. A similar proposal has been made at Duke University. Developments such as the above fly in the face of considerable creative work which has been done in the above-mentioned institutions, particularly in the preparation of teachers of English and the development of an English curriculum. It will not be possible to discuss all of these developments in this chapter although I would hope to make reference to a number of them, particularly in the American context, which is the one I know best. My own view is that we are on the threshhold of a pendulum swing to a new and more humanistic tradition in teacher education since I am also convinced that the public will not be deluded much longer that the methods for producing products of superior quality in the military-industrial complex can be transferred to the preparation of persons to teach and engage in the other helping professions, without considerable damage to the human values and human relationships which must be a part of the work of such professionals. In the wide-ranging discussions which took place in the Commission on Teacher Education at the Third International Conference on the Teaching of English, at the University of Sydney in August,

1980, it seemed clear that the experiments in 'competency-based teacher education' which have been going on in the United States for the past dozen years have been damaging to the professional preparation of teachers even though lauded by many researchers, deans and faculty members in teacher education and members of the public. This is why part of the story of teacher education in English in the United States over the past several years may be worth the telling. Perhaps the telling of it may also be a push to the pendulum for a swing back toward a more humanistic view. Pendulum swings have been a significant characteristic of American education in past years and after more than a decade of 'systems approaches' to ensure 'accountability' and movements called 'back to the basics', many teachers and parents, not to mention pupils, seem ready for a change.

Teacher Education: The National Council of Teachers of English

If one is to understand developments in teacher education in English in the United States, one must look carefully at the work of the National Council of Teachers of English (NCTE) in this area. No better chronicle exists than that written by Alfred H. Grommon[1] of the efforts in teacher education in English in the years before the formation of the National Council of Teachers of English, up through its beginning in 1912, and on through its history of influence until the heyday of the involvement of the Federal government in curriculum development in teacher education in the late 1960s.

Beginning in 1965, the Modern Language Association of America, the National Council of Teachers of English and the National State Directors of Teacher Education and Certification co-sponsored the English Teacher Preparation Study which was directed by William P. Viall, Executive Secretary of the National State Directors of Teacher Education and Certification. The document which emerged came to be known as the *Guidelines* and shall be so referred to in this chapter. NCTE's Committee on Preparation and Certification of Teachers of English had long urged that a national study of teacher education in English, built upon the recommendations and the expertise of scholars and teachers, could produce guidelines which would strengthen teacher preparation in English in the United States at all levels. Over a thousand state education department officials, representatives of certificating bodies, professors of English and education, representatives of other educational organizations, and spokespersons for the schools met in regional and national conferences across the country to set up guidelines for more effective elementary and secondary school preparation. The study actually went on for three years and the results are published in the *English Journal* of April 1968.[2] In general, the three-year-long English Teacher Preparation Study did not attempt to suggest the advocacy of one kind of classroom or school organizational model or another, but rather emphasized the importance to the future of the teacher's preparation of specific aspects of English subject matter and related fields. Nor did the English Teacher Preparation Study propose any specific arrangement of courses within a programme or a number of 'hours' in English or education required for adequate preparation. The *Guidelines* themselves contained agreed-upon areas which the beginning teacher should have studied, and also suggested directions — as well as diversity and depth — in further in-service study. The *Guidelines* were (in part) as follows:

1. A teacher of English at any level should have personal qualities which will contribute to his/her success as a classroom teacher and should have a broad background in liberal arts and sciences.

2. a. A programme in English for the elementary school teacher should provide a balanced study of language, literature, and composition above the level of freshman English. In addition, the programme should require supervised teaching in English, language arts methods, including the teaching of reading, and it should provide for a fifth year of study.

   b. The programme in English for secondary school teachers of English should constitute a major so arranged as to provide a balanced study of language, literature, and composition above the level of freshman English. In addition, the programme should provide supervised teaching and English methods, including the teaching of reading at the secondary level and it should provide for the fifth year of study, largely in graduate courses in English and in English Education.

   c. The teacher of English at any level should consider growth in his/her profession as a continuing process.

3. The teacher of English at any level should have the understanding and appreciation of a wide body of literature.

4. The teacher of English at any level should have skill in listening, speaking, reading and writing and an understanding of the nature of language and of rhetoric.

5. The teacher of English at any level should have an understanding of the relationship of child and adult development through the teaching of English.

6. The teacher of English at any level should have studied methods of teaching English and have had supervised teaching.

Viall, 1967[3]

As Jenkins[4] has pointed out, widespread progress in adopting these changes was slow. State boards of education and administrators of teacher certification agencies in state departments of education were slow in many states to accept the *Guidelines*. There was, after all, a historical division between those persons in various areas of professional education and teacher education and those associated with subject matter groups. Also, many were suspicious that at the time the *Guidelines* were developed they reflected a stampede by various members of the English teaching community to propose a model of English which would fit the conception of the discipline borrowed from the sciences in order to gain access to the largesse of Federal funds available for curriculum development and in-service teacher education.[5]

At this point in time it seems clear that the development of the *Guidelines* was a significant mark in the development of teacher education in English in the United States since it was the first time that comprehensive recommendations were offered to teacher education institutions and to accrediting agencies. Recommendations such as these are often obsolete as soon as they are published. Priorities in teacher education change rapidly and the *Guidelines* were only recommendations for minimum essentials. The whole exercise did bring together and focus a variety of opinion on the preparation of English teachers which had never been done before, and such organizations as the Conference on English Education, consisting mostly of teacher educators and supervisors in English within the National Council of Teachers of English which had formed in 1963, did keep such guidelines under constant review in the future.[6]

Continuing its work on attempts to influence policy and practice in the preparation of teachers of English, the National Council of Teachers of English Committee on Teacher Preparation and Certification, chaired by Richard Larson (1976) developed a statement 'recognizing that much has happened to the world since 1967', and 'seeking to reaffirm those parts of the 1967 *Guidelines* that still apply, to strengthen the positions taken in the earlier guidelines about the essentials of teacher education and to reflect the changes that have taken place in our profession since 1967', and developed new recommendations for teacher education in English.[7]

The Statement on the Preparation of Teachers of English (hereafter referred to as the *Statement*) was divided into four parts. First was an introduction which identified some of the developments to be taken into account presently in the preparation of teachers. Part I identified the essential knowledge, skills and attitudes that were to be developed by teachers of English. Part II was concerned with the experiences the Committee considered essential to the development of a well-qualified teacher. Part III presented 'some questions that a statement of this sort cannot resolve — unavoidable questions that teacher trainers and planners of curriculum attach to themselves'.[8]

Although it is not possible to make a detailed comparison in this chapter, it is of more than passing interest to note some of the differences between the *Guidelines* proposed in the 1967 English Teacher Preparation Study and the recommendations proposed for the 1976 *Statement* on the preparation of teachers of English. The 1967 *Guidelines* give little attention to students. The 1976 *Statement* noted the changes taking place in the student population:

> And our students are changing too. (We include here not only children and adolescents, but also students in four-year and community colleges). Physically, students are maturing earlier, they vote earlier, many are more alert to the social, political, and economic events that shape our world. Many are reared as much by media as by parents and schools. Many have lost respect for authority that students used to have. In addition, more of our students are adults — people who have interrupted their studies and have now returned to them with fresh energy and a broader perspective than they had when younger. Our student body, therefore, is more complex than a few years ago.[9]

Between 1960 and 1967 a major influence on teaching English was the United States Office of Education, which spent hundreds of thousands of dollars in the attempt to strengthen teachers' command of their 'discipline', to familiarize them with new materials and to let them work with 'disadvantaged students' by the funding of curriculum centres and summer fellowships for experienced teachers. For the most part, they were to learn what had been defined in the late 1950s and early 1960s as the new discipline of English, the familiar tripod curriculum comprising language, literature and composition.[10] The introduction to the *Statement* notes that:

> Today that metaphor (the tripod) has all but disappeared as a definition of English; our subject is viewed not only as a body of knowledge and as a set of skills and attitudes, but also as a process, an activity — something one does (i.e., one uses and responds to language, in a variety of ways and in variety of contexts). In the mid-60s, English was viewed as an academic discipline, whose mastery was a sign of one's intellectual development. Today many teachers agree that English is also a means by which students grow emotionally; they respond to their experiences and learn about their worlds, their attitudes, and themselves by using language about these subjects.[11]

The introduction to the *Statement* also noted the increasing interest in 'open classrooms' and a desire to recognize individual differences among students and to deal with them. 'Divergent thinking' and 'creativity' among students are values and goals applauded in much professional writing about the teaching of English.[12] Also, in contrast with the 1967 *Guidelines* the introduction to the *Statement* noted the trend towards 'field-based' programmes in teacher education, including large amounts of experience in schools in the pre-service programme proposing that prospective teachers be placed more in schools where they can serve as 'apprentices in a variety of ways and thus learn a profession from skilled, experienced, and imaginative teachers who are practising with children'.[13] In addition, the *Statement* noted a shift in the concern of the Federal government in the United States from allocating money for curriculum development and in-service teacher education, as had been done in the 1960s, to specific proposals for 'accountability' in the 1970s. As the report noted:

> The government's . . . attention was to employ ways of enforcing accountability: towards ways of assessing, through precise specification of desired behaviour in students and measurements of student's accomplishments whether the teacher had done the job the public is paying for. The interest in accountability may have been nurtured in Washington but it has been picked up by the state and local governments, with the result that in 1976, 'accountability' is the leading watchword in education.[14]

Approximately 10 years ago, Hook[15] and his colleagues reported their findings about a wide-ranging study of undergraduate English teacher preparation in the state of Illinois. When taken together with the ETPS Guidelines Study, the Illinois Statewide Curriculum Study Centre in the Preparation of Secondary School English Teachers (ISCEPET) revealed rather common teacher education programme inadequacies as identified by teachers in Illinois and other parts of the United States. Some of these inadequacies were as follows:

> 1. Reading, composition, literature for adolescents, grammar, history of language and related work in linguistics. (Illinois English Teachers, Grades 7, 8, and 9).

> 2. Grammar (the English language and composition) Illinois Teachers, Grades 10, 11, and 12. Language preparation in general (English department chairpersons in English).

In a recent study, (1980), Fagan and Laine compared the priorities that the Illinois English teachers noted above as deficiencies in their preparation in 1969 with a group of Pennsylvania English teachers who graduated from Pennsylvania State University in 1979. Fagan and Laine found that:

> 1. As one might infer, the professional qualifications for teaching English in the teacher shortage era of the 60s to the oversupply of the 70s were pronounced ... only 38 per cent of the Illinois respondents had majored in English and 6 per cent had no college degree ... slightly more than one third had degrees in fields other than English. The Pennsylvania respondents in contrast were all college graduates with majors in English.

> 2. Graduates of the Pennsylvania programme felt reasonably secure about their preparation in composition, grammar, adolescent literature, reading, and linguistics, although the teachers in both studies identified the teaching of composition as a major programme concern.

> 3. Thirty-five per cent of the Illinois teachers felt their 'least successful' area of teaching was composition. They also felt that a new approach was needed in teaching grammar.

> 4. In the 1969 Illinois study, adolescent literature and reading or children's literature and reading tended to be considered in the same area as reported by both elementary and secondary teachers, although only 25 per cent of the Illinois sample had had such courses. Apparently none of the senior high Illinois sample had had courses in adolescent or children's literature.

5. Prospective Illinois English teachers in 1969 followed a professional programme characterized by a general methods course, possibly some reading and adolescent literature. About 25 per cent of the sampled respondents had some composition or teaching of composition (about 20 per cent of those responding) a grammar course and survey course in American or English literature or period courses.

6. Prospective Pennsylvania teachers, in contrast, in 1979 followed a professional programme characterized by prescribed courses in: special methods, reading, adolescent literature, composition, linguistics (which included prescriptive, descriptive, and transformational grammars); other prescribed courses with alternatives, that is Milton or Chaucer; (journalism) or mass media analysis (theatre); speech communication, film educational measurement and supporting courses in American English literature.

Fagan and Laine point out that:

> From the Pennsylvania respondents' perspective, English teacher preparation programmes are more restricted and specified; yet they are broader in the sense that delivery systems and audiences or the content of the discipline are intrinsic targets for the programme.[16]

In a large measure, then, with respect to this study, some movement can be seen from the English Teacher Preparation Study *Guidelines* of 1967 to the 1976 *Statement* in at least some American institutions, that is, moving from one general methods course and survey courses in English and American literature and period courses and courses in traditional grammar, to require special methods in the teaching of English, and requiring courses in composition, reading, adolescent literature, history of the language, linguistics, drama and speech as well. Insofar as the content and academic preparation of English teachers is concerned, other studies document changes in the professional educational aspects of the programme.

Performance based teacher education

In the early 1970s Performance Based Teacher Education (PBTE) also known as Competency Based Teacher Education (CBTE) began to develop as a direct result of the general application of 'systems approaches' to all education stemming from recommendations by various members of Congress, of certain leaders in the United States Office of Education and the educational measurement community, that the education community had not been sufficiently accountable in the past, and that a systems approach to teacher education would bring about this needed accountability.[17] Performance Based Teacher Education centres on the specification of com petencies that teachers should acquire in order to perform certain tasks. Competency is to be determined at various points in the preparation of teachers in three general areas:

1. The specification of knowledge which will be imparted to the teachers in training.
2. The evaluation of their teaching behavior according to certain prescribed criteria.
3. Assessing the knowledge of the pupils taught by the student teacher or teacher.

A number of states has adopted Performance Based Teacher Education programmes; many have not. Writing in the mid-1970s, Jenkins (1977) commented on PBTE as follows:

The subject fields have resisted the approach, and in many instances the objection has been vociferous. Subject matter specialists oppose PBTE because of its limited philosophic and knowledge base. They feel that PBTE threatens to trivialize the curriculum by fragmenting their subjects. They oppose the heavy career or vocational orientation that it seems to suggest, an orientation that for some is a healthy and realistic antidote to the traditional academic emphasis of the curriculum.[18]

Jenkins goes on to point out that many English teachers have continued to oppose PBTE because of its concentration on the cognitive aspects of learning, while many of the important objectives of English programmes continue to be found in the affective domain. Supporters of PBTE propose that the approach can assist English teachers in making their objectives precise and therefore make accountability more possible by specifying how teaching is related to the pupils' achievement.

The analysis of results of PBTE programmes continues to be mixed. In a summary of all Performance Based Teacher Education done in the late 60s and early 70s, Heath and Nielson[19] concluded that 'an empirical basis for performance based teacher education does not exist' and that 'continued research on such sterile definitions of teaching seemed unlikely to provide a basis for training teachers'. They also noted that performance based teacher education models do not recognize two important types of variables. These are what is to be *taught* and also *who* is to be taught. Other practioners have reached different conclusions. Dickson[20] noted that although there are varying degrees of commitment to the practice of Performance Based Teacher Education, there is evidence that aspects of the movement continue to have an impact on teacher education, e.g., objectives for teacher roles have continued to be stated in behavioural terms. These specifications of teacher roles, which he feels have been brought about by PBTE, and have also sensitized teacher educators to the need to be practical provide a theoretical base for decisions in school. Further, Piper and Houston[21] compare PBTE and the movement known as Minimal Competency Testing which has grown up in a number of states, concluding that:

> The MCT movement for teachers is very different from the CBTE. The CBTE and MCT emphasize exit requirements but that is where the similarity ends. CBTE emphasizes professional practice in the classroom to improve student learning. MCT for teachers emphasizes minimal cognitive knowledge.

In a penetrating analysis of what may be the basic deficiency underlying PBTE, Popkewitz, Tabachnick, and Zeichner[22] proposed that much of the difficulty in attempting to establish PBTE as well as some other similar types of behaviouristic curriculum reform methods in professional education comes directly from a research paradigm which is almost universally used in the United States to study the effects of teacher education. They also proposed that the dominant research paradigm in teacher education is the empirical analytic model. This sees the purpose of inquiry as being to discover a deductive system of propositions or scientific laws which can be used to predict and explain human behaviour. Similarities are noted to the physical sciences, and human behaviour, which is assumed to have characteristics which exist independent of, or external to, the intentions and motives of the people involved in the action. The researcher's task is then to assume a position of distance from the studied phenomena to guarantee neutrality and to control subjectivity. They further propose that the empirical-analytic paradigm in teacher education research is expressed in three interrelated questions about the effects of programmes about prospective teachers. The first question has to do with the study of the ways that one can influence prospective teachers' classroom behaviour through such activities as micro-teaching or the use of the Flanders' interaction analysis programme, both of which specify 'desirable teaching behaviour'. Training programmes are then developed to teach behaviour and to measure the effects. The belief is that by changing the teachers' overt external behaviour, one can affect the quality of teaching as a whole, since it is believed that teaching is seen as a sum of various, discrete, overt, external behaviours.

Another related research question, according to these researchers, involves the attempt to identify empirical links between specific patterns of teacher characteristics or teaching behaviour and favourable student learning outcomes, such as high achievement and favourable student attitudes. These teacher variables are then identified as competencies to be developed in teacher education programmes, and the task of the researcher is viewed as discovering the laws governing these pedagogical acts. These are known as 'teacher effectiveness studies' and there are literally hundreds that have been conducted in the last few decades and have been catalogued in several major reviews.[23]

A third research question noted by Popkewitz *et. al.* concerns the effects of participation in a teacher education programme on attitudes and behaviour of prospective teachers. The idea is to study the impact of teacher education programmes on teachers' self-concepts. For example, the procedure would be to administer a self-concept inventory before and after the programme and then determine differences in scores obtained. Conclusions would then be drawn about the effect of the process on teacher self-concept which would be drawn from this before and after testing. The assumptions are that the effects are separable from each other and that they can be observed and described in precise, behavioural terms. Also, another assumption is, that each effect is attached to a separate, distinct cause and that a deductive set of propositions can link causes and effects in such a way that the behaviour of future teachers can be controlled and predicted through the appropriate design of teacher education programmes. As Popkewitz *et. al.* point out:

> All three questions about effects emerged from similar commitments to an empirical analytic paradigm. The studies attempt to predict and explain specific behaviours which are thought to be

causally linked through the testing of specific hypotheses. The operational categories used for analysis are usually determined *a priori* without reference to the specific event under study. In doing so, the analytic categories that the research subjects use to order their world are often not considered.[24]

As Popkewitz, Tabachnick, and Zeichner indicate, many of those persons conducting the studies referred to above propose that we now have enough sound knowledge to construct sound accountability programmes in teacher education. Popkewitz, *et. al.*, however, are concerned that although there have been hundreds of studies conducted on the impact of teacher education using this empirical analytical paradigm, these studies have depended almost entirely on the administration of pre- and post-test questionnaires and surveys, and that we have almost no studies on the *processes of teacher education as it unfolds over a period of time*. 'Almost unanimously, reviewers lament the lack of useful research in this category'.[25] Popkewitz, Tabachnick, and Zeichner go on to note that without case studies of teacher education or ethnomethodological research in teacher education, it is difficult to develop any theory or theories of teacher education. It is erroneous to assume that one can simply proliferate research studies using conventional experimental paradigms and by so doing build a theory. Historically, we have had no theory developed from the accumulation of data derived by the use of this paradigm.[26]

Despite the endorsements of PBTE, noted above, it is difficult not to agree with these researchers in their conclusions about the types of effects of much of the current research in teacher education — specifically some of the research on teaching and on the effects of competency based or performance based teacher education. This peculiar situation has been brought about entirely by the fact that most persons who have been doing the research on teaching and most of the work on PBTE have in their own training as educational researchers been steeped primarily in the uses of the empirical-analytic model referred to above, and have not deemed it appropriate to use, or do not know how to use, case studies or ethnomethodological research in studying teacher education. In fact, there are substantial numbers of people on teacher education faculties today who are vehemently opposing ethnomethodological research in any aspect of education, and view it as a threat to established courses and programmes. Part of the problem is that many of the opinion leaders and various segments of the teacher education community have publically endorsed programmes of performance based or competency based teacher education and have claimed that such programmes can be used to make teacher education 'accountable' in the present era of 'accountability' and have therefore set up what turned out to be unfortunate expectations in the public mind. What has happened is that in some teacher education courses and programmes which have been studied as examples of competency based and performance based teacher education, the results have shown it to be more and more irrelevant to the actual concerns of teachers in training. A recent article by Dunn[27] points out in considerable detail a number of the 'imperfections' which exist in competency based teacher education programmes. One of the major problems Dunn is concerned with is that of what happens to students who have been judged to be deficient in such a system and are given special feedback in order to 'recycle them' to ultimately achieve 'mastery learning'.[28] Dunn goes on in the article to demonstrate that the more conscientious the instructor is who attempts to assist students who do not meet minimum standards of competency, the more stressful is the situation for both the students and the instructor. Dunn notes that many of the students who lack 'significant prerequisites' are admitted to teacher education programmes. Dunn describes the situation in part as follows:

> It seems obvious that CBTE programmes place too much emphasis on 'recycling' procedures after students have failed to reach the appropriate criterion level on the initial attempt, and not enough emphasis on determining whether students have pre-requisites necessary for likely success on the initial attempt. Greater attention to prerequisites will be very consistent with the systematic approach to instruction (i.e. competencies would be analysed to determine prerequisities, diagnostic tests to point out the students who do not have the prerequisites, and then they would receive instruction on these prerequisites). The reasons for not doing what seems to be so sensible are quite complex . . . one basic instructional/learning problem affecting attempts to design and implement an overall PBTE instructional system is that there are marked limitations in the different components. First, a precise list of important competencies (in this case, teacher competencies) does not exist.[29]

Dunn proposes that CBTE and the other applications of

systems approaches have limitations of the sort referred to above. He feels, however, that they should not be abandoned — rather that the necessary research and curriculum development should be done so that these approaches can be perfected. Thus Dunn's article is written from the point of view of one who is apparently in favor of CBTE, but is concerned about the mental health of students who are caught between the Scylla of 'recycling' in the system and the Charybdis of 'mastery learning'.

The person in the process

Dunn's article demonstrates that we do have in American education an unbroken line of concern for the development of the person as pupil and the person as teacher. Such a concern goes back at least to progressive education movements of the 1920s and 30s and undoubtedly was in existence before it. It may well be that we are seeing the pendulum begin to swing from an excessive preoccupation with an empirical-analytical model which has led us to Performance Based Teacher Education (as well as other accountability movements) of the 1960s and 70s to a more person-oriented teacher education. We have been distracted for more than a decade from making constructive changes in our own teacher education programmes either on the basis of our own knowledge of what needs to be done, or better yet on the existing research of the ethnomethodological variety which would help us deal more creatively and constructively with the variables of what is to be taught and who is to be taught. Of course, we need also to conduct the ethnomethodological research which will allow us to incorporate the social, cultural, political and humanistic aspects of teacher education which have often been left out of many existing programmes.

Also, we need to personalize the mechanisms of teacher education so that we are taking account of the human beings in them. As previously mentioned, we have in the educational traditions of the Western democracies a heritage of concern with the personal growth model of education dating from the progressive education movement. We have in American teacher education, for example, the study by Hart (1934), who secured questionnaire replies from 10 000 high school seniors who were asked to describe both the best and least liked teachers they had ever had. They were asked to designate also the most effective teacher they had ever had; and four out of five of the students declared the best liked teachers were also the best teachers. Three out of four teachers then in the school were described as resembling the best liked teacher more than the least liked ones, showing that the preponderance of the affective variances between teachers and pupils were attractions. Hart developed a composite picture of the best liked and least liked teachers on the basis of replies from 3 725 of the 10 000 high school seniors. The nine most frequently mentioned reasons for liking the teacher best were that the teacher:

1. Was helpful with school work, explained lessons and assignments clearly and thoroughly, used examples in teaching.
2. Was cheerful, happy, good natured, jolly, had a sense of humour, could take a joke.
3. Was human, friendly companionable, 'one of us'.
4. Was interested in and understood pupils.
5. Made work interesting, created a desire to work, made classwork a pleasure.
6. Was strict, had control of the class, commanded respect.
7. Was impartial, showed no favouritism, had no pets.
8. Was not cross, crabby, grouchy, nagging or sarcastic.
9. 'We learned the subject'.

In the Hart study teachers were liked best for their help in encouraging learning. By contrast, teachers were liked least because of the unpleasant effects they produced by being cross, grouchy, or sarcastic, by never smiling and by losing their tempers. 'Ineffectiveness as a teacher takes second rank in leading to rejection of the teacher by pupils'.

John Dixon[30] made the personal growth model of English a reality, if not an art form, in his book about the Dartmouth Seminar. We now need to develop a personal growth model of teacher education. Such a personal growth view of teacher education might well contain a view of the existential man or woman who hopes to become a teacher, internalizing or integrating a myriad of courses from the English and education departments in attempting to sort out the self appropriate for teaching from many possible selves. A personal growth model of teacher education will help our prospective teachers accomplish the task. We must resurrect the evidence for this personal growth model.

Evidence for a personal growth model of teacher education
Ethnographic studies of teachers teaching and teacher

education programmes have existed since the progressive era in education and form the basis for a new personal growth model of teacher education in many countries. In relatively recent times George B. Leonard in his book *Education and Ecstasy*[31] notes the importance of building education programmes on the work of Abraham Maslow of Brandeis University, who instead of studying neurotic and psychotic people, studied people who were happy and successful. Instead of looking at the low points of mental illness, Maslow examined the high points of human joy. Maslow came to use the term 'self-actualizing people' for these happy ones he studied. In studying the self-actualizing people, Maslow came to use terms like 'more openness to experience, increased integration, increased spontaneity', and noted that self-actualizers are both mature and childlike. They manifest what Maslow called a 'healthy childishness' and a 'second naïvete'. From this and other evidence, Leonard concludes that we should return to a study of 'ecstasy' and 'delight' in the human condition:

> One of the first tasks of education, then, is to return man to himself (and presumably woman to herself); to encourage rather than stifle awareness; to educate the emotions, the senses, the so-called autonomic systems; to help people become truly responsive and therefore truly responsible.[32]

In their book, *The Professional Education of Teachers*, Combs, Blume, Newman, and Wass[33] basing their work on 'perceptual' or 'transactional' psychology, show how the personal growth model or the self-actualizing model, or, as they call it, 'The self-as-an-instrument-model', can be developed within a programme of teacher education. They base their programme of teacher education on such areas of emphasis as the development of the teacher's self concept: the development of his or her abilities to achieve an understanding of the self-concepts of pupils, and the relationship of the content of the curriculum of the interests and needs of the pupils. They stress with prospective teachers such strategies as learning to communicate effectively, learning how to involve students imaginatively in the subject matter, the necessity of understanding the nature of learning and the development of an informed teacher in both subject matter and in professional concerns. They use observation techniques to develop sensitivity and also stress a counselling relationship between teacher educators and their students through work in small groups and flexible arrangements, involving work in schools, curriculum laboratories and small seminars. Their programme, which has been successfully used at the University of Florida for some years is a marked alternative to the competency based programmes described by Dunn and Dixson above.

Another such alternative is the programmes described by Gwyneth Dow[34] in her book *Learning to Teach: Teaching to Learn* which is a case study of an experimental course in teacher education conducted at the University of Melbourne in the mid-1970s. The course was developed to propose a new partnership between the schools and the university which would find ways to relate theory to practice, and which would help new teachers to take part in 'innovating in curriculum planning and school organization' when they took positions in Victorian schools, as well as those in other Australian states. Much of the book is drawn from diaries which the students in the course agreed to write as they went through the course. The goals stated by Dow (1979) show clearly the relationship between the programme she describes and that of Combs, *et. al.*, at the University of Florida:

> Looked at from the students' point of view, there were three postulates that guided our thinking and planning. The first was that for each student the problem of becoming a teacher was an intensely personal, individual matter. The second was that to become an effective teacher, the student needed to be scholarly not only in his teaching subject, but also in his approach to education. The third was that graduate students, especially those who were to be teachers, and therefore needed to think about democratic school practices, should have as much experience as we could give them in their thinking and acting autonomously during their training years.[35]

After five years of working with the students in 'Course B' at the University of Melbourne, Dow concludes in her book that 'students, in learning to teach, can learn to learn: indeed, they are forced to be more self-conscious and less self-centered about their own learning'.[36] The diaries of the students in 'Course B' show clearly the significant influences, not only of their experience in schools but of the kind of personal attention, counselling and direct instruction that they were given by the University staff as members in small groups. They worked with them continuously throughout the course rather than in purely individual courses conducted entirely within the university setting. George Henry has commented on this lack of continuing and sustaining contact between teacher education faculty and students which exists in many teacher education institutions:

> This tension along the boundaries of the conventional divisions of knowledge is due to more of the embarrassing overlapping of career walls on the one hand or to their arbitrary, institutional separation on the other; this tension reveals also the inability of thought, as now organized into a college curriculum, to deal with the explosion of knowledge. Bringing the self and the fruits of reason into alignment is the meaning of liberal education in the curriculum sense.[37]

As Gwyneth Dow's book illustrates, we can learn much from the diaries and other personal documents of teachers in training and teachers in service. We need to ask teachers and prospective teachers to keep journals and diaries. These assist them in formulating and reformulating their own views and philosophies. Many teachers in the National Writing Project in the United States who are beginning to engage in this practice have testified to the help they obtained from writing and from the way in which writing helps them in learning about themselves as teachers. We have not often used this practice in teacher education programmes but where we have the value seems clear. Such documents help us to gain insight into the complex processes of becoming a teacher and continuing to be a teacher in difficult times. We need more case studies like the case studies on teachers in the first year of teaching such as those in Kevin Ryan's book, *Don't Smile Until Christmas*[38] and Nicholas Otty's diary[39] of his experiences as a university student coming from an Oxbridge background to the teacher education course in language as he worked for the Diploma of Education at the University of London's Institute of Education. Another well-known study is William Waller's study of teachers teaching contained in his well known book, *The Sociology of Teaching*.[40]

In teacher education for the 1980s and beyond, our task seems clear. We need to somehow wipe away the effects of the 1970s where we attempted to develop teacher education programmes on an industrial model (the CBTE model) with specifications of behaviour laced onto a performance based programme in the name of accountability. If we expect that the public will know that we are a helping profession or a caring profession we can best be accountable by restoring the caring elements to teacher education programmes. We need to toss aside our preoccupation with accountability models. Dunn's study points out that the application of the CBTE model has resulted in damage to the self concepts of prospective teachers. We have the knowledge of how to restore these caring elements to all teacher education programmes even though we recognize that they are especially important in teacher education programmes in English. We have the research base and the research methodologies which will enable us to study both the effects of our doing so and the effects of our not doing so. I therefore propose a 'soft revolution', with a bow to Postman and Weingartner, a 'soft revolution' to affect a new personal-growth model in teacher education in English:

> The soft revolution is characterized by a minimum of rhetoric, dogma, and charismatic leadership. It consists of a point of view (and concomitant strategies) that are serious and also solid ... The central purpose of the soft revolution is to help all of us get it all together in the interest of our *mutual* survival. It may try to reform an existing system or to start a better one from scratch. When you are making a soft revolution, you will not be required to assume that you are absolutely right; nor that you are, in all respects more virtuous than those whose ideas you would like to 'disappear'. All that is required is your considered judgement that you may have a better idea ...
>
> When you are making a soft revolution, you do not always need a large organization. Sometimes five people doing the right thing the right way can do the job ... This implies that individual effort can make the difference to even twenty people.[41]

My own soft revolution is underway. I invite you to develop your own along the lines I have suggested. Please let me know your revolutionary results.

12   PAUL K. BROCK

Processes involved in curriculum change: a case study of New South Wales, Australia

There have been some recent attempts to adapt Thomas Kuhn's theories concerning the nature of scientific revolutions to the teaching of rhetoric in the English curriculum in North America. Janet Emig has referred to Howard Gruber's adaptation.[1] Ian Pringle and Aviva Freedman have discussed Richard Young's modifications of Kuhn's theory of 'paradigm shift'[2] and agreed that as far as the history of the teaching of rhetoric in North America is concerned 'a new paradigm emerges from the enquiries and controversies of the crisis state and with it another period of relative stability'.[3] I will review some developments in English curriculum in NSW, Australia, in the light of Kuhnian theory of paradigm shift and will refer in passing to an emerging school of educational philosophy which would appear to be offering insights that are most relevant to the English teaching profession as we move through the 80s. The reaction of English teachers and academics from Canada and the United States to the NSW data, some of which was included in a paper delivered to the Canadian Council for the Teaching of English Conference at UBC Vancouver in 1981, would indicate clearly that the NSW experience is representative of much of what has occurred internationally in English curriculum development.

Allen W. Imershein has developed a sociological theory of organizational change based upon Kuhn's notions of paradigm shift as developed in his *The Structure of Scientific Revolution*.[4] Kuhn argues that:

> ... scientific change advances by revolutions from one paradigm to another; this involves changing ways of thinking, of seeing the world (and data in particular) and of doing research. This shift in world view and scientific practices occurs at a point when a new paradigm is perceived not only to handle most of the already manageable research problems but also to handle recalcitrant problems which have precipitated a crisis and which remain unresolved despite the efforts of practitioners using the old paradigm; the perception of these unresolved anomalies typically sets the stage for paradigm revolution.[5]

Imershein also notes Kuhn's insistence that those operating within the paradigm do *not* 'learn a set of rules or abstract theories'[6] which they then apply, but rather are introduced to 'a common set of practices (and) instrumentations', 'which are provided by the current paradigm'.[7] This will be shown to be an extremely useful comment in the light of the history of English teaching in NSW.

Imershein then goes on to make four other important applications of Kuhnian theory. The first of these is that within the structuring of an organization the *crucial* element is not the 'technology' itself, but the participants' knowledge of *how to apply* that technology.[8] If we conceive of the English teaching profession as an 'organization' and appropriate curriculum theory as the 'technology', Imershein's comment will be shown to have relevance to the NSW situation, especially after the promulgation of the revolutionary English syllabus for Years 7-10 which was issued in 1971 and became 'law' in 1972.

Secondly, Imershein asserts that it is not necessarily valid to assume that activities are carried out under the guidance of 'rules or norms' (or syllabus directives!). Participant behaviour may rather be a consequence of one's 'relying upon tacit knowledge'.[9] He suggests thirdly that 'general principles for organizational action can be employed only when *defined within a context of practice*',[10] for the replacement of one paradigm by another there must be what he terms 'exemplars'. If there are no practical exemplars handed on to those who are to be participants in the new paradigm, then there can be no order. Finally, what must be provided by any organizational paradigm are not only 'exemplars' of organizational tasks and procedures, but also exemplars for roles to be enacted in particular ways, in particular settings and in particular relation to the roles.[11] This observation will be shown to have significance in explaining the initial fate of the 1972 'new English' curriculum, yet it will be argued conversely that eventually the English curriculum in NSW benefited from the Committee's refusal to provide such exemplars.

Kuhn insists that before a reigning paradigm can be challenged, its operation 'must be perceived to be inadequate by a majority of its members'.[12] In science, where reform comes through research and publication, the repudiation of 'ruling' theory is relatively rapid — in the field of English teaching it is notoriously slow and the 'exemplars' are clung to tenaciously! Take the issue of the importance of teaching Latinate formal grammar as a prerequisite for improved usage. Matthew Arnold observed a century ago that:

> Young men whose knowledge of grammar, or the minutest details of geographical and historical facts, and above all, of mathematics, is surprising, often cannot paraphrase a plain passage of prose or poetry without totally misapprehending it, or write half a page or composition of any subject without falling into gross blunders of taste or expression.[13]

Inspectors of schools in Australia in the late nineteenth century re-echoed him.[14] The 1911 NSW syllabus made it clear that teachers ought not to feel compelled to teach formal grammar in order to improve the children's writing.[15] The Newbolt Report of 1921 endorsed Ballard's research which demonstrated that the concentration on learning formal grammar laws and systems could impede composition. British reports repeated the message.[16] Linguistic research since the 1960s has discredited the omnipotence claimed for Latinate grammar.[17] Yet the available evidence shows clearly that a significant number of NSW teachers continued to believe the old myths and practise them.[18] The gap between research and classroom practice has helped to assure the permanence of the reigning paradigm.

Perhaps Ivan Illich's notion of the 'institutionalizing of values'[19] is pertinent to an understanding of the failure of such knowledge to unsettle the ruling paradigm. He argues that institutions such as schools end up serving their own infrastructural 'staff' needs, rather than those whom the institutions appear to be serving. Thus while nineteenth century Australian inspectorial reports point regularly to the uselessness of so many classroom activities (e.g., the rote learning of vast slabs of poetry and prose, endless recitation of the rules of parsing and analysis etc.) the inspectors persistently refused to urge the abandonment of such exercises, perhaps because of a fear of losing the comfort of the classroom discipline and order that these structures helped to create and maintain.[20]

English teaching in NSW grew out of a nineteenth century British tradition with very little, if any, significant North American influence. The predominant American rationalist paradigm has never won support in the NSW English curriculum.[21] The ruling paradigm for NSW secondary English was dominated by 'heavy' literature, grammar and 'formal' written expression. The classical traditionalists looked down with disdain on English literary studies both in the UK and Australia in the nineteenth century. A most influential academic 'great' at the University of Sydney, Charles Badham, epitomized such disdian for the vulgar vernacular, judging English 'literature' to be so vastly inferior to classical studies that he considered it to be a corrupter of educated taste.[22] That these classicist roots went very deep is illustrated by an official report on the 1951 Leaving Certificate English results by the Chief Examiner, the Professor of English at the University of Sydney, A.G. Mitchell. In accounting for the significant decline that year in the standards of metropolitan candidates' results compared with rural candidates, Mitchell declaimed that a decline in Latin studies was a very significant factor.[23] Later research not only utterly discredited this statement of 'fact', but also proved that the so-called decline was nonsense. The city candidates were unlucky to have had a large part of their paper marked by a hard marker and the converse occurred for the country students![24]

Imershein's contention that what *really* controls the maintenance of a paradigm is not a set of rules, or theory but rather a 'common set of practices, instrumentations' is certainly relevant to the history of the English curriculum in NSW. Theoretically, one might have expected that the respective English syllabuses would have been the effective regulators of English teaching. Not so! For example the 1911 syllabus (which remained in force until replaced in 1944) certainly did not prescribe the enormous concentration on parsing and analysis that occupied so much time in English classrooms. Explicit prescriptions stressing the importance of *spoken* English in the 1944 and 1953 syllabuses would not appear to have been widely implemented — there were no marks for oral English in the public exams. The dominant exemplars that dictated classroom practice were the demands of the external examinations, long-established text books and English teaching 'folklore' irrespective of syllabus principles and rules.

Many teachers from the 1920s to at least the 1950s (if not later), had probably never read a syllabus. For example, Phyllis Kittson, co-founder of the NSW English Teachers Association in 1961, and a figure of major importance in the state's English curriculum development, commenced her teaching career in 1931, yet did not even *see* a copy of an English syllabus until her appointment to the English staff at Sydney Teachers' College in 1953![25] Other former leaders in the English teaching profession agree that such ignorance was widespread.[26]

The public examination system virtually cemented the components and 'exemplars' of the dominant paradigm. Up until 1965 there was an Intermediate Certificate exam at the end of the third year in secondary schools, and the Leaving Certificate exam at the end of the fifth. The former was replaced by the School Certificate exam after four years (in 1965) and the latter by the Higher School Certificate after six years (the first exam being in 1967). There is no need to repeat the widespread criticisms that abound in English curriculum writing with regard to the effect of such examinations on the teaching and learning of English. For far too long the strategies for maximizing written examination performance have been the exemplars that have defined the 'context of practice' within the established paradigm of English teaching/learning.

The NSW experience demonstrates the power of the examination. For example, an analysis I have made of English Syllabus Committee minutes between 1950 and 1955 reveals that over 90 per cent of these are explicitly and directly concerned with examination issues. Since the introduction of the Higher School Certificate, the examination system has distorted the Senior school (Years 11 and 12) curriculum. The first and second courses were designed specifically for students intending to pursue tertiary studies in English. This would be a very small proportion of the total candidature. Yet in 1979, for example, approximately 22 000 out of 35 000 students took this course. The third course would be far more suitable for the vast majority of these students but, because of the differential marking scales and matriculation criteria, students are loath to take it. On the other hand the unreliability of marking procedures at the top level (the *first* English course) has dissuaded gifted English students from taking that course which was designed specifically for their needs and interests. In the 1950s and early 1960s, between 5 and 5.5 per cent of the student candidature undertook the Honours Course. In 1967, the first year of the *new* system (before the syllabus became constricted by the exam) 12.5 per cent presented for the top course.[27] This progressively withered away to 3.8 per cent in 1979 and barely 3.9 per cent in 1980.

The responses of Australian teachers of English to the 1972 UNESCO Survey showed that the overwhelming majority perceived the system of formal external exams to be hindering the proper teaching of English.[28] Yet, despite an apparent majority desiring reform the NSW Higher School Certificate examination persists. Why? Two major factors are the massively *centralized* system of curriculum design and evaluation that operates in NSW, and the HSC being tied to tertiary education matriculation and faculty entry standards. The degree of centralization is often a source of surprise, if not amazement, to British or American visitors to NSW, a state twice the size of California and sixteen times as large as England! The HSC English curriculum is laid down for nearly 450 government and non-government schools in NSW by a central committee of professors of English, representatives from the Department of Education, academics from tertiary institutions and a few practising teachers, all but one of whom are drawn from Sydney metropolitan schools.

In 1971, under the chairmanship of Graham Little, the junior secondary (Years 7-10) English Syllabus Committee published a radically new syllabus for implementation in 1972. Limitations of space prevent a thoroughly detailed examination of this document. A South Australian Syllabus appeared also in 1971 and these were the first to implement the general thrusts of John Dixon's *Growth Through English*. The New South Wales document drew upon the understanding of the relationship between language, learning and experience that was developed in James Britton's *Language and Learning*. Little had been profoundly impressed by James Moffett's *Teaching the Universe of Discourse* and his accompanying handbook for teachers *A Student-Centred Language Arts*

Curriculum, Grades K-13. The Syllabus Committee sought to re-define English in a way that would restore integrity to the subject at a time when it was in danger of disintegration. The minutes and Little's early drafts reveal clearly that he feared that things were falling apart; that the centre might not hold and that 'mere anarchy' might indeed be 'loosed upon the world' of the English classroom.[29] Little was determined to establish a 'centre' for English.

The final document is a statement of aims and objectives complemented by a series of non-prescriptive Notes which amplify the syllabus on such issues as language, talking, listening, reading, literature and mass media, as well as providing a bibliography. The words of Marjorie Greene that 'if all knowing is a kind of doing and (as) human doing is always value-bound, then knowledge is as well'[30] could be inscribed as a motif to this syllabus which opens with the bold assertion that English is 'action-knowledge' and not merely 'knowledge-about':

> This syllabus assumes that English for twelve to sixteen-year-olds should be an active pursuit: a matter of pupils developing competence by engaging in an abundance of purposeful language-activities, enjoyable because they are appropriate to needs, interests and capacities. The competence sought is no mere utilitarian skill, but involves essentially human qualities of thought and feeling, because it is by language that we organize our human experience.[31]

Here, as elsewhere, Moffett's influence can be strongly felt. The syllabus shares his insistence that 'students learn essentially by doing and getting feedback on what they have done'.[32] Thus all objectives of English in this NSW syllabus are defined as ability to do something: 'to listen, read, speak and write.' These words mirror Moffett's statement of the basic principles underpinning his *A Student-Centred Language Arts Curriculum, Grades K-13* that 'if the goals of the curriculum are to help learners think, speak, listen, read, and write to the limit of their capacities, then the most reasonable premise is that *they should do exactly those things*'. (italics mine).[33]

The last two sentences of the Introduction point to values, cultural realities, and an understanding of the relationship between language experience and personal development that vastly exceed the parameters of any narrowly utilitarian approach to education. The very last sentence did not appear in any of the earlier drafts. Little himself added it after a draft document had been circulated to teachers for comment. Several respondents had indicated concern that the previous paragraph, as it then stood, could have been interpreted to constitute an endorsement of the strong American tradition of behaviourism expressed at that time in a proliferation of programmed-learning materials and kits, and to which Little was strenuously opposed.[34]

In some ways the 1972 syllabus can be seen to be implementing the kind of curriculum that the Reconceptualist movement later in the 70s called for in its vigorous reaction to behaviourist models such as have tended to dominate American education since the 1920s, when financially successful theories of scientific economic management were lifted from the commercial world and applied to education. Taking their inspiration from the rationalism of the biological and physical sciences, later theorists developed programmes within a behaviourist paradigm . These shared a central tenet that 'everything essential to human behaviour must in principle be understandable in terms of discrete independent elements and be formalized'.[35] Unmeasurable and unquantifiable qualities such as discrimination, sensitivity, exploration of experience, and creativity, that are called for in English teaching under the 1972 Syllabus in NSW, held no place of esteem in the canons of behavioural predictability and 'instruction'.

It would therefore appear useful to make some passing and brief reference to the Reconceptualists. What unites them, despite their individual differences, is their determination to rebut behaviourist, materialistic paradigms of education. Their writings certainly buttress the kinds' of assumptions underpinning the 1972 syllabus. Mann, whose reconceptualism emerges from the perspective of literary criticism speaks for many of his colleagues when he criticizes those educational leaders who have succumbed to the myth of scientific materialistic 'objectivity' in their efforts to win respectability.[36] Of course, the use of any umbrella term like reconceptualist is dangerously simplistic; Reid's functionalist sociological perspective contrasts sharply with the Marxist positions of Apple, Greene and Mann, who argue strongly for profound changes in educational power structures. One common theme running through Pinar's collection of reconceptualist writings is that the search for *meaning* should be absolutely central to the educational process. As William A. Reid expresses it:

> The function of a humane study is to explain, interpret and evaluate a specific type of human activity and achievement in terms by which it is given meaning, significance and value. [37]

The 1972 syllabus certainly places great emphasis on this search for the interpretation, explanation and evaluation of meaning in and through language:

> The terms *meaning, form* and *values* are used to sum up what is centrally involved in the appreciation and good use of language in any situation. They are also inseparable in the sense that English in Years 7-10 is not concerned with form without meaning, or with values that are not established by consideration of the actual language used. [38]

The syllabus then goes on to use this 'Meaning-Form-Values' triad as the central perspective of integration to hold together the myriad facets of English.

A significant development in the Reconceptualist counter-attack to American educational behaviourism was the publication in 1979 of Elliot W. Eisner's *The Educational Imagination*. Just as the writings of Britton and Moffett in the late 1960s and the 70s drew inspiration from the philosophies of linguistics of authors such as Cassirer, Vygotsky, Polanyi, and Langer, so perhaps English curriculum developers of the 80s, especially in the United States, may draw inspiration and support from Eisner's educational theory based on his philosophy of aesthetics. At the end of this decade Janet Emig may be able to include Eisner's name in her list of those writers in the fields of philosophy, sociology, literature and linguistics whom she considers, constitute the 'tacit tradition' underpinning contemporary developments in rhetoric. [39]

Eisner most vigorously denounces what he sees to be the reigning American paradigm's narrow concept of learning and it failure to attempt to teach and reward knowledge in the auditory, sensual, allegorical, metaphorical and, in general, the aesthetic and non-discursive modes of learning. He is particularly critical of the system's failure to recognize that there are extremely valuable educational experiences that can be neither pre-planned nor quantified and 'measured'. The 1972 NSW syllabus certainly attempts to foster such modes of learning.

Another theme developed by Eisner is pertinent to a consideration of some of the ways in which the new NSW English curriculum broke new ground. Eisner argues that one of the effects of the dominant American paradigm has been to reduce the 'creative' role of the individual teacher and to produce 'teacher-proof' materials for direct implementation in the classroom. He calls for greater professional responsibilities to be given to the individual teacher so as to permit teachers to interpret general aims and objectives creatively. He suggests ways in which the teacher's task should be a creative one.

The very kind of creative autonomy advocated by Eisner in 1979, was *prescribed* by the NSW 1972 syllabus, which handed over the responsibility for developing curriculla to the individual English teacher. All teachers were directed to conduct 'responsible experiments' and they were given the hitherto unheard-of official directive to 'develop their own courses according to the needs of their pupils and to evaluate their success'.[40]

The Imershein-Kuhn version of paradigm shift provides a useful perspective for reviewing briefly the fate of the 1972 syllabus since its promulgation. Kuhn insists on the necessity of a paradigm's providing 'exemplars' and plays down the importance of participants' comprehending the paradigm's underpinning theory. The little research that has been undertaken since 1972 indicates that the new curriculum has not been implemented widely.[41] It has already been suggested that the exemplars that have historically defined the context (in Imershein's terminology) of English teaching have been the external examination system, classroom textbooks, and teacher 'folklore'. The external examination in its traditional form was phased out in 1975. While the whole thrust of the 1972 syllabus was to lead teachers away from a dependence on traditional textbooks, some teachers carried on regardless with these well-worn tomes. They could do so with no fear of being penalized by any new examination system that might try to enforce the new rationale. One of five overall strategies suggested for teacher consideration by the syllabus was 'theme teaching'. Book publishers eagerly latched on. Soon the schools were flooded with new thematic textbooks. The election in 1972 of the first Labor Federal government in twenty-three years saw massive increases in the allocation of funds to schools in all Australian states for textbook purchasing. Rapidly, almost uncontrollably, 'theme teaching' became the new English orthodoxy for many teachers of English.

Postle's research on paradigm shift initiated by a central authority concluded that:

> paradigm shift is unlikely where exemplars provided by the central authority are inadequate or inconsistent, for the recipients of the change are likely to interpret any proposals into the ongoing operations of the current paradigm. [42]

That such failure of paradigm shift occurred between 1972 and 1978 seems highly likely if Watson's research is representative. Little and his committee had deliberately refrained from detailing specific kinds of implementary strategies and exemplars as advocated by Imershein:

> The roles to be enacted must be provided primarily in the form of concrete examples which can be known and used in the fashion specified . . . Concrete examples are precisely what Kuhn specifies as central to scientific paradigms; so it should be with organizational programmes. [43]

I believe that Little was correct — despite Imershein's remarks. He was convinced that such specificity would have been widely interpreted as prescriptive and would have undermined a fundamental assumption of the syllabus that each individual teacher must exercise his or her professional judgement in developing implementary strategies according to the specific needs, interests and capacities of the particular pupils in each individual situation.

Nevertheless, the committee was acutely aware of the dangers of issuing such an innovative document demanding new degrees of teacher creativity and requiring teachers to have a familiarity with the new theory of language acquisition and development underpinning the syllabus, without an adequate programme of teacher in-service training. The minority of English teachers who were members of the NSW English Teachers' Association had been well prepared for the new curriculum. Through its newsletters, journals, conferences and sponsorship of visits to Australia by overseas teachers and scholars, the NSW ETA had brought constantly before its members those developments in English curriculum upon which the 1972 syllabus was based. Little therefore recommended to the NSW government that it should use some of the $1 million saved by the Department of Education's decision to abolish the external exam in Year 10, to establish in-service programmes at state and regional levels in order to assist teachers. He was ignored.[44] As David Homer has observed 'the problem (has always been) that at no time have teachers fully had the rationale of the approach explained to them, a communication problem inherent in Australian Education Departments'.[45] Consequently confusion tended to reign for the next five or six years. At one extreme, many teachers refused to change; at the other a mish-mash of quasi-sociology, permissiveness and 'anything goes' proliferated. Many climbed on the bandwaggon of working doggedly through the new 'theme' textbooks. Such procedures enabled teachers to avoid studying the new syllabus and implementing the aims and objectives of a child-centred developmental curriculum. New wine was poured into old wineskins — and old wine was camouflaged within new wineskins.

It has been only since 1978 with an upgrading of the importance of the NSW Directorate of Studies, which has the responsibility of establishing state-wide curriculum developmental and in-service programmes, that the English teaching profession in NSW has begun to come to grips seriously with the syllabus. State-wide and regional conferences have enabled large numbers of English teachers, especially departmental heads, to study the rationale deeply and to design programmes for implementing the curriculum to meet specific and local 'needs, interests and capacities'.[46] So a decade after its promulgation, the 1972 syllabus is now being closely explored and creatively implemented on an ever-increasing scale throughout NSW.

Obviously there are many 'factors that influence schooling which have their sources far from the school or district', as Eisner observes.[47] Elsewhere I have detailed many of these factors operating in NSW and the negative influence they have had in reinforcing an irrelevant paradigm.[48] Factors such as political forces; ignorance of research conclusions; a misinformed public; bureaucratic inefficiencies; competing institutional power structures; influence of tertiary educational control over secondary educational curriculum; economic recession, and public service promotional structures have all served to inhibit paradigm shift.

This chapter has not attempted to provide a thorough historical review of English curriculum development in NSW. While such a history would provide some depressing aspects of change and 'non-change', there is much, particularly associated with the 1972 syllabus, that has been invigorating and impressive. Though Kuhnian perspectives of paradigm shift help to explain some of the processes that have inhibited change and consolidated the reigning paradigm, they do not account for much of the imaginative and creative educational growth that has taken place as a result of a syllabus committee's determination to implement progressive English curriculum theory, and its faith in the long-term ability of the teaching profession to 'own' and implement such curriculum theory, theory which is suffused with the kinds of assumptions about education that one finds in the emerging reconceptualist tradition. Perhaps Howard Gruber is correct when he observed that the '(Kuhnian) notion of paradigm does not deal with the psychology of creative individual thought'.[49] It hardly needs to be said that the advocacy of liberal humanistic education long predates any Reconceptualist school of the 1970s. Graham Little, the 'creative individual' thinker freely acknowledges to have been influenced deeply by Matthew Arnold's *Culture and Anarchy*.[50] It is therefore appropriate to conclude this review of some features of English curriculum development in NSW by referring back to Arnold's concept of 'culture' — one could substitute 'the theory and practice of English teaching' for the word 'culture' — and find in Arnold's words a cogent directive to all those responsible for the development and implement- ation of an English or Language Arts curriculum, to undertake:

> . . . a pursuit of our total perfection by means of getting to know on all matters which most concern us, the best which has been thought and said in the world; and through this knowledge, turning a stream of fresh and free thoughts upon our stock notions and habits, which we follow staunchly but mechanically, vainly imagining that there is a virtue in following them staunchly which makes up for the mischief of following them mechanically.[51]

13 IAN PRINGLE

English as a world language — right out there in the playground

On the whole, the worlds of English education and of 'Teaching English as a Second Language' have been largely that: separate worlds, each revolving in its independent orbit. How many teachers of English Language arts even know of the existence of the vast TESL/TEFL industry? I suggested at the Third International Conference on the Teaching of English in Sydney that those of us who work in the first-language field should pay much more attention to what is going on in the second-language field. In this chapter I want to examine this claim in more detail.

There are two reasons for my concern. The first is the simple practical one: for various reasons, English teachers these days have to teach students for whom English is not the first language, and they have to do so on a scale and in numbers unimaginable a couple of decades ago. Many teachers naturally feel some need for help in a kind of work for which nothing in their teacher training and their previous professional experience has prepared them.

There is, however, a far more important reason. The demographic shifts which have catapulted second-language students into first-language schools in such numbers have also occasioned vast expenditures on research into second-language learning. The discoveries made possible in this way offer important insights not only into how second languages are learned, but also, simply, into how language is learned. It is clear today as perhaps never before that there is a commonality which underlies these two disciplines. By looking at second language research we can certainly find advice to help us help second-language learners. We can also find striking confirmation of some of the most impressive of recent work in the first-language field. And by looking at both first and second language learners in the light of this research, we can approach our primary task, that of helping first-language learners to learn, with new assurance.

English and its new learners

One of the reasons why those of us who teach English can feel a certain glow not merely of satisfaction but actually of importance as we do so is the immense importance of English as a world language. Not only does it have the second largest number of native speakers of all world languages, surpassed only by Mandarin Chinese; it is also by far the most widely used second language in the world. To be sure, much of what is entailed or implied by the latter fact has not traditionally been of very great concern to those who teach English to students for whom English is the first (and usually the only) language. It has been enough for us to wrestle with our own version of what English education might be in an Ll (i.e., first-language) context, and to do our best to bring it about.

All of a sudden, that is no longer the case. It used to be that we had virtually no students in our classrooms for whom English was not the mother tongue. In some parts of the world — the Empire, as we used to say — education in English was available at least to some of the indigenous peoples, but for the majority English-speaking countries, what went on educationally in the rest of the Empire was not of much interest. Of course, in the majority English-speaking countries there were sometimes children of an indigenous people — Maoris, American Indians, Inuit, Aborigines — who would find their way into English classes; in others, the children of an earlier wave of European colonizers might have to be contended with — the French in Canada, the Spanish in the South Africa, the Celtic-speaking people of Britain. And occasionally, a child of a different race or culture altogether would turn up in a school. Traditionally, the latter children were ignored, if not by individual teachers, at least by policy makers. They were so few that no special attempt had to be made to help them to assimilate linguistically: somehow they seemed to do it all by themselves. As for the children of a displaced colonial power — the Canadian French, the

American Chicanos — they usually seemed to have acquired enough English on the streets to be able to get by at least in the lower levels of the education system. It often seemed to be the case, however, that a majority of them could succeed only at that level: their mean school-leaving age was characteristically lower, and their success rate in school also was typically not very good. Much the same generalizations seemed to be applicable to the children of minority indigenous peoples when they were educated in the majority language schools; Maori children, for example, simply did not continue beyond compulsory school-leaving age in the same proportions as their *Pakeha* compatriots.

As for the native children in those countries where the colonizing English-speaking population was only a very small minority, the traditional view used to be that there was no need for the children of the colonized population to master English. If they were the children of the privileged classes of their own society, there was no practical reason for them to have absolute mastery of English; and often, indeed, their characteristic mistakes proved to be rather charming (not to say convenient). And if they were not members of the privileged classes, then it was still less important that they should master English: the work they would do in their own society later did not make perfect English a necessity.

What I have just been describing is oversimplified, perhaps a parody; but in any case, insofar as it reflects any reality, it reflects the realities of an earlier age. The Second World War ushered in the post-colonial era. In those parts of the Third World which were formerly British colonies, the situation and status of English have changed in very fundamental ways.[1] Until recently, however, those changes were far removed from the concerns of classrooms in the English-speaking world. If, all of a sudden, we find ourselves having to deal with 'English as a world language' on a daily basis, the change is due not to changes in the political status of former British colonies, but to an unparalleled series of population movements which may constitute the greatest demographic upheaval of all time, surpassing even the European emigrations of the eighteenth and nineteenth centuries.[2]

In the majority English-speaking countries, the details of these changes must be immensely complicated in all cases, and they clearly differ from one country to another.[3] Canada and the United States have long been hospitable to non-English-speaking immigration. However they have responded to it in different ways. The traditional policy in the United States has always been one of assimilation, and this was usually achieved within one generation, because the Anglophone (i.e., English-speaking) population has always vastly outnumbered all non-Anglophone immigrant groups, and has also wielded all the political power. Canada, on the other hand, has always been much more tolerant of the survival of immigrant languages and cultures. This is due above all to the absolute intransigence of the Canadian French and to some extent of the Canadian Ukrainian populations, both of which have steadfastly refused to give up their language and culture, thus giving an example of language maintenance and cultural survival to other groups. It is due also to the fact that the monolingual Anglophone population in the country, already much smaller in absolute terms, is proportionately smaller still than that of the United States and has therefore had to share political power with groups speaking other languages. Not only has this meant a characteristically different response to recent immigrations; it has also meant the maintenance of the language and culture of previous immigrations. Within a hundred and sixty kilometres of the city of Ottawa, for example, are stable communities in which the Kashubian dialect of Polish is still the first language of the community, though the immigration which established the community took place before 1890. If it is justified to talk of the American 'melting pot', Canada is by contrast a cultural and linguistic mosaic. Nonetheless, both Canada and the United States have felt the effects of recent population shifts. What is most noticeable in the shift in public policies in Canada is not that non-English-speaking immigration has continued, but that for the first time non-white immigration has occurred in significant numbers.

In Australia, what is noticeable is the dramatic shift in immigration policy from an almost total restriction to English-speaking immigrants of British origin before the Second World War to a welcoming of white immigration from all Europe subsequently, and, most recently (and most astonishingly, for those who know something of the history of Australian racial attitudes), the recent acceptance of numbers of non-white immigrants. Even New Zealand, which resisted non-English-speaking and non-white immigration even longer and more effectively than Australia, has always been willing to make one particular exception, and in recent times to honour it: it has regarded itself as having a special responsibility for the Polynesian peoples of the Pacific. In addition, it has allowed small numbers of non-English-speaking immigrants to come since the Second World War, although it has made plain its preference for those whose origins (in Holland, Denmark and Yugoslavia) promise easy and rapid assimilation. And in the most astonishing of all developments, as the Empire has imploded, Britain itself has found in its midst a very substantial non-white and non-Anglophone population: Harold Rosen has reported recently that in London schools alone, children speak over a hundred different languages.[4]

In the decade after the Second World War, the shifting patterns of immigration were only beginning, and newcomers were usually assimilated much as they had always been. By the late 1960s, however, many factors combined to swell that small trickle into a flood: in the target countries, newly enlightened attitudes towards peoples of different languages and cultures and new doubts about the validity of traditional racist attitudes; in the source countries, greater personal wealth and better information about prospects elsewhere, undoubtedly helped by the new mobility within the countries of the European Economic Community. These combined with the increased ease, speed, safety and the relative cheapness of travel to make vast population shifts possible. Throughout the 1970s they came, in increasing numbers. And there they are, right out there in the playgrounds, speaking 'English as a world language', those infinitely various approximations to English which are so characteristic of its use as a second language, and which used to be so safely removed from our schools.

In some places, the change has been phenomenal. In the city of Toronto (which now has the fourth-largest Italian-speaking population in the cities of the world, surpassed only by Rome, Milan and Turin), over 50 per cent of the elementary school population speaks a language other than English as a first language. In Vancouver, the number is something like 40 per cent and rising fast. The great challenge to English education in the 1980s, greater than the problems caused by demands for 'basic' teaching; for teacher accountability; for system-wide competency testing; by censorship of works of literature; by the strains caused by shrinking and ageing populations and a period of particular bloody-mindedness on the part of many governments; greater too than the more positive challenges of responding to recent research into the acquisition and development of writing abilities, and of the importance of talking in the learning process — the greatest challenge of all is going to be coming to terms with bilingualism, with English as a world language in the English classroom. Evidence for this need has never been before in such obvious and demanding numbers.

Bilingualism and bilingual education

Bilingualism is an extremely complicated phenomenon, potentially as various as the number of ways any two or more of the world's more than four thousand different languages can come into contact. Any generalization, consequently, can only be tentative. However, the types of bilingual situations that are most directly relevant to teaching English as a second language in English-speaking countries can be loosely grouped into four patterns, with minor variations within different countries, and with the implications of some of the differences clearer if we consider bilingual situations involving languages other than English.

In the commonest kind of pattern, English is the majority language, and is sociologically and politically dominant. This is the pattern in Canada, for example, where the Anglophone population considerably outnumbers the Francophone population and is dominant politically, commercially and linguistically. The relations between English and Spanish in the United States and between English and Maori in New Zealand are similar. It happens to be the case that in Canada, French and English are both official languages, so that there are constitutional guarantees of the rights of French and Francophones.[5] But even with this protection, the sociolinguistic consequence of the relations between the two languages is essentially the same as they are in United States and New Zealand, where constitutional guarantees of minority language rights have historically been non-existent. The consequence is that the children of the minority group have to become bilingual, whereas the children of the dominant group do not.

The ways in which this can happen are various. In Canada the range of acquisition of English by Francophones varies from a level of fluency which is completely indistinguishable from the English of Canadian monolingual Anglophones, to a characteristically heavily-accented kind of Canadian French

English which preserves all kinds of interference from French, and is usually learned from other Francophones in Francophone and bilingual communities rather than recreated anew in every generation by direct contact with Anglophones. It should be noted that this situation exists in large measure even in those parts of the country where the population is almost uniformly Francophone, and so far it seems to be persisting despite the stringent language legislation put into effect in the 1970s in the province of Quebec to protect the status of the French language there.

The personal consequences for the children of the minority group are similar in all such situations. Because the communities into which they are born are pervasively bilingual, they learn both languages simultaneously from early childhood. The range of uses of their first language is sometimes severely restricted because the functions which would be served by shifting styles in a monolingual community are served by shifting to the majority language. However, their exposure to the majority language is also abnormal, largely because they learn it from other bilinguals in the same minority group. The strength of both languages is thus apparently somewhat attenuated. This seeming deficit of course correlates with membership in a socio-economically deprived stratum of society, and so the schools, with the middle-class values they always assume, are usually not particularly well-equipped to address the educational needs of these children. Disadvantaged socio-economically and linguistically from the start by virtue of the fact that they are born into a stratum whose difference is signalled by their use of the minority language, they tend to fall further and further behind during the school years. This, in turn, ensures that their deprived socio-economic status will be passed on to the next generation.

In a second kind of pattern, English is the dominant language, but is spoken by only a very small minority of the total population. This is the kind of situation that applied in the Empire: in India, for example, only the British originally spoke English as their only language, but by virtue of their political power and the education system they imposed, English became the dominant language of the country, though very much a minority language. The situation changed somewhat in India after independence. It persists, however, in other parts of the English-speaking world. Within Canada, the same relationship holds between English and indigenous languages in remote areas: the Inuit (Eskimos) of the Ungava Peninsula, in the North of Quebec, for example, have chosen English as their language of official contact with the Federal government; consequently English has traditionally been the language of education in their communities, and though this has now changed, with more and more of the instruction taking place in Inuktitut (Eskimo), and English now taught as a subject, it remains the only language through which they can keep in contact with the rest of Canada. In a somewhat similar way, English is the dominant language, though a minority language, of many of the Pacific Islands; for example, a recent article describes in detail the situation in American Samoa.[6]

In this situation too, the majority of the population has to learn some English; however, in contrast with the first, for most purposes it is easy to function in the society without using English at all, and consequently the extent to which English is mastered by those for whom it is not a native language is characteristically much less, and the characteristic errors are in fact created anew by each new learner rather than perpetuated within the community.

The situation in Western Europe constitutes another variation of this pattern. There too English is very commonly taught in school systems, with teaching beginning at an early age and continuing with an intensity (and a level of success) unknown in foreign-language teaching in Anglophone countries. The motivation for teaching English is not quite as simple as it is in the Ungava Peninsula or Samoa, but the task of learning is doubly easier, firstly in that the children's first language is much more closely related to English than Eskimo or Samoan or any of the Aboriginal languages of Australia; and secondly in that the children's first language is one which is the vehicle of a European high culture having much in common with the English cultural tradition. On the other hand, the situations are similar in that the number of native speakers in the community is very small, and fluency in English is not necessary for daily life.

In such situations, bilingualism does not entail any weakness in the first language. In the second language, the success rate can vary depending on the educational system. A recent article spells out in detail some of the consequences of this sort of situation for learning English as a subject in India.[7] The dramatic success of French language acquisition in South East

Asia, however, by children who attended French language schools, and the equally impressive success in English acquisition in German, Danish, Swedish and Norwegian schools in Europe, testify that the acquisition of the second language can also seemingly approach native competence in this situation.

The third kind of situation is the opposite of the first: the English are the minority group, outnumbered by speakers of another language, and sociologically inferior to them. This is the situation which recent language legislation in Quebec is attempting to bring into effect for that province, without regard to the rest of Canada. If it is successful, it will presumably mean that the Anglophone population will have to be bilingual, whereas the Francophone population will not. It will take a generation to see whether or not this result has been achieved, but to date all the evidence suggests that it will. The results for the English of Quebec will probably not be as severe as the traditional situation has been for the French of Quebec, since the Anglophone population still has contact with the huge surrounding Anglophone populations in Canada and the United States.

The fourth kind of situation has English as the majority and dominant language relating not to a uniform population of speakers of one other language, but rather to a range of different languages. The number of speakers of these different languages is variable; communities can be large or small; they may live in urban ghettoes or in isolated rural enclaves; they may be communities which are the result of recent migrations, or of early migrations which established a community which survived; or of a historical policy of restricting indigenous peoples to reserves. In Canada this is the relation of English to the recent immigrant communities, which are largely urban, as well as certain older urban communities (e.g., Chinese). It also applies to hundreds of small rural communities across the country which have Ukrainian, Kashubian, Icelandic, German and Gaelic etc. as a first language, and also to the majority of indigenous Amerindian languages, of which about sixty survive, with numbers of native speakers varying from about fifty for Sarsi to about 60 000 for Cree and Montagnais-Naskapi. Obviously, these languages differ enormously in their similarity to English and in the similarity of the culture they embody to mainstream Canadian culture. Their speakers differ as well in their readiness to abandon their minority language. And the languages differ considerably in the extent to which they are literate, uniform and standardized. The implications of this sort of bilingual situation for the education of minority group children also vary rather dramatically. We shall return to this question.

Just as bilingual situations differ in the number of languages involved, and relations between them, so too a number of different kinds of bilingual education programmes have evolved to try to address these various needs. Following James Cummins we can distinguish seven types of bilingual education programmes:[8]

1. *Immersion programmes*. In these the children of the linguistically dominant group receive most or all of their education in the language of the linguistically subordinate group. The most extensive and best-documented studies of immersion programmes deal with the teaching of French by immersion to Anglophone children in Canada.

2. *Functional bilingual programmes*. Such programmes in Canada have involved teaching in Ukrainian or German to children who are of Ukrainian or German heritage but whose dominant language is English. The aim is to make them functionally bilingual in what in Canada is called a 'heritage language'.

3. *Language shelter programmes*. In these the children of minority groups are taught in their first language (e.g., in French in Canada), and it is the medium through which they learn the language of the linguistically dominant group, as one subject among others.

4. *Transitional bilingual programmes*. These address the problem of the mismatch between home language and school language in minority populations (whether of recent immigrant origins or of enclavic populations). Their aim is to help the children of the minority group learn the majority language as quickly as possible, usually so that they can be assimilated into the main educational stream. Teaching of the second language starts in the first language, but as soon as possible instruction in the majority language takes over.

5. *Culturally sensitive instruction in the majority language only*, with the first language taught as a subject, and with literacy in the first language as one of the goals of education.

6. *Instruction in the majority language only*, but with serious attempts to make the majority population appreciate the benefits of multiculturalism.

7. *Submersion*. This is the opposite of the immersion programmes: children who speak a language other than the majority language

are simply thrown into the classroom in which education in the majority language is taking place. There, if they are lucky, they swim; otherwise they sink. Submersion has been the traditional practice in majority English-speaking schools, both with indigenous children and with non-Anglophone immigrant children.

The ongoing research into bilingual education has focused chiefly on only two of these different possibilities: immersion and submersion. First of all, the Canadian immersion programmes. In the most extreme and most dramatic of these, English-speaking children enter kindergarten after their fifth birthday in a half-day programme in which all the teaching takes place in French, a language which at this stage they do not understand. In Grade 1 the following year, instruction continues to be entirely in French: it is in French that they learn to read and write, to follow teachers' instructions, to do arithmetic, to spell, to put their snowsuits on. In a subsequent year, sometimes in Grade 2, but at all events no later than Grade 4, some instruction in English is introduced, perhaps only thirty minutes daily at first. Gradually, the amount of instruction offered in English increases, until at about the eighth year the proportion is typically fifty-fifty.

The effects are astounding. You have to appreciate that since French is the language of a linguistically subordinate minority in Canada, traditional modes of French teaching have been very ineffective. Instruction in French as a second language has long been compulsory for Anglophone children throughout much of their education, and the results have been abysmal. Canadian Anglophone children have no more reason to learn French than upper-class British children have to learn Cockney, or Anglophone children in Texas and New Mexico to learn Spanish. In this kind of bilingual situation, it is the minority group that has to do the adjusting.

Children in early French immersion programmes, however, do not know that they are learning the unknown language of a minority group: they think that they are going to school. And so they are. But in the process they learn French to an extent that has hitherto been virtually impossible for Anglophone children in Canada. From a very early stage, their accents are impeccable. In reading and listening in French they attain native-like skill. Their speaking and writing skills are below the mean levels of native speakers — but are still greatly superior to the results achieved by any other kind of instruction.

However, this gain in second language ability is achieved at no cost to first-language skills. Understandably in the early grades their command of written English is below that of children being educated in normal English language programmes: they invent new phonetic spellings for English words on the basis of French spelling conventions, for example. But as soon as English is introduced, they begin to transfer to it skills acquired to handle French: the speed with which they learn to read in English is particularly striking. The differences between French immersion children and children in English programmes disappear by Grade 4, at the latest. And from that point on, French immersion children typically outperform children in the English programmes in various English skills, in which they tend to stand above the national norms for their grade level. Still more surprising, they tend to outperform the students in the English programme in mathematics and science, even though they have been taught these subjects entirely in French but are tested in English. In addition, researchers have detected attitudinal and affective changes which are judged to be desirable.

On the face of it, these impressive results would seem to point to an obvious solution to the problems caused by non-English-speaking children in our classrooms. If immersion teaching of French to monolingual English Canadian children is so clearly beneficial, why not teach English to ESL children in the same way?

The trouble is that almost all the research that has been done on such programmes when the children are members of a linguistically *subordinate* community suggests that the effects are just the opposite. Instead of doing better than monolingual children, they do worse, and instead of gaining near-native command of a second language with no expense to their first language, they tend to lose their first language without acquiring anything like native mastery of the second.[10] Intuitively, this seems to be right. It certainly coincides with the typical pattern when indigenous children are thrust into classrooms in which education is taking place in English as majority language. That, after all, constitutes an immersion in English for the minority language children, and usually they do not do as well as Anglophone children: once submerged, they tend to sink lower and lower.

The studies show, on the contrary, that such children do better if they are educated in their first language. Moreover, it has been repeatedly demonstrated that when it comes to learning the second language, the amount of education given in it does not correlate directly with the level of attainment reached. For example, in one Canadian study, Francophone students receiving 80 per cent of all their education in French and 20 per cent in English did just as well in English as students receiving 20 per cent of their education in French and 80 per cent in English. However, the level of French (i.e., first-language) achievement of the former group was significantly superior.[11] Thus there is no obvious disadvantage to their English if the time devoted to it is low, but there is a real disadvantage to their first language, and to their general academic achievement, if the time devoted to their first language is low.

On the face of it, these results suggest that the most desirable approach to education for minority children of immigrant origin must be to provide them with an opportunity to receive education in their first language. Of course, such a decision might be terribly expensive. In Toronto, when parents were asked if they would like their children to receive classes in their native languages (as a subject, not as the medium for all education), parents speaking twenty-eight languages replied in such numbers that the Board of Education considered itself justified in setting up classes in those languages.[12] That in itself is a costly enough undertaking. To offer them instruction through the medium of their first language might be more than most jurisdictions can accept. It is the Swedish solution: in Sweden, municipalities are obliged by law to provide mother-tongue instruction if minority children or parents request it. Obviously, this increases the net cost of education considerably. But even when such solutions are not possible, there can be other costs in bilingual education. For example, in Ontario approximately 28 000 students are currently enrolled in French immersion classes at the elementary level. This means that, since all those who teach French immersion classes are native speakers of French, some 700 teaching positions which would have been taken up by Anglophone teachers if the French immersion programmes had not been instituted, have been assigned to Francophone teachers. Apart from the resentment this can cause through the loss of career-advancement opportunities, it has also had subtler effects, such as an increase in the mean age of the Anglophone teachers.

Moreover, where minority language children are concerned, it is still not clear that L1 instruction is necessarily the best solution. Whereas the data for French Canadian and Amerindian children show that they are clearly disadvantaged if they are placed in a *de facto* immersion in the majority language, there are other data which show that other bilingual minority children, especially if they were born in Canada, may in fact outperform even the monolingual majority children with whom they compete if they are placed in the same sort of *de facto* immersion in majority language. For example, a study in Toronto schools in 1971 which examined the proportion of French Canadian 'other' bilingual and Anglophone children in different sorts of classes, showed that the French group had the highest proportion of children in low academic special education classes at the elementary level, the highest percentage in special vocational programmes at the secondary level, and the lowest percentage in the high academic five-year secondary programmes. The English-speaking children occupied a middle position. However, the 'other' bilingual children had the lowest percentage in elementary special education classes, the lowest percentage in special vocational programmes at the secondary level, and the highest percentage in high academic five-year secondary programmes.[13] These results do not suggest that there is any particular academic need to provide first-language education for minority children, unless they are members of a fairly large-sized subordinate group in a stable bilingual situation.

How can we make sense of such apparently contradictory results? Research into second-language education suggests that three factors are of paramount importance; there is a fourth, however, which is perhaps more important than any of the other three.

The first factor has to do with the nature of the 'input' on the basis of which the second language is acquired. This term is due, in this sense, to the work of the American linguist Stephen D. Krashen, who has formulated a theory of second-language learning which makes a distinction between 'learning' a second language and 'acquiring' it. Second-language 'learning' is due to direct teaching; for example, to direct instruction in the grammar of the second language. Second language 'acquisition', however, is due to comprehensible input — that is, it is due to an unconscious understanding of language which grows when the student's attention is focused not on the language, but on its meaning. Krashen hypothesizes that these two processes are largely independent. He also hypothesizes that what is 'learned', in his sense, can be accessed for linguistic performance only when certain very narrow conditions are met: the students must have enough time to think of the rules they have been taught; they must in fact do so (this does not necessarily follow from fulfilment of the first condition); and they must not be in an emotional state which prevents them from doing so. These conditions can be met in test situations; however, they cannot normally be met in situations where the use of language is normal (as it is not in test situations).

In normal situations, learners have to fall back on what they have acquired on the basis of Krashen calls 'comprehensible input'. According to this hypothesis, second-language learners acquire a working knowledge of the structure of the target language by focusing not on form, but on meaning.

The empirical evidence for this group of hypotheses about second-language learning and acquisition is impressive.[14] By themselves, they go a long way to explain the different results between French immersion and subordinate minority second-language education programmes. The French immersion students have the advantage that they are a segregated group within the classroom; everybody in the same class is at approximately the same level in relation to the teacher. Because the teachers are working in this sort of sheltered environment, they can tailor the 'input' they are providing very directly to the students' abilities as they develop: the input is comprehensible. This is true from the beginning, as a matter of fact. The teachers understand English; consequently they are able to understand children's questions and responses, and of course they can and do rely on gestures and on any other possible technique to convey to the children the meaning that is also being conveyed in the unknown language. Because the situation is meaningful, communication takes place; in the process, the language is acquired.

The submersion of minority group children is often exactly the opposite. In the first place, they are not segregated. They are, therefore, competing with majority language children who have a much fuller and stronger command of the majority language. The teaching which is going on is addressed for the most part to the level of understanding of the majority language children. Handicapped at the start by their less than perfect command of the majority language, the minority language children thus fall further and further behind. They do not receive enough comprehensible input to master the second language, because the classroom situation is not designed to make the input comprehensible to them.

The second factor is closely related to this. For the majority language children learning a minority language, as in the Canadian French immersion programmes, the second language is only the language of the classroom. It is not even the language of the school, for the school as a whole functions in a predominantly monolingual community. The children play in English outside the classroom, and of course they live in English in their own homes and in their community; their parents read to them in English; they hear English radio programmes; they watch English television and films. For such children, bilingualism is what W.E. Lambert has called 'additive' bilingualism:[15] it adds to the very broadly-based competence in the first language a very high level of bilingualism in the second. For the subordinate minority language children, however, the situation is quite different. For them, bilingualism is what Lambert has called 'subtractive' bilingualism: it deprives them of the opportunity to build up in their first language that range of linguistic competence which is acquired by the input from the whole community in monolinguals, and it also deprives them of a chance to equal the competence of the majority language children amongst whom they are submerged.

The difference between these two types of bilingulism can be attributed to the third factor which has been the concern of James Cummins. Cummins has elaborated a theory of language acquisition which suggests that learning to use the first language in its full range of communicative potential (including such functions as gaining knowledge, applying knowledge, classifying, abstracting, generalizing, etc.) establishes cognitive abilities which are not limited only to the language in which these abilities are acquired. Cummins thus sees the part of language that surfaces in performance as the tip of an iceberg of linguistic competence. For the bilingual child in an additive situation, the unseen part of the iceberg generates not one set of linguistic performances, but two. To the external observer, it seems that the child is using two unrelated linguistic codes. Cummins' claim is that they both depend on the same psychological and cognitive abilities.[16]

What happens in the subtractive kind of bilingual situation, then, is that the child is deprived of the chance to build up full cognitive competence in either language. The justification for first-language education for such children, then, is that, to quote Merrill Swain, 'education in the first language appears to promote precisely those aspects of proficiency which are central to progress and achievement in academic settings.'[17]

But a mystery still remains to be solved. If submersion can have such long-term deleterious effects on the children of subordinated minority groups in the kind of stable bilingual situations that obtain between French and English in Canada; between Spanish and English in the United States, between Finnish and Swedish in Sweden; between Amerindian languages and English in both Canada and the United States; then why is it that the children of some immigrant groups in cities like Toronto perform even better than their monolingual Anglophone classmates? Still more to the point, why is it that in those parts of Canada which are pervasively bilingual but where education in French has always been available to Francophone children, the French-speaking population continues to be a linguistically subordinate group, whose children continue to be disadvantaged?

To my knowledge, the available research has not addressed this question at all. I would suggest, however, that the answer is not to be sought in the psychology of bilingualism. Instead, it should be sought in politics. The factors that create and maintain disadvantaged groups in society have little to do with language, as such, for all their complex effects on language. They have to do with power and with the maintenance of certain groups in positions of privilege. The disadvantaged position of the Spanish-speaking population in the United States is not a consequence of bilingualism; it is due to the same factors which put unilingual black children in a disadvantaged position. The factors which put Amerindian children, Francophone children, and some immigrant children at a disadvantage in Canadian schools but do not disadvantage other immigrant children, are also not due primarily to bilingualism as such, but to such factors as socio-economic stratification and to racism. And surely the same is true in Britain, Australia and New Zealand, and everywhere else where minority groups are clearly at a disadvantage.

Towards some conclusions

What then are the implications for those of us who teach English as a majority language in English-speaking schools? First, it is clear that bilingualism is not necessarily bad: the common attitude that being bilingual is itself a disadvantage, so that schools and communities should suppress minority languages for the good of their speakers, is flatly contradicted by the results of the Canadian French immersion studies, by the results of the Canadian 'heritage language' programmes, which are essentially another kind of immersion programme, and by the impressive achievements of certain Canadian-born non-native-speakers in the Toronto school system. All these results suggest that bilingualism is very much to the advantage of such children. For majority-language children in a predominantly monolingual culture, immersion can provide a high level of fluency in a second language, and with it access to another culture, with all the benefits that implies. In certain circumstances, it can do so even for minority-language children.

On the other hand, it is clear that bilingualism is not something that is achieved easily. It is commonly asserted that children can pick up two or more languages effortlessly in early childhood, and of course to all appearances this is true. I have observed it in my own (predominantly French-speaking) household; indeed, owing to a series of circumstances, at the age of three my younger son was fluently bilingual (at a three-year-old level) in French and Vietnamese, and able to function adequately (though not so fluently) in English as well. Nonetheless, it takes eight years of classroom exposure to French in French immersion classrooms to get Canadian Anglophone children to attain the level of French they attain — a level which, impressive as it is, is still not as high as that of Francophone children in French-language programmes. Consequently if there is any justification for transitional bilingual programmes it will have to be recognized that they need many years to accomplish what they are supposed to do. A few weeks, a month, even a year, is certainly not enough.

Thirdly, the case for language shelter programmes teaching through the medium of a minority language is very clear when the minority language is spoken by a fairly sizable bilingual community that is in a subordinate position, and where the relations between the dominant and the subordinate groups are fairly stable. Language shelter programmes will at least give them an education which ensures the greatest level of cognitive development possible, insofar as this is a product of education in any language.

Fourthly, there is a case for language shelter programmes also for immigrant and enclavic populations when it is clear that they are likely to be permanently at a disadvantage socioeconomically. On the other hand, when they are not, when there is a high level of literacy in either the native language, the majority language, or both, in the home; when parents have strong expectations that their children will succeed, and there is nothing in majority attitudes which prevents them from doing so, then language shelter programmes are not necessary. For such children, language maintenance programmes may be desirable for other reasons; for example, they may help to assure recent immigrant populations that they are genuinely welcome and that it is the expectation of the host country that they will integrate comfortably into the society of their new country without renouncing their background. However, since they are not necessary, if the cost of putting them into effect is judged to be too high, there is still no reason why the children should suffer academically. This is the case even where their command of the majority language is less than that of monolingual native speaker. This is often the case in Canada with certain long-established enclavic populations like the Ukrainians and the Chinese, and it appears likely to continue to be the case with the Vietnamese. This does not prevent any of them from becoming dentists, doctors, lawyers, engineers or anything else they may want to be. Having an accent, then, is not necessarily a disadvantage.

This conclusion may be cold comfort for teachers who find themselves facing classes three-quarters full of children of migrant origins for whom English is a second language. It is, however, soundly based. To expect children to master English quickly is unrealistic in even the most favourable situations. To expect them to acquire it without a trace of an accent is also unrealistic (although peer-group pressure will hasten the process, if they socialize with English-speaking children). The truth of the matter is that, when circumstances are less than ideal (which is always), it is unrealistic to expect teachers to do everything that might be done to assimilate migrants in ways that do not disadvantage them and yet leave them indistinguishable from native speakers.

On the other hand, there is one very clear implication for teachers. They should trust the children to learn: there is nothing that the human brain is better equipped to do, and one of the things it learns best, given the right conditions, is language.

This implication returns me to my other theme: the implications of recent work in second-language education for the first-language field. The great strength of much of the recent work in second-language education is the care which has gone into the design of the research studies investigating what goes on, and the intelligence with which these results have been examined. Again and again, the results in the second-language field seem to be pointing educators towards the same directions as the foremost researchers in the first-language field have indicated.

Consider, for example, the input hypothesis. Krashen himself has pointed out how neatly his theory fits the research evidence which relates to learning to write.[18] Just as the grammar which is taught in second-language classes can be tested in test situations but apparently has no effect on language acquisition, so also all the evidence relating to the usefulness of grammar teaching aimed at the improvement of writing abilities shows that there is no carry-over effect at all, even when tests show that the grammar has been learned. The obvious conclusion us is that the ability to produce written discourse depends on comprehensible input: that by reading a great deal, and reading not to see how the surface of the language works, but to get at the meaning beyond it, children can acquire that feel for written discourse which is necessary if they are to be good writers.

Equally, Krashen's theory fits very neatly with the underlying assumptions of the 'Language across the curriculum' movement. Insofar as students fail to acquire mastery of that special variety of English which is school language, or the specialized language of a specific discipline, they fail because schools fail to make that language available to them in a form which makes it possible for them to acquire it. If they are to acquire it, rather than simply learn it as something they can parrot back without understanding, then they must acquire it incidentally, while their attention is focused on something other than the language, namely, on meaning.

Furthermore, the model of linguistic competence which

James Cummins has elaborated with respect to the second-language learning also relates directly to recent work in first-language education. In the first place, his theory that there is a 'linguistic threshold' which specifies the minimal exposure necessary before a second-language learner can begin to handle the second language again parallels the underlying assumptions of the 'Language across the curriculum' move-ment. The threshold hypothesis assumes that those aspects of bilingualism which might positively influence cognitive growth are unlikely to come into effect until the child has attained a certain minimum or threshold level of competence in his second language. So it would seem to be with growth towards mastery of specialized sub-varieties of one's own language. Schools may be too impatient to test for, or to presuppose, competence which is in fact being acquired, but in which the threshold level that would make testing a sensible activity has not yet been attained.[19]

At the same time, Cummins' 'developmental interdependence' hypothesis confirms the insights of recent work on the importance of talking, especially expressive talking, and above all expressive writing, in the first-language field. The relevant feature of the developmental interdependence hypothesis is that the bilingual child's first language has functional significance in the developmental process, and for this reason should be actively promoted in schools. This clearly relates to the monolingual child's development of the ability to use what Margaret Donaldson has called 'disembedded' language, the kind of language in which meaning is found in the autonomous text rather than in a combination of the text and the whole communicative situation of which it is part.[20] Britton, Barnes, Martin, Tough and many other authorities have stressed that the ability to use language in this way grows out of talk — expressive talk about everyday events — in the course of which meaning is gradually shaped and grows into coherence in extended conversations. What is wrong with submersion for bilingual and minority children is that it deprives them of the ability to use their first language in this way at the developmental stage at which it must happen if the next cognitive stage is to be attained.

Finally, the failure of certain non-Anglophone immigrant children to progress in either language shelter or submersion programmes probably relates to the implications of Gordon Wells' most recent work on the acquisition of literacy. Wells has discovered that two factors above all correlate with the success of first-language children in acquiring literacy skills in their first two years of school. The more important is the children's understanding of the purposes of literacy when they start school. Almost as important, however, is the nature of the interactions between the children and those who look after them in their pre-school years. Those parents or guardians who are most likely to accept and develop conversations started by children are also most likely to see their children succeed in school.[21] Insofar as there is something other than socio-economic factors, simple racism, and excessive restriction of expressive use of the first language, which can explain why some minority language children actually thrive in submersion programmes, it is no doubt to be sought in cultural values such as these in the home situation. It is just as clear that one reason for the success of Canadian French immersion programmes is precisely that they are valued so highly in the homes.

In such ways as these, then, recent work in the second-language field confirms the strongest tendencies in the first-language field. Again and again, starting from different concerns, proceeding in ways and using techniques of verification which are sometimes quite different from what is normal in the first-language field, those working in the second-language field have made discoveries and elaborated theories which serve to corroborate, strengthen and expand recent tendencies in English education. To be sure, the links I am sketching at this stage are only hypothetical. The second-language research was not undertaken to investigate questions of concern in the first-language field, and more formal research will be needed before the strength of the commonality between the two fields is clearly established. Nonetheless if, starting from such different points, we find so much in common, the chances are so much the better that we are indeed heading in the right direction, concerned as we are on both sides to make education in English as meaningful and rich as possible for the children entrusted to us, whatever their home language may be.[22]

NOTES

1 James Britton

[1] Michael Polanyi, *Personal Knowledge*, Routledge and Kegan Paul, 1958, pp. 100-1.

[2] Wallace Stevens, *Collected Poems*, Faber and Faber, 1955, p. 130.

[3] Robert Graves, *The Common Asphodel*, Hamish Hamilton, 1949, p. 1.

[4] L.S. Vygotsky, *The Psychology of Art*, MIT Press, 1971, p. 48.

[5] See in particular, Susanne K. Langer, translator's preface to Ernst Cassirer, *Language and Myth*, Dover Publications, undated, pp. vii-x.

[6] From Tolstoy, *Collected Works*, 30, 1951, quoted in Vygotsky, p. 36.

[7] Peter McKellar, *Imagination and Thinking*, Cohen and West, 1957, p. 26.

[8] I.A. Richards, *Principles of Literary Criticism*, Routledge and Kegan Paul, 1934, pp. 212-13.

[9] A.R. Luria and O.S. Vinogradova, 'The Dynamics of Semantic Systems', *British Journal of Psychology*, 50, 1958, pp. 89-105.

[10] Michael Oakeshott, *The Voice of Poetry in the Conversation of Mankind,* Bowes and Bower, 1959, p. 61.

[11] Vygotsky, p. 257.

[12] W.H. Auden, *Collected Shorter Poems*, Faber and Faber, 1950, pp. 122-3.

[13] W.H. Auden, *Making Knowing and Judging*, the Clarendon Press, 1956, p. 9.

[14] With acknowledgements to Sheila Williams and Gary Stokes of Grande Prairie Composite High School, Roberta Neal of Countesthorpe College and their respective teachers.

[15] Denys W. Harding, 1962, 'Psychological Processes in the Reading of Fiction' in Margaret Meek, Aidan Warlow and Griselda Barton (eds), *The Cool Web*, Bodley Head, 1977, p. 60.

[16] W.H.N. Hotopf, whose book *Language, Thought and Comprehension*, Routledge and Kegan Paul, 1965, is a patient and detailed study of Richards' life work, concludes that Richards, in a variety of ways underestimates the social dimension of experience: 'Richards' real concern is indeed with the individual and this frequently shows itself in hostility or suspicion concerning society' (p. 240).

2   Bruce Bennett

[1] Wallace Stevens, *Collected Poems of Wallace Stevens*, Faber and Faber, 1945.

[2] I.A. Richards, *The Philosophy of Rhetoric*, Oxford University Press, 1950, p. 90.

[3] e.g., by Ernst Cassirer, *Language and Myth*, Harper, 1946, translated by Susanne Langer and Winifred Nowottney, *The Language Poets Use*, the Athlone Press, 1962.

[4] *Ibid.*

[5] Terence Hawkes, *Metaphor*, Methuen, 1972.

[6] *Ibid.*, p. 2.

[7] Northrop Frye, *The Educated Imagination*, Canadian Broadcasting Commission, 1963.

[8] *Ibid.*, p. 11.

[9] Holton, Gerald, *The Scientific Imagination: Case Studies*, Cambridge University Press, 1978. See alsl: 'Metaphors in Science and Education' in W. Taylor, (ed) *The Metaphors of Education*, (forthcoming).

[10] George Lakoff and Mark Johnson, *Metaphors We Live By*, University of Chicago Press, 1980.

[11] See Bruce Bennett and Adrienne Walker, 'The Development of Writing Abilities 15-18', *English in Australia*, 44, June 1978. *What Do Pupils Write?* Education Department of Tasmania, 1975. *32 Voices*, Education Department of Western Australia, 1977.

[12] Liam Hudson, *Contrary Imaginations: A Psychological Study of the English Schoolboy*, Pelican, 1967.

[13] *Ibid.*, p. 59.

[14] Janet Emig, 'Children and Metaphor', *Research in the Teaching of English*, 6, 2, 1972, p. 163.

[15] H.R. Pollio, J.M. Barlow, H.J. Fine, M.R. Pollio, *Psychology and the Poetics of Growth: Figurative Language in Psychology, Psychotherapy and Education*, Lawrence Erlbaum, Hillside, New Jersey, 1977.

[16] *Ibid.*, p. 169.

[17] *Ibid.*, p. 184.

[18] J.W. Chapman, 'The perception and expression of metaphor as a function of cognitive style and intellectual level', Unpublished

doctoral dissertation, Georgia State University, 1971. Cited in Pollio *et. al.*, pp. 85-8.

[19] *Ibid.,* p. 89.

[20] *Ibid.*, p. 170.

[21] *Ibid.*, pp. 175-6.

[22] See B. Bennett, D. Bowes, C. Jeffery, S. McPhail, A. Sooby and A. Walker, 'An investigation of the process of writing and the development of writing abilities 15-17', Report to the Education Research and Development Committee, Canberra, 1980; and Bruce Bennett, 'Writers and their Writing, 15-17', in Aviva Freedman, Ian Pringle and Janice Yalden (eds), *Learning to Write: First Language, Second Language*, Longman, (forthcoming).

[23] Eleven of these case studies were published by the English Department, University of Western Australia and were included in the Report to the Education Research and Development Committee.

[24] R.B. Schonberg, 'Adolescent thought and figurative language', Unpublished doctoral dissertation, University of Tennessee, 1974, quoted in Pollio *et. al.*, p. 185.

[25] C.M. Porter, 'Figures of speech, divergent thinking and activation theory', Unpublished doctoral dissertation, North Texas State University, 1969, quoted in Pollio *et. al.*, p. 89.

[26] Bennett *et. al.*, Chapter 9.

[27] A·case study approach to research is strongly advocated by Donald Graves. See 'An examination of the writing processes of seven-year old children', *Research in the Teaching of English*, 9, 3, 1975, pp. 228-31; and 'Writing research for the eighties: what is needed', *Language Arts*, 58, 2, 1981.

[28] These two were not among the case studies published with the report of the University of Western Australia writing research project.

[29] These findings have been cast in doubt however by R. Ashton and K.D. White, 'Sex differences in imagery vividness: An artifact of the test', *British Journal of Psychology*, 71, 1980, pp. 35-8.

[30] See James Britton, Tony Burgess, Nancy Martin, Alex McLeod and Harold Rosen, *The Development of Writing Abilities (11-18)*, Macmillan, 1975, Chapter 4 and *passim*.

[31] James Moffett, 'Integrity in the Teaching of Writing', *Phi Delta Kappan*, 61, 4, 1979, pp. 276-9.

[32] Jerre Paquette, 'The influence of the sense of audience on the writing processes of eight adolescent boys', Unpublished doctoral thesis, University of London Institute of Education, 1981.

[33] Nancy Martin, 'Scope for Intentions' in Freedman *et. al.*

[34] Pollio *et. al.*, Chapter 9. The authors recommend a series of workbooks, *Making It Strange*, Synectics Inc., New York, Harper and Row, 1968.

[35] See Paul Foot, *Red Shelley*, Sidgwick and Jackson, 1981.

3   Douglas and Dorothy Barnes

[1] This paper is based on material collected for the 'Versions of English' project, which is based at the University of Leeds and supported by a grant from the Social Science Research Council.

The project is concerned with the kinds of English experienced by different groups of students in the last year of compulsory education and the following year: it is based on information collected in the North of England from six schools and four colleges of further education (equivalent to the community colleges of Australia). We set out not only to describe the different versions of the subject that we observed and recorded in classrooms, but also to understand how each version was justified by those who taught it, how it was related to its institutional context — which here includes examination requirements — and how it was experienced by students.

All six of the schools were co-educational and comprehensive; in all of them English was taught in the fifth year to sets organized according to previous academic success — but not always success in English — and we obtained permission to work with a top, middle and bottom set in each school. The material we are using in this paper is drawn from eighteen fifth year courses, taught by seventeen teachers; we are not using material from sixth forms and colleges of further education. A curriculum is not a simple unproblematic activity: what you are told depends on whom you ask, amongst other things. Thus we decided to collect information from a range of sources:

a. Documents at national and local level, including examination syllabuses and papers.

b. Documents at institutional level, such as schemes of work.

c. Teachers' and lecturers' statements about their teaching and antecedents, gathered both informally and by structured interview and questionnaire.

d. Classroom observation (153 hours in all).

e. Classroom materials, students' written work, teachers' comments.

f. Interviews with a third of the students in each class.

We expect the sources to differ one from another: part of the interest lies in tracing the process by which purposes originated in various contexts, some of them outside schools, are progressively re-interpreted until they gain meaning in exchanges between teachers and pupils.

We should like to acknowledge the contributions of our collaborators Stephen Clarke and John Seed to the work reported here.

[2] P. Bourdieu 'The school as a conservative force: scholastic and cultural inequalities', 1966, in J. Eggleston, (ed) *Contemporary Research in the Sociology of Education*, Methuen, 1974.

[3] The 'Ordinary Level' of the General Certificate of Education, intended originally for the top 20 per cent of the ability range, is a required qualification for higher education and for many careers. The Certificate of Secondary Education is the standard leaving certificate. Though its highest grade is equivalent to GCE Ordinary Level, CSE tends not to have so high a standing in the eyes of the public. Alternative examinations called sixteen plus which seek to interrelate GCE and CSE grades, have been on trial since 1974.

[4] In the lessons we observed being taught to classes preparing for coursework assessment, the bottom sets spent 71 per cent of their time preparing to write and writing, which can be compared with 21 per cent for the top sets.

[5] These figures may overestimate the personal by placing fiction in that category; we found, however, that a large proportion of the stories were written in the first person, and that stories about loneliness, the sufferings of old people, relations with the opposite sex, and the personal results of prejudice and violence were very common indeed.

[6] B. Bernstein, 'Class and Pedagogies: Visible and Invisible' in *Class, Codes and Control*, III, Routledge and Kegan Paul, 1975.

[7] What found when we interviewed pupils that less than a quarter said that they liked writing about themselves, whereas a greater number — about a third — said that they disliked it, the majority of the latter coming from lower sets. This is a finding that teachers of English would do well to ponder.

[8] F. Inglis, 'Against Proportional Representation' in *English in Education* 9:1, 1975.

[9] See Bourdieu.

[10] This excludes the very substantial amount of writing about literature which was done by pupils in top sets.

[11] The textbook is: J. Atherton, *Guidance and Practice in English*, Hulton, 1978.

[12] Peter Medway displays the perspectives of one such pupil, Barry, in Chapter 3 of P. Medway, *Finding a Language: Autonomy and Learning in School*, Writers and Readers Publishing Co-operative in association with Chameleon Books, 1980.

4   John Dixon

[1] F.R. Leavis, *Education and the University*, Chatto and Windus, 1943.

[2] L.C. Knights, 'In Search of Fundamental Values' in 'The Critical Moment', *Times Literary Supplement*, 26-7 September 1963, reprinted (1964) by Faber.

[3] See the discussion of staging points in narrative in L. Stratta and J. Dixon, *Achievements in Writing 16 +*, Schools Council, 1980.

[4] John Brown and I discuss these points in more detail in our forthcoming Schools Council *Report on Evidence of Response*.

[5] See James Moffett's handbook for students and teachers, *Active Voice*, Boynton-Cook, 1981.

[6] See the *Evidence of Response* report for more detailed examples and discussion.

[7] *Ibid*.

[8] See *Criteria for Writing in English*, a discussion booklet series based on CEE cross-moderation exercises, SREB/Schools Council, 1981.

5   Nancy Martin

[1] Nancy Martin, *What Goes on in English Lessons: Case Studies from Government High Schools in Western Australia*, Education Department, Western Australia, 1980, pp. 1-3.

[2] George A. Kelly, 'A brief introduction to personal construct theory', in Bannister, D. (ed), *Perspectives in Personal Construct Theory*, Academic Press, 1970.

[3] M. Parlett, D. Hamilton, 'Evaluation as Illumination' in D. Tawney (ed), *Curriculum Evaluation Today: Trends and Implications*, Macmillan Research Series, 1976.

[4] A. Bussis, E. Chittenden and M. Amarel, *Beyond Surface Curriculum: An Interview Study of Teachers' Understandings*, Westview Press, 1976, pp. 14-18.

[5] See Martin, *op. cit*.

6   Margaret Gill

[1] D. Holbrook, 'An Unmitigated Disaster', *The Use of English*, 28, 2, 1977, p. 49.

[2] P. Abbs, 'English in Crisis', *The Use of English*, 24, 2, 1972, p. 122.

[3] National Association for the Teaching of English Submission to the Bullock Report, *English in Education*, 7, 2, 1973, p. 75.

[4] Case study as a research technique provides data which is both generalizable and specific, typical and unique. Like good fiction it asks the question 'This is so, is it not?' But it does more

than that. In some areas it may provide information that is not available any other way. In fields which are in a constant state of flux, where the chance of finding enduring relationships is minimal, and where the number of variables to be controlled is almost infinite, there is little to gain and much to lose from a heavy investment in geographically extensive sample surveys. Since we cannot filter the uniqueness out of any educational situation, we are, as researchers, better advised to accept the inevitability of ambiguity, and to aim for impressionistic data, for insights, for clarifications, for ways of looking at things, rather than for theorems, laws, constants and calculuses (W.A. Reid, 'What is Curriculum Research?' in P.H. Taylor and J. Walton, (eds), *The Curriculum: Research, Innovation and Change*, Ward Lock Educational, 1973 p. 96).

In other words, the intention is to describe and interpret, rather than to measure and judge. There *are* occasions when educational research must measure and judge, must answer the questions, *how* generalizable? *how* typical? The aim on this occasion is to illuminate some of the ways teachers define English in practice. The account is drawn from three case studies, part of a larger research study which examines the nature of curriculum change in English at classroom and national levels. My debt to the teachers and their students is, once again, acknowledged.

5 The Bullock Report (1975), *A Language for Life*, Report of the Committee of Inquiry appointed by the Secretary of State for Education and Science, HMSO p. 143-5.

6 Bourdieu, P. and Passeron, J.C., (1970), *Reproduction in Education, Society and Culture*, English edition, Sage Publications, 1977.

7 This remains so even in times of economic recession. Anne's students did not talk about fears of unemployment, they talked of modified career choices. For example, 'I'm choosing pharmacy, rather than teaching, because I've heard it's hard to get jobs in teaching now'.

8 An interesting fact emerged from a survey designed to discover which unit had been most popular. There appeared to be no consistency in the students' preferences until it was realized that they had all liked *least* whichever unit they took in third term, i.e. the term in which they were preoccupied with external exam requirements!

9 The choice of this particular context for English Literature presents a specific and problematic situation which provides a restricted picture of Tom's English teaching, and an equally restricted version of English Literature teaching. My intention is not to generalize from either of these phenomena, but to

consider a larger curriculum issue which Tom's situation exposes.

[10] Bourdieu and Passeron's interpretation, 1970, p. 142 of the role of the examination system in society is relevant:

In fact the examination system is not only the clearest expression of academic values and of the educational system's implicit choices: in imposing as worthy of university sanction a social definition of knowledge and the way to show it, it provides one of the most efficacious tools for the enterprise of inculcating the dominant culture and the value of that culture. As much as or more than through the constraints of curriculum and syllabus, the acquisition of legitimate culture is regulated by the customary law which is constituted in the jurisprudence of examinations.

[11] F. Inglis, *The Englishness of English Teaching*, Longmans, 1969, p. 19.

[12] The Bullock Report, p. 131.

[13] Briefly, it was rejected by the examination board on the grounds that it was likely to be too difficult to mark and moderate; might not gain recognition (with university admissions committees); would create too many administrative problems, and, finally — the ultimate deterrent — would be too costly.

[14] For example, S. Bowles, and H. Gintis, *Schooling in Capitalist America*, Routledge and Kegan Paul, 1976.

7 C.T. Patrick Diamond

[1] D.E. Hunt, 'Teachers are Psychologists, Too: On the Application of Psychology to Education', *Canadian Psychological Review*, 17, 3, 1976, pp. 210-18.

[2] G.A. Kelly, *The Psychology of Personal Constructs*, Norton, 1955.

[3] D. Bannister and F. Fransella, *Inquiring Man: The Psychology of Personal Constructs*, Penguin, 1980, p. 86.

[4] D.M. Wegner and R.R. Vallacher, *Implicit Psychology: An Introduction to Social Cognition*, Oxford University Press, 1977.

[5] H.C. Triandis, *The Analysis of Subjective Culture*, Wiley, 1972.

[6] S. Delamont, *Interaction in the Classroom*, Methuen, 1976.

[7] G.H. Mead, *The Philosophy of the Act*, University of Chicago Press, 1934.

[8] A.J. Rosie, 'Teachers and Children: Interpersonal Relations and the Classroom', in P. Stringer and D. Bannister, (eds), *Constructs of Sociality and Individuality*, Academic Press, 1979.

[9] P. Salmon, 'Children as Social Beings: A Kellyian View', in

Stringer and Bannister.

[10] C.T.P. Diamond, 'The Constructs, Classroom Practices and Effectiveness of Grade 10 Teachers of Written Composition', Unpublished doctoral dissertation, University of Queensland, 1979.

[11] A.T. Ravenette, 'Personal Construct Theory: An Approach to the Psychological Investigation of Children and Young People', in D. Bannister, (ed), New Perspectives in Personal Construct Theory, Academic Press, 1977.

[12] See A.T. Ravenette, 1964, 'Some Attempts at Developing the use of Repertory Grid Techniques in a Child Guidance Clinic', paper, Brunel University, 1964, and D. Bannister, and J. Agnew, 'The child's construing of self', in A.W. Landfield, (ed.), Nebraska Symposium on Motivation, 1976, University of Nebraska Press, 1977.

[13] L. Davies, 'The View from the Girls', Educational Review, 30, 2, 1978, pp. 103-10.

[14] J. Britton, 'Writing to Learn and Learning to Write', in The Humanity of English, NCTE, 1972, p. 52.

[15] See the Bullock Report, HMSO, 1975.

[16] N. Bennett, et. al., Teaching Styles and Pupil Progress, Open Books, 1976, p. 150.

[17] N. Martin, 'Encounters with 'models'', English in Education, 10, 1, 1976, pp. 9-15.

[18] F.D. Flower, Language and Education, Longman, 1966, p. 160.

[19] C. Adelman and R. Walker, 'Developing pictures for other frames', in G. Chanan, and S. Delamont, (eds), Frontiers of Classroom Research, NFER, 1975, p. 230.

[20] C.H. Ehman, 'A Comparison of Three Sources of Classroom Data: Teachers, Students and Systematic Observation', paper, Minneapolis: AERA, 1970.

[21] H.H. Remmers, 'Rating Methods in Research on Teaching', in N.L. Gage, (ed), Handbook of Research on Teaching, Rand McNally, 1963.

[22] J.B. Goldberg, 'Influence of Pupils' Attitudes on Perception of Teachers' Behaviours and on Consequent School Work', Journal of Educational Psychology, 59, 1968, pp. 1-15.

[23] G.V. Glass, 'Teacher Effectiveness', in H.J. Walberg, (ed), Evaluating Educational Performance, McCutchan, 1974, p. 26.

[24] B. Rosenshine, Teaching Behaviours and Student Achievement, NFER, 1971, p. 177.

[25] M. Donaldson, Children's Minds, Fontana, 1978, p. 68.

8 James Moffett

[1] Norbert Weiner, The Human Use of Human Beings, Doubleday Anchor, 1954.

[2] I have dealt more fully with these techniques in 'Writing, Inner Speech, and Meditation', in *Coming on Center: English Education in Evolution,* Boynton Cook, 1981.

9   Roslyn Arnold

[1] James Britton, *Language and Learning*, Penguin 1970.

J.L. Britton, T. Burgess, N. Martin, A. McLeod and H. Rosen, *The Development of Writing Abilities (11-18)*, Macmillan Education, 1975.

James Britton, 'Shaping at the Point of Utterance', in Freedman, Aviva and Pringle, *Reinventing the Rhetorical Tradition*, CCTE, 1980.

Janet Emig, *The Composing Processes of Twelfth Graders*, NCTE Research Report 13, 1971.

Janet Emig, 'The Tacit Tradition: The Inevitability of a Multi-Disciplinary Approach to Writing Research' in Freedman, Aviva and Pringle.

Donald H. Graves, 'An Examination of the Writing Processes of seven-year-old Children', *Research in the Teaching of English* 9, 1975, pp. 227-41.

Donald H. Graves, 'Patterns of Growth in the Writing Processes of Young Children', paper delivered at CCTE Conference, 'Learning to Write', Ottawa, 1979.

N. Martin, P. Darcy, B. Newton and R. Parker *Writing and Learning across the Curriculum 11-16*, and associated pamphlets, Ward Lock, 1976.

N. Martin, *The Martin Report — What Goes on in English Lessons*, Cast Studies from Government High Schools, Education Department of Western Australia, 1980.

James Moffett, *Teaching the Universe of Discourse*, Houghton Mifflin, 1968.

James Moffett and Betty Jane Wagner, *Student-Centered Language Arts and Reading, K-13*, Houghton Mifflin, 1976.

James Moffett, *Coming on Center — English Education in Evolution*, Boynton/Cook, 1981a.

James Moffett, *Active Voice — a Writing Program across the Curriculum*, Boynton/Cook, 1981b

[2] J.Z. Young, *Programs of the Brain*, Oxford University Press, 1978, p. 10.

[3] Moffett, 1981a, p. 84.

[4] Moffett, 1968.

[5] David Dirlam, 'The Changing Wisdoms in Children's Writing' unpublished article, talk to New York State Education Department Conference on Writing Education, 1980.

[6] Moffett, 1981b.

[7] I am indebted to James Moffett, Patrick Diamond, Paul

Richardson and Ken Watson for their helpful comments on this chapter.

10   Margaret Meek

[1] A comparable experience a decade later is described by Marian Glastonbury in *The English Magazine*, April 1982.

[2] See D.P. and L.B. Resnick, 'The Nature of Literacy' in *Harvard Educational Review* 47, 3, 1977, pp. 370-85.

[3] See Louise M. Rosenblatt, *The Reader the Text the Poem*, Southern Illinois University Press, 1978.

[4] The phrase comes from Jonathan Culler, *Structuralist Poetics*, Routledge and Kegan Paul, 1978, which not only makes clear the links literary theory has with the linguistic studies of Saussure, but also relates this general statement to the diversity of the writings in this field.

[5] J. Culler, 'Prolegomena to a Theory of Reading' in S. Sulieman and I. Crossman, (eds) *The Reader in the Text*, Princeton University Press, 1980.

[6] See Frank Smith, *Reading*, Cambridge University Press, 1978, Frederick U. Gollasch, *Language and Literacy: the selected writings of Kenneth S. Goodman*. Routledge and Kegan Paul, 1982.

[7] Wolfgang Iser, *The Act of Reading*, Routledge and Kegan Paul, 1978.

[8] See Gollasch.

[9] M.A.K. Halliday, *Learning How to Mean — Explorations in the Development of Language*, Arnold, 1975.

[10] See Arthur N. Applebee, *The Child's Concept of Story*, University of Chicago Press, 1978.

[11] I. and P. Opie, *The Lore and Language of School Children*, Oxford University Press, 1969.

[12] Denys Harding, 'The Bond with the Author', in M. Meek, A. Warlow, G. Barton, (eds) *The Cool Web*, Bodley Head, 1977.

[13] James, Britton, *Language and Learning*, Allen Lane, 1970.

[14] It is *The Unvanquished* by William Faulkner. The passage was chosen by Harold Rosen for the first conference of the London Association for the Teaching of English in 1949 when the topic was 'comprehension'.

[15] See Resnick.

[16] R. Barthes, *Le Plaisir du Texte*, Sevil, 1973.

[17] See Seymour Chatman, 'Story and Discourse' in *Narrative Structure in Fiction and Film*, Cornell University Press, 1978.

[18] *Ibid*.

[19] G. Ginette, *Narrative Discourse*, Blackwell, 1980.

[20] See Culler.

[21] R. Barthes, 'Sur la lecture' in *Le francais aujourd'hui*, 32, 1976.

[22] Wayne Booth, *The Rhetoric of Fiction*, University of Chicago Press, 1961.

[23] See Iser.

[24] Raymond Williams, *The Country and the City*. Chatto and Windus, 1973.

[25] M. Meek, *et. al.*, *Achieving Literacy: a kind of evidence*, Routledge and Kegan Paul, (forthcoming).

[26] Zuetan T. Toderow, *The Poetics of Prose*, Blackwell, 1977.

[27] The words are those of my colleague, Judith Graham.

[28] Roy Schafer, 'Narration in the Psychoanalytic Dialogue' in W.T. Wilson, (ed), *On Narrative*, University of Chicago Press, 1981.

[29] See Kermode in Schafer.

[30] Ted Hughes, 'Myth in Education' in *Children's Literature in Education,* I, 1970, pp. 55-70.

[31] See Iser.

[32] L.S. Vygotsky, 'Play and its role in the mental development of the child' from *Soviet Psychology*, 12, 6, 1966, reprinted in J.S. Bruner, H. Jolly, and K. Sylva, (eds), *Play*, Penguin Books, 1976, p. 549.

11   Robert E. Shafer

[1] Alfred H. Grommon, 'A History of the Preparation of the Teachers of English', *English Journal*, 57, 1968.

[2] William P. Viall, *et. al.*, 'English Teacher Preparation Study: Guidelines for the Preparation for Teachers of English and Composition', *English Journal*, 57, 1968.

[3] *Ibid*.

[4] William Jenkins, 'Changing Patterns in Teacher Education', in James, R. Square, (ed), *The Teaching of English, Part I, The 1976 Yearbook of the National Society for the Study of Education*, 1977.

[5] Robert E. Shafer, 'The Attempt to Make English a Discipline', *The High School Journal*, 52, 7, 1969, pp. 336-51.

[6] Michael F. Shugrue and Eldonna L. Everetts, 'Guidelines for the Prepartion of Teachers of English', *English Journal*, 56, 1967, pp. 884-95.

[7] Richard Larson, *A Statement on the Preparation of Teachers of English*, National Council of Teachers of English, 1976, p. 192.

[8] Larson, p. 196.

[9] *Ibid*., p. 200.

[10] Robert E. Shafer, 'The Changing Program in English', *Audio Visual Instruction*, 10, 4, 1965, pp. 276-80.

[11] Larson, p. 197.

[12] *Ibid*.

[13] *Ibid*.

[14] *Ibid.*

[15] J.N. Hook, *Illinois Statewide Curriculum Study Center in the Preparation of Secondary School English Teachers: Final Report*, Department of Health, Education and Welfare, Washington, 1969.

[16] E.R. Fagan and C.H. Laine, 'Two Perspectives of Under-graduate English Teacher Preparation' in *Research in The Teaching of English*, 14, 1, 1980, pp. 67-72.

[17] Stanley Elam, *Performance Based Teacher Education: What is the State of the Art?*, American Association of Colleges for Teacher Education, Washington, 1971.

[18] Jenkins, p. 270.

[19] Robert W. Heath, and Mark A. Nielson, 'The Research Basis for Performance Based Teacher Education', *Review of Education Research*, 44, 4, 1974, p. 475.

[20] George E. Dickson, 'CBTE Revisited: Toledo Program Remains Strong', *Journal of Teacher Education*, XXX, 4, 1979, pp. 17-19.

[21] Martha K. Piper, and Robert W. Houston, 'The Search for Teacher Competence: CBTE and MCT', *Journal of Teacher Education*, XXXI, 5, 1980, pp. 37-40.

[22] Thomas S. Popkewitz, Robert B. Tabachnick, and Kenneth M. Zeichner, 'Dulling the Senses: Research in Teacher Education', *Journal of Teacher Education*, XXX, 5, 1979.

[23] N. Gage, *Teacher Effectiveness and Teacher Education*, Pacific, 1972; M. Duncan and B. Biddle, *The Study of Teaching*, Holt, Rinehart, and Winston and D. Medley, *Teacher Competence and Teacher Effectiveness: A Review of Process-Product Research*, American Association of Colleges for Teacher Education, Washington, 1977.

[24] Popkewitz *et. al.*, p. 54.

[25] *Ibid.*

[26] *Ibid.*

[27] Thomas G. Dunn, 'Understanding and Coping with CBTE Limitations', *Journal of Teacher Education*, XXXI, 4, 1980, pp. 27-33.

[28] *Ibid.*

[29] *Ibid.*

[30] *Ibid.*

[31] *Ibid.*

[30] John Dixon, *Growth Through English*, National Association for the Teaching of English, 1967.

[31] George B. Leonard, *Education and Ecstasy*, Delacorte Press, 1968.

[32] *Ibid.*

[33] Arthur W. Combs, Robert A. Blume, Arthur J. Newman, H.C.

Wass, *The Professional Education of Teachers: A Humanistic Approach to Teacher Education*, Allyn and Bacon, 1974.

[34] Gwynth Dow, *Learning to Teach: Teaching to Learn,* Routledge and Kegan Paul, 1979.

[35] Combs *et. al.* p. 8.

[36] Dow, p. 241.

[37] George Henry, 'A Way of Preparing an English Teacher', in Stanley B. Kegler, (ed), *A Changing Role of English Education*, National Council of Teachers of English, 1965, pp. 53-4.

[38] Kevin Ryan, *Don't Smile Until Christmas*, University of Chicago Press, 1970.

[39] Nicholas Otty, *Learner Teacher*, Penguin Books, 1972.

[40] Willard Waller, *The Sociology of Teaching*, John Wiley, 1965.

[41] Neil Postman and Charles Weingartner, *The Soft Revolution: A Handbook for Turning Schools Around*, Delacorte Press, 1971, p. 4.

12   Paul K. Brock

[1] J. Emig, 'The tacit tradition; the inevitability of a multi-disciplinary approach to writing research' in A. Freedman and I. Pringle, (eds), *Reinventing the Rhetorical Tradition*, L + S Books, 1980, pp. 9-18.

[2] A. Freedman and I. Pringle, 'Epilogue: Reinventing the Rhetorical Tradition' in Freedman and Pringle, 1980, p. 176.

[3] *Ibid.*

[4] A.W. Imershein, 'Organizational Change as a Paradigm Shift' in *The Sociological Quarterly*, 18, 1977, pp. 33-43, and 'The Epistemological bases of social order: towards ethnoparadigm analysis' in D. Heiser, (ed), *Sociological Methodology*, Jossey-Bass, 1976.

[5] Imershein, p. 33.

[6-11] inclusive *Ibid.*

[12] This account of the Kuhn-Imershein paradigm is in G. Postle, 1979 'Curriculum Change in Queensland Primary Schools: A Paradigm Analysis' (unpublished). I am indebted to Postle's account of the paradigm and the record of his efforts to apply it to a school curriculum under a central authority.

[13] P. Smith and G. Summerfield, (eds), *Matthew Arnold and the Education of the New Order*, Cambridge University Press, 1969, p. 233.

[14] See D.B. Homer, 'Fifty years of purpose, and perception in English teaching (1921-71): an overview with special reference to the teaching of poetry in early secondary years'; Unpublished thesis, University of Melbourne, 1974, pp. 39-40, and *Victoria — Second Report on the Board of Education*, 1864.

[15] The 1911 English syllabus says of 'Composition', *inter alia*, 'Apart from incidental work, formal instruction in the theory of expression will scarcely be needed. In any case it is doubtful whether such instruction is effective in securing a good style of composition'. *NSW Department of Public Instruction — Courses of Study for High Schools, 1911.*

[16] See Hadow, 1926; Spans 1939; Norwood, 1941; Newsom, 1963 and, especially, the Bullock Report, 1975, pp. 162 *ff.*

[17] Much of the research supporting this is referred to in A. Wilkinson, *The Foundations of Language*, Oxford University Press, 1971.

[18] See Homer, *The Teaching of English,* Australian UNESCO Seminar, AGPS, Canberra, 1973, p. 94; K.D. Watson, 'Now you see it, now you don't — The New English in NSW Secondary Schools' in *the Teaching of English*, ETA of NSW 37, September 1979, p. 47; K.D. Watson, 'The New English', Unpublished thesis, University of Sydney, 1978.

[19] I. Illich, *Deschooling Society*, Penguin Education, 1971, p. 3.

[20] Homer, p. 99.

[21] It is notable that from the first time that any behavioural-objective/operant condition/programme-learning approach to the teaching of English was ever proposed in NSW, it met with strong opposition. NSW State Archives 7/6303. Professor A.G. Mitchell, chairman of the English syllabus committee in 1953, maintained his strenuous opposition, as did subsequent syllabus committees. (Mr Graham Little in a recorded talk he called 'Reminiscences' in May, 1980, in Canberra).

[22] Homer, p. 33.

[23] *Minutes of the Board of Secondary School Studies*, 12 March 1952, filed in NSW State Archives 7/6307, p. 425 ff.

[24] *Minutes*, 20 November 1952, pp. 594-607. (The documents are filed using a *reversed* pagination method).

[25] Interview with Miss Kittson conducted by author in 1980.

[26] Interviews (1980) with Mr Arthur Ashworth, former head of English department, Sydney Teachers' College and president of NSW English Teachers' Association and Mr Don Bowra, former inspector of schools, chairman of English syllabus committee 1961-69 and founding member of NSW English Teachers' Association, Sydney.

[27] A.M. Hellyer, 'The Wyndham Report: A social and education evaluation compiled from published comment', Unpublished thesis, University of Sydney, 1976, p. 138.

[28] UNESCO Seminar, p. 84.

[29] Yeats' poem, 'The Second Coming'.

[30] M. Greene, *The Knower and the Known*, Faber, 1966, p. 180.

[31] *Syllabus in English Years 7-10*, NSW Secondary Schools Board,

1971, p. 2.

[32] James Moffett, *A Student-Centred Language Arts Curriculum, Grades K-13*, Houghton Mifflin, 1968, pp. 31-2.

[33] *Ibid*.

[34] See Little.

[35] G. Selden, 'Curricular Metaphors: from Scientism to Symbolism', *Educational Theory*, 25, 3, p. 25.

[36] J.S. Mann, 'Curriculum Criticism' in W. Pinar, *Curriculum Theorizing: the Reconceptualists*, McCutchan, 1975, p. 147.

[37] W.A. Reid, *Thinking about the Curriculum*, Routledge and Kegan Paul, 1978, p. 108.

[38] NSW syllabus, p. 2.

[39] See Emig.

[40] NSW syllabus, p. 2.

[41] See Watson, 1979 and 1978.

[42] Postle, p. 15.

[43] Imershein, p. 37.

[44] See Little.

[45] Homer, p. 216.

[46] NSW syllabus, p. 8.

[47] E. Eisner, *The Educational Imagination*, Macmillan, 1979, p. 277.

[48] P.K. Brock, 'Some factors inhibiting the development of English Studies with particular reference to NSW' in *Australia and New Zealand History of Education Society (ANZHES) Journal*, 11, 2, 1982.

[49] H. Gruber, *Darwin on Man*, Basic Books, 1974, p. 256.

[50] G. Little, in a communication to the author, Canberra, December 1981.

[51] M. Arnold, *Culture and Anarchy*, Cambridge University Press, 1950, p. 6.

13 Ian Pringle

[1] For a survey of some of the different sorts of language policies involving English as an official exoglossic minority language for educational and related purposes in the post-colonial age, see Roger T. Bell, *Sociolinguistics: Goals, Approaches and Problems*, Batsford, Chapter 7, 1976. For a fuller discussion, see J. Fishman, 'National Languages and Languages of Wider Communication in the Developing Nations', in W.H. Whitely, (ed) *Language Use and Social Change: Problems of Multilingualism with Special Reference to Eastern Africa*, Oxford University Press, 1971, pp. 27-56.

[2] Perhaps, in a long-term view, it will prove rather to have been part of the same upheaval. The recent movements of non-white peoples are mostly indirectly due to European colonialism, and

for the rest, the emigrations from southern and eastern Europe may be merely an extension or replication of earlier emigrations from western and northern Europe.

[3] It is important to note that it is not only the English-speaking world that has been affected by these unparalleled population shifts. In much of western Europe, in particular, the effects of the same changes have been very marked; it has been estimated recently that by the year 2000, approximately one-third of the European school population will have an immigrant background. (Cf. M. Chaib and J. Widgren, *Invandrarbarnen och skolan*, Wahlstrom and Widstrand, Stockholm, 1976).

[4] Harold Rosen, 'Language Diversity: The Demands of the School', *Highway One*, 4, 3, Fall, 1981, pp. 34-46.

[5] In Canada, as in most officially bilingual countries, there is a substantial body of law defining the rights and privileges of the official languages and their speakers. Because of the Federal nature of the Canadian state, some of these laws are enacted at the Federal level, while others are enacted at the provincial level. The Federal government controls dealings with the Federal bureaucracy, in which the government is committed in principle to dealing with Canadian citizens in their first language (although in fact this commitment cannot be upheld in parts of the country where Anglophone or Francophone populations are almost nonexistent). Other levels of political activity fall within provincial jurisdiction, notably education. In the Provinces of Quebec, Ontario and New Brunswick, publicly supported education systems offer complete education through to the end of the tertiary level in either official language; in most of the rest of the country, education in French for Francophone children is a rare exception. For an extensive if slightly dated discussion of the linguistic situation in Canada, see W.H. Coons, D.M. Taylor and M.A. Tremblay, (eds), *The Individual, Language and Society in Canada*, the Canada Council, 1978.

[6] Richard B. Baldauf, Jr., 'The Language Situation in American Samoa: Planners, Plans and Planning', *Language Planning Newsletter*, 8, 1, February 1982, pp. 1-6.

[7] S. Nagarajan, 'The Decline of English in India: Some Historical Notes', *College English*, 43, 7, November 1981, pp. 663-70.

[8] J. Cummins, 'The Language and Culture Issue in the Education of Minority Language Children', *Interchange*, 10, 4, 1980, pp. 72-88. See also W.F. Mackey, 'A Typology of Bilingual Education', *Foreign Language Annals*, 3. 1970, pp. 596-608.

[9] For a little more detail on types of French immersion programmes and their effects, see Swain, Merrill, 'French Immersion: Early, Late or Partial?', *Canadian Modern*

Language Review, 34, 4, 1978, pp. 577-86, and James E. Alatis, (ed) 'Bilingual Education for the English-Speaking Canadian', *Georgetown University Round Table on Languages and Linguistics 1978, (International Dimensions of Bilingual Education)*, Georgetown University Press, 1978, pp. 141-54, and the (copious) references there.

10 Such effects have been demonstrated with Spanish-speaking and Navajo-speaking children in the United States, Finnish-speaking children in Sweden, French-speaking students in Canada, and in many other cases. For detailed references see James Cummins, 1980 'The Construct of Language Proficiency in Bilingual Education', in Alatis, pp. 81-103; 'The Cognitive Development of Children in Immersion Programmes', *Canadian Modern Language Review*, 34, 5, pp. 855-83; and Swain, Merrill, 'Bilingual Education for Majority and Minority Language Children', *Studia Linguistics*, 35: 1-2, 1981, pp. 15-32.

11 R. Hébert, *et. al.*, *Rendement académique langue d'enseignement chez les élèves franco-manitobains*, Saint Boniface, Manitoba: Centre de Recherches du College Universitaire de St. Boniface, 1976.

12 The languages in question are Albanian, Arabic, Armenian, Bengali, Chinese (Cantonese and Mandarin), Croatian, Dutch, Estonian, Filipino, Gaelic, German, Greek, Gujerati, Hungarian, Hebrew, Hindi, Italian, Japanese, Korean, Latvian, Macedonian, Ojibwa, Persian, Polish, Portuguese, Punjabi, Russian, Serbian, Serbo-Croatian, Slovenian, Spanish, Ukrainian, Urdu and Vietnamese. It may be noted that there is no direct correlation between the strength of parental demand and the size of the local community of native speakers.

13 E.N. Wright, *Programme Replacement Related to Selected Countries of Birth and Selected Languages*, Research Report 99, Toronto Board of Education, 1971.

14 For details, see Stephen D. Krashen, 'The Input Hypothesis', in Alatis, 1980, pp. 168-80; 'The 'Fundamental Pedagogical Principle' in Second Language Learning', *Studia Linguistica*, 35:1-2, pp. 50-70; and *Second Language Learning and Second Language Acquisition*, Pergamon Press, 1981.

15 W.E. Lambert, 'Culture and Language as Factors in Learning and Education', in A. Wolfgang, (ed), *Education of Immigrant Students,* Ontario Institute for Studies in Education, 1975, pp. 55-83.

16 The fullest exposition of Cummins' theory is that in Alatis.

17 Studia Linguistica, 35:1-2, p. 27.

18 Stephen D. Krashen, 'The Role of Input (Reading) and Instruction in Developing Writing Ability', Unpublished paper

delivered at Carleton University, Ottawa, Fall 1981.

[19] At least in some fields, it is in fact quite certain that they do this, as Aviva Freedman and I have been able to show. See 'Writing in the College Years: Some Indices of Growth', *College Composition and Communication,* 31:3, 1980, pp. 311-24.

[20] Margaret Donaldson, *Children's Minds,* Fontana/Croom Helm, 1978.

[21] Gordon Wells, *Learning through Interaction: The Language of Development,* Cambridge University Press, 1981.

[22] I have to acknowledge my gratitude to Professor Stephen Krashen, a visiting professor in Ottawa during the Fall term of 1981, and to my colleagues Professor Aviva Freedman and Professor Janice Yalden; my discussions with these three authorities have helped me to sharpen the ideas in this paper, even if they could stand some more sharpening. I would also like to express my gratitude to my wife, Marie-Victoire (herself a French immersion teacher), and to our children Antony and Marc David; between the three of them these authorities have also taught me much about bilingualism and education, as well as much more.